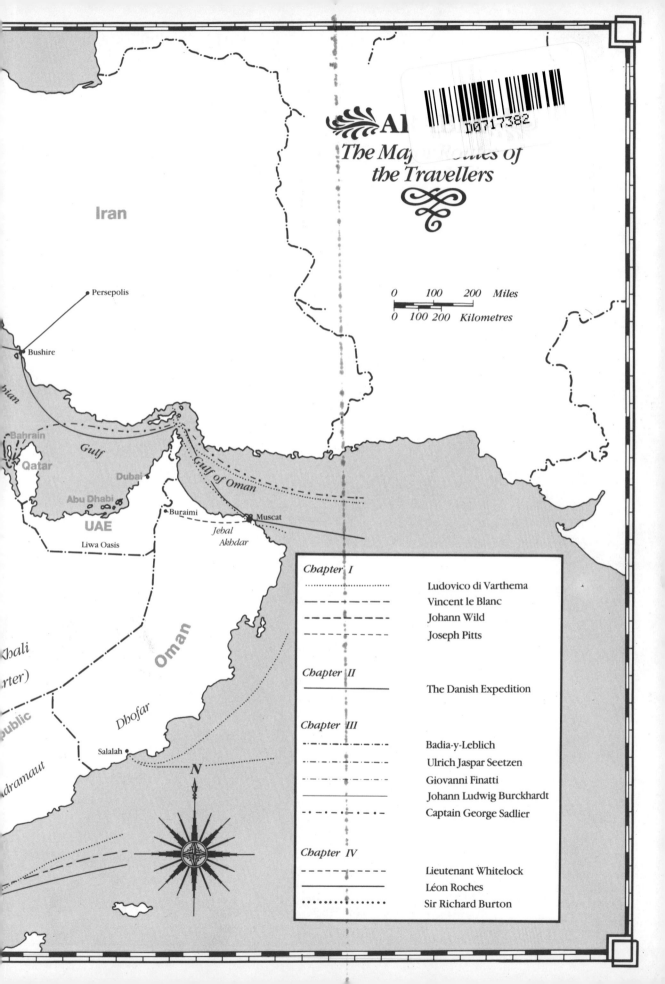

ARABIAN
TRAVELLERS

CEL

ARABIAN TRAVELLERS

RICHARD TRENCH

MACMILLAN
LONDON

To Jock Murray

Title page: *Islamic tiles depicting the Kaaba in Mecca.*

First published by
MACMILLAN LONDON LIMITED
4 Little Essex Street London WC2R 3LF
and Basingstoke

Associated companies in Auckland, Delhi, Dublin,
Gaborone, Hamburg, Harare, Hong Kong,
Johannesburg, Kuala Lumpur, Lagos, Manzini,
Melbourne, Mexico City, Nairobi, New York, Singapore
and Tokyo

ISBN 0-333-42889-7

Designed and produced by Robert Adkinson Limited,
London

Editorial Director	Clare Howell
Editor	Sydney Francis
Art Director	Christine Simmonds
Designer	Paul Morgan
Cartography	MJL Cartographics

Phototypeset by Dorchester Typesetting Group Limited,
Dorchester

Illustrations originated by East Anglian Engraving
Limited, Norwich

Printed and bound in Italy by Sagdos, Milan

CONTENTS

FOREWORD

Above: *Wilfred Thesiger in the Empty Quarter in 1958, photographed by bin Kabina.*

I have read Richard Trench's comprehensive book with great interest. What interested me especially was to discover the many and varied motives that prompted the men he discusses to explore Arabia. As the last in this long line of Arabian explorers, I have been asked to write a foreword explaining what induced me to travel in the Empty Quarter. I have tried to do so.

In 1945, the Locust Research Centre offered me the opportunity to travel in and around the Empty Quarter of Arabia to collect information on potential outbreak centres of the desert locust. That I knew nothing about locusts did not matter, what did matter was that I was already an experienced desert traveller.

I was born in the Legation in Addis Ababa in 1910, the first British child to be born in Abyssinia. Before I was eight I had travelled across deserts with camels, and I had seen something of the barbaric splendour of the Abyssinian Empire. After this, life in England seemed very tame. Unlike my contemporaries, I had no interest in cars, aeroplanes, wireless or indeed any of the material manifestations of our civilization. I craved for adventures in savage lands. During my second year at Oxford, I returned to Abyssinia and attended the coronation of the Emperor Haile Selassie, and then spent a decisive month hunting big game in the Danakil country. Two years later I returned to Abyssinia, and, using camels, explored hitherto unknown regions of the Danakil Desert. Three previous expeditions had been wiped out by the Danakil who rated a man's prowess by the number of men he had killed and castrated. During those nine months I had experienced the fascination of exploration and known the excitement of living among dangerous tribes.

The following year I joined the Sudan Political Service and served for three years in Northern Darfur. The largest district in the Sudan, it was bordered on the west by the French Sahara, and to the north merged with the Libyan Desert. The District Commissioner and I were the only two Europeans in the district. We had a lorry and a pick-up, the only cars in the district, but we seldom used them, riding everywhere on our camels. I always travelled light, accompanied only by three or four retainers, lived on the local food, and slept on the ground. I soon acquired an affection for the tribesmen we administered, several of whom became my friends.

In 1938 I spent three months in the Sahara, travelling to and from the Tibesti mountains, across deserts where no car had as yet been. It was summer and hot, but pressed for time and with two thousand miles to cover, we rode long hours, often thirteen or fourteen on end. The very hardships and privations of this journey drew me and my five tribal companions close together in happy comradeship. The Sahara had, however, been explored, its tribes had been pacified and were being administered, while Bagnold had recently been exploring in cars the sand sea of the Libyan Desert. Here there was nothing left for me. Only the Empty Quarter of Arabia still offered the final challenge of desert exploration. I had believed that access to it was impossible for me since I had no connection with Arabia. Now suddenly and quite unexpectedly it was within my reach. I accepted the job at once without even asking about pay or any conditions of employment.

For two years I worked for the Locust Research Centre during which time I crossed the Empty Quarter with a few chosen companions from the Rashid tribe, returning to Dhaufar through the desert borderland of Oman, a region at that time more inaccessible to Europeans than Tibet. Satisfied with the information I had collected, the Locust Research Centre offered me employment elsewhere. I refused. I was determined to remain with the Rashid, and with them to continue my exploration of the Empty Quarter and of the interior of Oman, ruled by its xenophobic Imam. Already I was the first European to have visited the Liwa oasis, unexplored as yet, though it was only sixty miles from the Trucial Coast, and to have seen the fabled quicksands of Umm al Samim. But it was the companionship of certain individuals among the Rashid, rather than the satisfaction of exploring the unknown, which drew me back to that harsh land. Without the presence of those Bedu, the deserts of southern Arabia would have been as meaningless to me as the Antarctic; these journeys a mere penance.

I went to Arabia resolved to meet the challenge of the desert on equal terms with the Arabs who lived there. I wanted no concessions. I wished only to live with them as they lived and to win their acceptance. I sought nothing else. I certainly had no intention of writing a book. It was only ten years after I had left them that I was persuaded to do so. I took nothing with me other than my rifle, a compass, my camera and my watch, a few drugs and a couple of books. I wore their clothes and went barefooted as they did. Under no circumstance would I have taken a radio. While I was with them I only wanted to escape from the outside world. Their fascination for me was that they knew no world other than their own.

These Bedu lived a life that was scarcely possible, travelling sometimes for ten days or more across immense sand dunes from one well to the next; then if their camels foundered they were faced with certain death. Hunger, verging on starvation, and almost incessant thirst were their daily lot. They were generally without shelter even in summer, and in winter they endured the bitter cold as they slept on the bare sand, covered only with their loin-cloths. And always their rifles were at hand and their eyes unceasingly searched the horizon for tribal enemies. Any of them could have found employment in the towns of the Hadramaut; all of them would have scorned this easier life of lesser men. They met every hardship and challenge with the proud boast 'I am a Bedui'. It was the freedom of their lives they valued above all else. This and the well-being of their beloved camels.

I knew when I went there that I could not compete with them in physical endurance; they, after all, had been born to this life, but with my family background, with Eton and Oxford behind me, I did expect to excel them in civilized behaviour. It was humiliating to find how often I failed to measure up to their standards. Among these desert nomads I encountered a nobility, not only of individuals, but of these people as a whole. Few in numbers they yet ranged far afield and everything that happened, whether in the foothills of the Yemen or hundreds of miles away on the borders of Oman, was eventually known and discussed. 'What is the news?', invariably this question followed the formal greeting, and 'God blacken the face of so and so' was the inevitable condemnation passed on anyone whose behaviour had merited censure.

Bedu hospitality was past belief. Often it exasperated me, when, for instance, my companions fed our scanty rations or gave the little water we had with us to chance-met strangers. Then we might pass an encampment and a man would hail us and kill a camel to feed us, sending us off in the morning having half convinced me that we had conferred a kindness on him by accepting his hospitality. Their generosity with any money they had acquired was equally lavish. Then, too, there was their courage, their patience, their pride in themselves and their tribes, and their loyalty to each other, and to me, often at risk of their lives, a man of another faith from an unknown land. As a result of their raids they had little regard for human life and, to settle a blood feud, killed without mercy, but they would never torture a man. They were horrified when I told them that the Danakils castrated the dead and dying, 'they must be animals', they said. Always I shall remember their kindness and thoughtfulness and be proud that they accepted me as a friend.

I would have remained indefinitely with the Rashid, but circumstances beyond my control eventually barred my access to them. Ibn Saud had protested at my unauthorized travels in territory he claimed as his, and the Sultan of Muscat was increasingly indignant at my repeated penetration into inner Oman. And always the forthcoming activities of the oil companies loomed like a dark cloud on my horizon. Prospecting parties moved in a year or two after I had left and their activities have in themselves destroyed for ever the immemorial life of the desert Arabs.

WILFRED THESIGER
London
June, 1986

INTRODUCTION

To Herodotus, it was the southernmost place on earth. To eight hundred million Moslems it is the very centre of the universe, where Adam and Eve were exiled after the Fall. Arabia's dimensions are enormous: a million and a quarter square miles of peninsula, one thousand across by one and a half down, flanked by two fingers of the Indian Ocean, the Red Sea and the Arabian Gulf. It lies across the route from Europe to India, at the crossroads of three continents.

On the western edge of the Peninsula the ground rises up into mountain ranges stretching from the Hejaz in the north to the Yemen in the south, hemming in the coastal belt, the Tihamah, which runs alongside the Red Sea. East of the mountains, in the very centre of the Peninsula, is the Jebal Tuwagq, a fertile crescent of oasis palm gardens supporting the central oasis towns of Hail, Buraydah, Unayzah and Riyadh. Radiating from it are three great deserts: the Nafud to the north, with its oasis port of Hail; the Dahna to the east with its oasis archipelago around Riyadh; and finally the Empty Quarter, the Rub el-Khali, to the south, two hundred thousand square miles of desert within desert, which not even the Bedouin themselves had crossed until the twentieth century.

In the middle of the mountain range stretching from the Hejaz to the Yemen lies Mecca, a trading town protected by a ring of mountains, where the frankincense trail from the Yemen divided west to Cairo, north to Damascus and east to Baghdad. According to the Moslems who lived in the city, Mecca was founded by Hagar, lover of Abraham and mother of Ismail, who found water there. She called the waterhole the Well of Zem-Zem. Abraham and Ismail, seeing the water as a sign from God, built a shrine out of black stone, the Kaaba. Ptolemy, who drew a map of the world in the second century, called it Makorba, and through it Aelius Gallus' Roman legions must have passed on their long and ragged retreat from what they so inappropriately called 'Arabia Felix', the first of the great powers to be defeated by the deserts that the Romans called 'happy'. Here in AD 610, amid the dust and the sand, the flies and the camels, the merchants' stalls and the three hundred and sixty idols, a man named Mohammed received a message that there was no god but God, a revelation which came to him, according to his widow, 'like the breaking of dawn'.

Left: *The Prophet's Tomb and Great Mosque in Medina in the nineteenth century, from a sketch by Sir Richard Burton.*

9

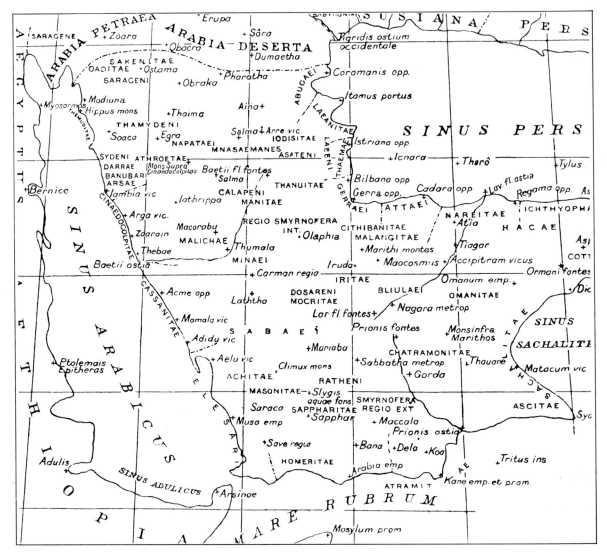

'There is no god but God' became the first pillar of wisdom. The second was to pray, the third to give alms and the fourth to fast. Persecuted, the Prophet fled to the second Holy City of Islam, Medina. He returned to Mecca victorious in AD 630 and added a fifth pillar of wisdom, that all should make the pilgrimage to Mecca once in a lifetime, and that no unbeliever should ever set foot in the Holy City. It was not just the barren landscape that served to enforce the holy writ; the people of the Peninsula, the Bedouin who valued pride above pain, freedom above security, reinforced the edict. Did not Strabo say that of all the nations upon earth, only the Arabians disdained to send ambassadors to Alexander the Great?

The history of the Bedouin in the centuries that followed was a continual assertion of that pride and freedom; through war and raiding, alliances and trade, tribes grew and withered, their strength dependent on their numbers, their military might and their attraction to lesser tribes and factions who gathered around them. It was pure feudalism, with the Bedouin as the warrior caste and the oasis-dwellers as the serfs.

Only two towns were large enough to escape this Bedouin servitude, Mecca and Medina, whose size and religious prestige allowed them some control of

Above: Ptolemy's Arabia Felix. Improving on the ideas and methods of Hipparchus and Eratosthenes, he divided the world into parallels of latitude and longitude.

the deserts around. But even they were rarely independent; their very size forced them to rely on Egypt for grain. Economic dependence turned inevitably into political dependence, and the Holy Cities became part of the growing Egyptian domain.

Once only in these centuries did Christendom have any direct contact with the Holy Cities, in the last years of the twelfth century when Renaud de Chatillon, a supposed crusader, led an expedition to loot Medina. The Bedouin waited until the Christians were only a day from the city then fell on them. The survivors were taken to Arafat, just outside Mecca, where they were stoned to death.

When Egypt was annexed by the Ottoman Empire in 1517, Medina, Mecca and the surrounding territory became part of the Caliphate. Though Turkey had pretentions to the whole of Arabia, in practice Turkish rule rarely extended beyond the walls of Medina and Mecca and their ports of Yanbu and Jeddah. Outside that rectangle the Bedouin ruled.

For only one month of the year was there peaceful access across those lawless drylands, in the Haj (pilgrimage) season when the pilgrims crossed the deserts, their eyes fixed on Mecca, escorted by hundreds of Turkish soldiers. Largest of these great pilgrim caravans was the Damascus caravan, forty thousand strong in the sixteenth century. It began in Constantinople, collecting tributary caravans from Anatolia, Russia, Kurdistan and central Asia on the way. From Damascus it travelled forty days and nights across the Syrian and Nafud deserts to Medina, the way ahead lit by torches hanging from high poles at the head of the caravan. Second in importance was

Above: *The* ihram, *the two simple pieces of seamless cloth that the believer puts on after the ritual washing which the pilgrim must undergo before entering the holy ground around Mecca.*

Right: *Detail from 'Encampment of the Aulad Sa'id, Mount Sinai' by David Roberts.*

the Cairo caravan, packed with pilgrims from all over north Africa, trekking forty days and nights across the Sinai Desert and Hejaz mountains, marching to the tunes of pipes and drums and bringing with it the new covering for the sacred Kaaba, the yearly present (until 1927) of the people of Egypt to the Holy City. Next in size came the Baghdad caravan with its gigantic Shiite contingent from Persia. Finally there was the local caravan traffic from Muscat, the Yemen, Hail and Riyadh. And all the time the caravans were arriving there would be a steady stream of thousands coming by sea to Jeddah and Yanbu on ships unchanged since the voyages of Sinbad.

The arrival of the great caravans coincides with the first twelve days of the Moslem year (eleven days shorter than the Christian year). Before entering the holy land around Mecca, the pilgrims wash, shave and change into the *ihram*, the two pieces of simple seamless white cloth (one wrapped around the loins, the other around the neck and left shoulder), which the pilgrim must wear to enter the Holy City. Once inside, the pilgrim first finds a guide, who instructs him in the rites and gets him lodgings, then makes his way to the Kaaba, the black stone cube which he circles seven times and kisses. From there he walks across the courtyard of the Great Mosque to the Well of Zem-Zem, where he drinks and washes, then makes the quarter-mile run from Mount Safa to Mount Marwa just outside the city, which he repeats six times, allegorizing Hagar's search for water and redemption. The pilgrim stays in Mecca eight days, praying and fasting. On the ninth day the whole city migrates to the plain of Arafat, a natural amphitheatre set among rocks, and listens to the holy man, the Imam, preach at the same spot where Mohammed made his last sermon before his death. As the sun goes down and the sermon ends, the pilgrim races six miles to Muzlalifa where, on the tenth day, he collects forty-nine pebbles, flinging them in seven sequences of seven, at the Pillars of Mena. On the final day he sacrifices a sheep, distributing the surplus meat to the poor. The pilgrimage over, the pilgrim has become a Haji.

With so many millions passing along the caravan routes into the Holy City, Mecca became the intellectual hub of the Moslem world, drawing to it poets, philosophers, geographers, scientists and historians. Long before the Norman Conquest, men like Hamdani, Istakhri and Mukaddassi had described Mecca and the roads to Mecca. Ibn Haukal, who travelled for twenty-five years in the tenth century and whose *Book of Ways and Provinces*

Below: *The Great Mosque in Mecca.*

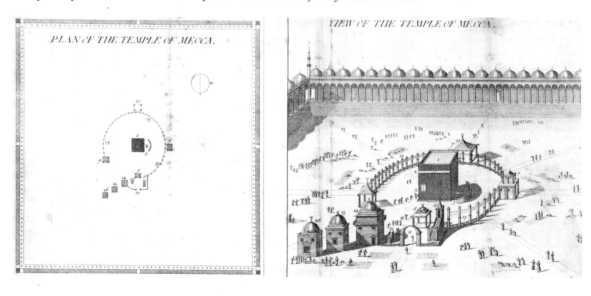

12

encompassed all that 'ever made geography of interest to either princes or peoples' called the Kaaba the 'navel of the world'.

Three hundred years later ibn Battuta, the most widely-travelled of all Moslem geographers, arrived in Mecca from Morocco aged twenty-one. Wanting to discover how small the world was, he extended his original six-month Haj into a twenty-four-year tour of Iraq, Persia, India, Russia, Turkey, Afghanistan, China, Indonesia and Africa. Altogether he made four visits to Mecca. On the second visit, coming across the Nafud from Baghdad, he nearly died of dysentry and, as a result, stayed in Mecca for two years. He was an intellectual snob, and his social calendar reads like a *Who's Who* in Arabic history, but he was no prude; he likened the Kaaba to a bride displaying all her naked majesty, and he always made sure he had a couple of slave girls in attendance to distract him from the rigours of the road. Back in Morocco, seventy-five thousand miles later, he discovered how small the world was when he met a man in his home town whose brother had given him hospitality in China.

The books these travellers wrote gave a clear and concise account of the geography of Arabia. But, except in a few monasteries, no one read their books. Europe looked on Arabia through hostile eyes. The Moslem geographers were ignored, many of their best treatises on Arabia remaining untranslated until the twentieth century.

Dismissing this vast stock of knowledge, Europe chose to regard Arabia as a 'huge white blot' on the map of the world: a far-away, distant and impenetrable place. Forbidden fruit, they yearned for it, yet it was qualitatively different from the more mundane blank spaces on the maps of Africa, South America and central Asia, the blank spaces that the young Joseph Conrad and a thousand other nineteenth-century boys dreamed of. There was not only a climate and people to overcome, but a religion too, and its very womb, the place where it was conceived, there in Mecca.

As for the Europeans who tried to fill that 'huge white blot', most of them had something in themselves to overcome too. Few were attractive characters; they were imperialists, sacrilegers, adventurers, romantics, opportunists, spies and simple searchers. Many arrived with a contempt for Islam, others arrived in the guise of children of Islam, still others came to exploit Islam. Yet virtually none left without a profound respect for it. Some, like Philby, became Moslems themselves; others, like Palgrave and Doughty, used Islam as a backdrop for their own inner journeys; and many, who remained unfulfilled after the experience, died by their own hands. What they all had in common was an obsession with Arabia, with the Bedouin and their nomadic society, and with themselves.

I

THE EARLY TRAVELLERS

It is no accident that the last of the great Moslem geographers, Hassan ibn Mohammed, ended up in the court of the Medici pope, Leo X, with a new name, Leo Africanus. A generation earlier the eight-hundred-year-old Moslem tide had reached its highest point when the armies of Islam crossed the Bosporus and captured Constantinople. It was now on the ebb, not to reassert itself, except in local turmoils, for four hundred years.

With European power dominating the trade routes and European thought the universities, a new type of traveller came into Arabia: the European of the Renaissance and post-Renaissance world. It was to be through these eyes, and these eyes alone, that Europe received its conceptions and preconceptions about Arabia. The Moslem geographers were forgotten.

The first of the New Men to come to Arabia was a soldier of fortune, Ludovico di Varthema, 'Gentleman of Rome', who left Italy in 1502, just four years after Vasco da Gama reached India by sea. He was a true Renaissance man. 'If anyone asks me the motive for my voyages, I can give them no better one than the desire for knowledge.' Knowledge was not all he desired though, and he liberally helped himself to the fruit of the countries he passed through, enduring 'hunger, thirst, cold, heat, wars, captivity, terrors', and much else on the way. Happy-go-lucky, sharp-eyed, quick-witted and without any trace of guilt or racism, it is impossible to dislike this narcissistic vagabond, and impossible to trust him.

From Rome Varthema sailed to Alexandria, Cairo, Beirut and Tripoli before landing on the Syrian coast at Latakia. From there he took a caravan to Aleppo and Damascus, a city of orchards bearing figs, oranges, apricots, mulberries and pomegranates. 'It is incredible and unbelievable how fair the

Left: *An Arab sheikh who escorted Sir David Wilkie on his expedition to the Dead Sea and Jordan in the nineteenth century. The Arab costume would hardly have changed since that worn in Varthema's day.*

15

city of Damascus is, and how fertile its soil,' he enthused. He stayed several months, learning the language and customs of the people sufficiently to pass as one of them. He visited the spectacular Umayyad mosque which he compared to St Peter's in Rome, the markets where he complained the peaches and pears were unripe, and the city wall from which St Paul had been lowered in a basket to escape the persecution of the Christians that he himself had initiated. Damascus could hardly have changed since ibn Battuta visited it two centuries earlier and wrote of the people strolling along the banks of the Barah on Saturday afternoons and lingering under the trees till nightfall. The red and white roses lining the streets were the prettiest that Varthema had ever seen.

He spent most of the time with the Mamelukes, the Circassian military caste of the Ottoman Empire, who gave him a tour of the city's bordellos. As for the women he met there, they 'beautify and garnish themselves as much as any'. Their clothes were of silk, their shoes were red or purple and they glittered with jewels and bracelets. 'They marry as much as they like and when they get weary of their husbands they just go to the *kadi*, the local judge, and get divorced.'

In the bordellos he met the Emir el-Haj, the commander of the military escort for the pilgrim caravan to Mecca. With a hefty bribe Varthema persuaded the Emir to give him a place on the escort, and with the new name of Yunis and the new persona of a European renegade in the service of the Mamelukes, he joined the caravan of forty thousand souls, thirty-five thousand camels and an escort of sixty Mamelukes. It was 11 April 1503.

The forty days that followed took on a routine. For twenty-two hours they marched across barren wastes. Then the Emir sounded the trumpet and the thirty-five thousand camels dropped down, first on their forelegs throwing the rider forward, then on their hind legs throwing him backwards. The pilgrim dismounted and unloaded 'to victuel himself and his animal', then

Below: Damascus in 1668, much as it would have looked when Ludovico di Varthema visited the city at the beginning of the sixteenth century.

Right: *'Dawn prayer outside the Great Mosque and Prophet's tomb in Medina' by Etienne Dinet, approximately four hundred years after Varthema first described the temple. (Mathaf Gallery, London)*

slept till the trumpet sounded again and the day began anew. After a while the pilgrims learnt to 'cat-nap' as they rode, gently swaying in time with the camels' steps.

It was not an easy journey. Thirty died of thirst, others were drowned in sinking sands, the caravan passing on as they slowly submerged 'not yet fully dead'. There were confrontations with Bedouin, but since the Bedouin had high-pitched voices and were 'despicable and of little stature', Varthema did not think much of them. Some sixty miles north of Medina, they came upon a colony of Jews living around an oasis amid the lava fields of Mount Khaybar. They were no different from any of the other Bedouin tribespeople Varthema met, 'of little stature, less than five or six spans high, with voices like women and black complexions'. They kept well away from the caravan and its escort, and 'scattered like wild goats' over the mountain. In the foothills was a waterhole and eight thorn trees 'in which we found a pair of turtle doves, which seemed like a miracle having been so long on a journey without seeing beast or fowl'.

Two days later Varthema arrived in Medina, providing the first description of the city through European eyes. There were about three hundred houses built of stone and brick. Apart from the rivulet of the Aynal-Zarka flowing through the palm trees and gardens of Kula, the land around was utterly barren. But the soul of the city was the Great Mosque, the Prophet's tomb.

> His temple is square, a hundred paces long and eighty wide, with two entrance gates. Along the sides are three levels of vaults, held up by four hundred columns of white bricks. . . At the far side of the mosque is a tower, about five paces in circumference, valuted on every side and covered in silk. It is protected by an intricately wrought copper grate, so you look at the tower as if through a lattice. On the left of the lattice is the gate to the tower, the way flanked by books.[1]

After three days constantly being cheated by the inhabitants the caravan moved on to Mecca. They were guided by a pilot with a ship's compass. One good well was passed before they entered a 'sea of sand', where the sand, as fine as flour, was frequently whipped up by winds into storms that reduced visibility to ten paces. Many died of thirst, and the survivors had to walk past the mummified corpses of those who had fallen before them. They spent three days in the 'sea of sand', then arrived at Jebal Warkan, one of the four hills of Paradise, where the Prophet contemplated after receiving his Message from Allah.

Ten days later, on 18 May 1503, after two more confrontations with the Bedouin, the caravan arrived in Mecca. 'Inside the city we found a marvellous number of strangers and pilgrims, some from Syria, some from Persia, some from India. Never before had I seen such a gathering of people all in one place.' With the thousands of others from the Damascus caravan he made his way to the Kaaba, which he compares to the Colosseum in Rome. The surrounding arcades sold only jewels and precious stones, the water of the holy Well of Zem-Zem tasted disgusting and the sermon on Arafat was impressive. He even spotted a couple of unicorns, probably oryx in profile. (Those who would dismiss Varthema's narrative on account of the unicorns would do well to remember the historian ibn Khaldun's defence of ibn Battuta's strange tales. A young child, put into prison with his father, asked about the different kinds of meat that were served to them. The father described cows, sheep and goats; but all the son could see were different species of rats, for rats were the only animals he had ever seen.)

All went well until Varthema was spotted by a Mameluke who had known him in Venice.

'What are you?'

'I am a Mohammedan.' (No genuine Moslem would ever call himself a Mohammedan, it would be like a Catholic calling himself a Papist.)

'That's a lie.'

'By the head of Mohammed, I am a Mohammedan.'

He persuaded the Mameluke that he was a Moslem convert and an artillery expert on his way to India to fight the Portuguese. The Mameluke, impressed, quickly offered him assistance in leaving Mecca in return for using his friendship with the Emir el-Haj to help the Mameluke smuggle fifteen camels laden with spices out of Mecca. As the caravan was preparing for departure Varthema was hidden in the Mameluke's house. The next day the trumpeter of the Syrian caravan gave notice of departure, with a proclamation of death for all those who had come on the caravan and refused to return. Varthema was 'marvellously troubled in mind'. Fortunately relief was at hand.

> While I lay hidden in the Mohammedan's house, I cannot express how friendly his wife was to me. My entertainment was furthered by a fair young maid, the niece of the Mohammedan, who was greatly in love with me. Alas, in the midst of these troubles and fears the fires of Venus were almost extinct in me; and so, with dalliance of fair words and promises, I kept myself in her favour.[2]

A few days later he left for Jeddah. The port was packed with pilgrims returning from the Haj. He remained there for fifteen days in the sweltering summer heat until he found an Arabian dhow to take him to the Yemen and Persia.

Eleven days later he arrived in Aden, which boasted five thousand families and five castles. The crew were stoned by the population when they landed and in the riot that followed twenty-four Yemenis were killed. Varthema, who entered the affray with characteristic gusto, was thrown into prison. He was lucky to miss the death penalty. After fifty-five days in chains, while a

Right: *Mamelukes, the Circassian military caste of the Ottoman Empire, which ended up almost destroying the empire it was created to protect, until being wiped out by Mohammed Ali in 1811.*

Left: *An Egyptian merchant on the caravan route to Sinai, the same route that hundreds of thousands of pilgrims have taken to Mecca.*

lynch mob outside demanded his death, he was taken before the Sultan at Rada, a small town in the north-east corner of the Yemen, but failed to convince the Sultan that he was a genuine Moslem, and was put back into chains. The Sultan had more pressing problems elsewhere and left Varthema in the care of the Sultana.

Varthema's only way out, as he saw it, was to feign madness. First he tried to convert a sheep, then he stabbed to death a donkey which refused to utter the testament of the Moslem faith: 'There is no god but God and Mohammed is his Prophet.' When Holy Men came down from the mountains to pronounce on his sanity, 'I pissed into my hands and hurled it in their faces, whereby they all agreed I was no saint but a madman.'

The Sultan returned, and to escape from both Sultan and Sultana Varthema persuaded them to let him return to Aden to consult a Holy Man. In Aden he found a sea captain willing to take him to Persia and India, and he passed his time before the departure visiting Sana'a, Lahej, el-Makrana and Yerim. From India he travelled throughout Asia collecting information on such diverse subjects as the Indian prince whose moustache was so long he had to tie it in a bow around his head, the cannibals of Java, the extravagant methods by which elephants copulate and the first rumour of the existence of Australia. He returned to Europe in 1508 after five years of adventure. Little is known of him after that date, but we may suspect, since the book which he wrote in 1518 is dedicated to Agnesina, Duchess of Tagliacozzo, that one kind of his adventures at least went on many more years.

The year that Ludovico di Varthema returned to Europe, a Portuguese sea captain, Gregorio da Quadra, arrived on the shores of Arabia. It was an inauspicious time. In 1504 the first Portuguese ships had arrived in the Red Sea and two years later they established their first base on the island of Socotra. Only a few months before da Quadra's arrival the Portuguese adventurer Afonso d'Albuquerque had occupied Muscat.

Above: *Afonso d'Albuquerque, who took Muscat from the Turks in 1507.*

Shipwrecked off the Yemen, da Quadra was imprisoned in a cistern in Zabid for five years, where he learnt fluent Arabic. He was released after one of the Yemen's almost seasonal revolutions, and taken by the new Imam in his entourage to the Holy Cities. In Medina his religious enthusiasm almost sent him back to prison for another five years when he shouted in front of the Prophet's tomb: 'Prophet of Satan, if you are the one these dogs are worshipping, show them that I am a Christian, and by the mercy of God I hope to see this house of abomination turned into a church for His praise, like Our Lady of Conception at Lisbon.' Fortunately his hearers chose to regard it as the ravings of a saint rather than a sinner. He left Medina for Basra (the first European to cross the Dahna, a huge region of dunes which forms a ring around the heart of Arabia), lived off locusts, was rescued by Bedouin and died a Capuchin friar.

Sixty years went by before another European set foot – or rather claimed to have set foot – in Mecca. born in Marseilles in 1554, Vincent le Blanc ran away to sea at the age of fourteen on the sailing ship *Lady of Victory*, bound for Alexandria. After berthing at Alexandria and sailing up the Nile to Cairo, the ship was delayed in Candia where the crew sold the cargo, pocketing the money. To escape prosecution for fraud they wrecked the ship. Le Blanc survived the catastrophe and was taken on board a Venetian merchantman on its way to Lebanon. There he left the sea with one of the ship's company, Cassis, and continued to Damascus, 'from thence commonly are set forth the caravans or land convoys for Medina and Mecca'. The two were planning to visit Jerusalem.

At Mezarib, two days from Damascus, they met Cassis' brother, a renegade who persuaded them to go with him to Mecca where he hoped to sell his merchandise at a high profit; le Blanc and Cassis could visit Jerusalem on the return journey. The three joined the Haj caravan 'of above twenty thousand camels, two leagues in length', and set out for Mecca.

It is debatable whether le Blanc really reached Mecca. However, his account of the desert journey, like the motives for his later life of travels, has a ring of truth about it. There are too many details that a half-educated boy could not have picked up from hearsay or from books, even if he never actually set foot in Mecca. Only someone who had been on a forty-day caravan trek could write that 'in the desert there are many fantasies and goblins seen, that strive to seduce the travellers and cause them to perish with hunger and despair,' and only someone who has never been on a caravan would dismiss it as fiction. The Bedouin call them *djinns*, manifestations of spirits. To Jungians they are the projections of one's own fears and subconscious, that must be confronted to be overcome; for once one has faced one's *djinns*, say the Bedouin, they disappear.

After fifteen days the caravan ran out of water. The strongest camels were concentrated into search parties and sent to look for waterholes. Le Blanc was with one such party. 'We came upon the sides of a little sandy hill, where we found a great store of little trees. . . . A little further we discovered an Indian cane with a flag at the end of it, which is a sign for water in these parts, and groping with our hands in the sand, we found a great piece of camel's leather which stopped the mouth of the well.'[3]

Right: *The desert djinns of 'heart-beguiling Araby', the European mirage that drew so many to Arabia. But she proved 'a hard, barren mistress and those who serve her she pays in weariness, sickness of the body and distress of the mind.' (Lord Belhaven).*

Continuing past Mount Sinai – 'The Arabians pay great reverence to Mount Sinai, and do not suffer beasts to feed thereon' – they reached the oasis of Jusoreh, whose inhabitants 'hide their secret parts with a linen cloth and are naked for the rest of their bodies'. One of the inhabitants at Jusoreh, appearing to be mad, walked up to Cassis and hurled a handful of lice at him. Cassis tore off his clothes in panic, whereupon the 'madman' picked up the clothes and ran away.

Some days later the caravan arrived in Medina, and from there made the last lap to Mecca, 'about the size of Rome and twice the size of Marseilles'.

> The Mosque or Temple of Mecca is a mass of stones, round and like St Sophia's in Constantinople. You ascend some fifteen or sixteen steps, and around are fair piazzas and galleries where merchants have their market. . . . The Mosque is gorgeously adorned, hung with tapisteries.[4]

At Mecca, le Blanc and Cassis successfully cheated Cassis' brother of his merchandise (justifying themselves on the grounds that the brother had sinned against Christ by becoming a Moslem) and took it to Jeddah. From there they sailed to Persia, where they sold the merchandise at a profit and travelled on together to Samarkand, Aden, East Africa and India. Nor did le Blanc's travels end there, but continued after he had married 'one of the most terrible women in the world' to Brazil, the West Indies and Guinea, before he finally returned to France and settled there at the age of seventy. 'Life', he wrote, 'is a perpetual voyage'.

Three more non-Moslems visited Mecca in the next century. The first, Johann Wild, arrived in 1607. Born in Nuremberg, he joined the Imperial

Below: Detail from 'The walled city of Jerusalem as seen from the Mount of Olives', painted by Luigi Meyer at the end of the eighteenth century. (Mathaf Gallery, London)

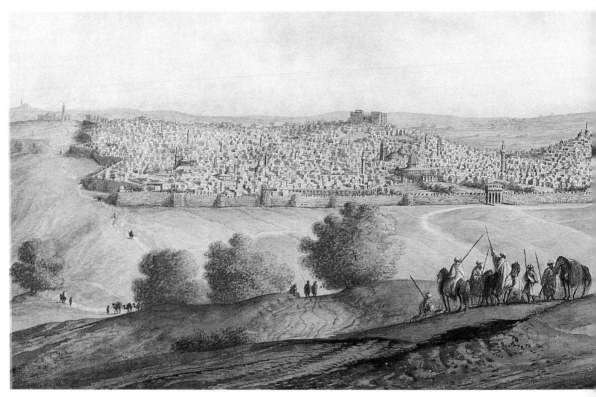

Hungarian Army and was taken prisoner by the Turks aged nineteen. After a freezing journey to Constantinople, so cold that the Danube was frozen and they crossed on the ice, he was thrown into a Turkish bath: a sensation Wild found even more unpleasant than the ice. Taken with his fellow prisoners to the city slave market he was bought by a Captain of the Janissaries. Within a few months of the purchase the Janissary was killed at the Seige of Gran, and after five months Wild found himself the servant of a Persian miser. 'He was an unmerciful dog, who did nothing but beat me, persecute me and humiliate me.' After a year together in Constantinople the unlikely couple sailed to Egypt to take the Haj caravan to Mecca.

The swarming mass of twenty thousand pilgrims leaving Cairo were to take a hundred thousand camels with them. The pilgrims must have looked out across the desert with all the optimism of the passengers on the *Titanic*. Each camel carried a tarred goatskin full of water: a hundred thousand waterskins. The camels were tied in lines, nose to tail. There were a hundred Mamelukes and six cannon in the escort. But there was a drought. The waterholes were dry. The camels collapsed with thirst, splitting the waterskins under their weight as they rolled over. Half way across the Sinai Desert the pilgrims began to panic. By the time the demented survivors arrived at Aquaba almost two thousand had died. The plain of the Hejaz, which they now faced, offered no relief. All the way the pathetic remnants of the once-proud caravan were attacked by Bedouin. Near Yanbo 'my master was wounded with an arrow, but the Devil would not take him all together, though I wish he had'. Johann Wild had witnessed the greatest caravan disaster of the century.

They arrived in Mecca where they spent twenty days, while the Persian recovered from his wounds. Wild, always more interested in people than in places, was most impressed by the procession to Arafat. 'You should see the stately way the people of Mecca marched to the mountain, their camels'

Left: *The slave market of the Orient, unchanged since Wild and Pitts passed through in the seventeenth century.*

flanks hanging with carpets, and the women and camel drivers singing all along the road.' Recovered from his wounds, the Persian miser took Wild to Jeddah where they embarked on a trading mission to Abyssinia. They returned via Jerusalem, where the Persian was so offended by Wild's interest in Christian rather than Moslem shrines that he sold him. Wild's new master was a kindly old Turk who gave him his freedom. In 1611 Wild was back in Nuremberg.

Alas, of the three non-Moslems who penetrated Mecca in the seventeenth century, the strangest is the one we know least about. He was an ex-Brahmin, born in Goa, called Mateo de Castro, who was converted to catholicism and ordained a bishop in Rome. Returning to Rome after quarrelling with his diocese in India, he visited Mecca in 1643. What he had quarrelled about, and how he – a Catholic bishop – had got into Mecca and what he observed there, are either lost or hidden in the archives of the Vatican. We are never likely to know.

None of the travellers since Varthema had come back with more than vague tales. No more was really known about Arabia than what Varthema had already written. It was not until the end of the century that a European traveller was to gather more detailed information.

Joseph Pitts, who combined all the natural and supernatural prejudices of the West Country Dissenter that he was, went to sea at fifteen on the merchantman *Speedwell*. When they were captured by corsairs off the coast of Spain, the terrified boy cried out to the captain:

'Oh, Master, I am afraid they will kill us and eat us.'

'No, no, child,' the captain assured him, 'they will carry us to Algiers and sell us.'

The captain proved right and the day after their arrival they were taken before the *dey*, who chose one-eighth for himself as the traditional customs duty. The rest, including Pitts, were taken to the slave market. Here the unfortunate boy was bought by a profligate and debauched Captain of Horse. The Captain, determined to atone for his sins by converting the Christian slave, beat the lad mercilessly.

After months of beatings the exasperated Captain gave up on Pitts. First he sent him back to sea in a corsair, then he sold him. Pitts ended up in Tunis where, walking through the streets in his European clothes, he met the British consul. When his new master had no further use for him and put him on the market, the consul managed to raise three hundred dollars for his release. The owner would accept nothing less than five hundred and sold him elsewhere. Not only was he still a slave, but his new owner was the very same Captain of Horse, who had rebought him in order to continue his efforts at conversion. Pitts burst into tears. 'I roared out to feel the pain of his cruel strokes, but the more I cried out the more furiously he laid on, and to stop the noise of my crying, would stamp with his feet in my mouth.'

Pitts finally gave in. 'Overcome with terror and pain I spoke the words, holding up the forefinger of my right hand.' He was utterly dejected. A day or so later, to make it all worse, the first letter from his father reached him. Keep close to God and never deny Him, the father urged, adding that he would rather hear that his son had died than that he had renounced his faith. God be merciful to sinners, Pitts prayed. Clearly God was, for suddenly Pitt's master was arrested for plotting to overthrow the *dey* and executed. Pitts was sold to a benevolent old gentleman who took him to Mecca for the Haj.

The first stage took them by sea to Egypt. The young Dissenter was unimpressed by the Egyptians. They 'scold like whores, but seldom care to fight', and were 'much addicted to the cursed and unnatural sin of sodomy'. From Egypt they went by sea to Jeddah (in easy stages because of the poor health of Pitts' master) and from there they rode two days by camel to Mecca.

> It was a sight indeed, able to pierce one's heart, to behold so many thousands in their garments of humility and mortification, with their naked heads, and cheeks watered with tears; and to hear their grievous sighs and sobs, begging earnestly for the remission of their sins.[5]

The city itself was so hot that people ran from one side of the street to the other to avoid the sun's rays. At night the population either slept on their roofs or took their beds out onto the street. Pitts slept on an open roof, covering himself with a damp cloth which he had to resoak in water every few hours.

Among the Hajis Pitts met was an Irishman who had been taken into slavery so young that he had not only lost his religion, but his language too. After thirty years of slavery on French and Spanish galleys, he had gone to Algiers rather than return to Ireland and renounce his faith. He was looked on by the other pilgrims as a great zealot, and once told Pitts that he felt God had delivered him from Hell into Heaven. 'I admired much his zeal but pitied his condition.'

Pitts, his old master (who had given Pitts his freedom in Mecca) and the Irishman left Mecca on the Cairo-bound caravan, Pitts complaining that the cost of renting camels was so high he ought to have been able to buy them. The first day was total confusion; gradually order was established, the caravan dividing into separate companies, each with its own emblem. Many of the camels carried bells on their necks and ankles that jangled as they walked, the goatskin water containers hanging from the sides of the camels flopping more loudly the emptier they got. Each night camels died, their flesh distributed to the poorer pilgrims; and always there were the Bedouin, ready to rob.

> When they see the Haji fast asleep (for it is usual for them to sleep on the road), they loose a camel before and behind, and one of the thieves leads it away with the Haji upon its back asleep. Another of them, in the meantime, pulls on the next camel to tie it to the camel from whence the halter of the other was cut; for if that camel be not fastened again to the leading camel, it will stop, and all that are behind will then stop of course, which might be the means of discovering the robbers. When they have gotten the stolen camel, with his rider, at a convenient distance from the caravan, and think themselves out of danger, they awake the Haji, and sometimes destroy him immediately; but at other times, being a little more inclined to mercy, they strip him naked, and let him return to the caravan.[6]

After ten more days the caravan arrived in Medina, where Pitts inspected the Prophet's tomb and his 'patroon' had a silk handkerchief stolen. They continued to Aquaba where many camels fell on the steep slopes, never to rise

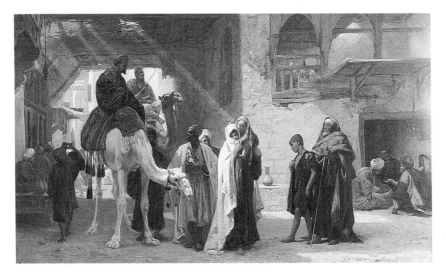

Left: *Detail from 'Mecca Pilgrims Passing Through the Bazaar at Suez' by Frederick Goodall, painted in 1864, the year of Guarmani's visit to Arabia. (Mathaf Gallery, London)*

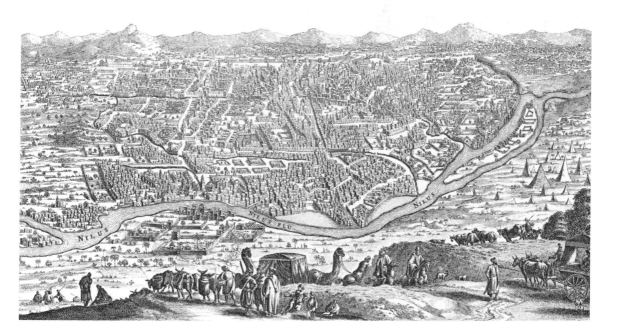

Above: Cairo in 1670,
*about the time of Pitt's
visit.*

again. Seven days before Cairo the caravan was met by friends and relatives of the Hajis, standing by the side of the way, yelling names at the thousands of undistinguishable shapes passing by in the night. Four days later the pilgrims were refreshed by Nile water, brought by camel to the caravan. The closer they got to Cairo the more people came out to meet them. Soon it was a triumphal procession. The journey from Mecca was over. It had taken forty days, 'and in all this way there is scarcely any green thing to be met with, nor beast, nor fowl to be seen or heard; nothing but sand and stones, excepting one place which we passed through the night. . . where were some trees, and, we thought, gardens'.

Passing through Alexandria on their way back to Algiers, Pitts met a seaman from an English ship who was an old schoolfriend. Pitts was anxious to escape, but although he was no longer a slave, any suspicion that he was going to renounce his new religion would send him straight back to slavery, and possibly death. Besides, he could not trust the Moslem Irishman. He did, however, manage to pass on a letter to his family, together with a Turkish pipe for his father and a silk purse for his mother.

Pitts returned to Algiers and lived with his 'patroon' for six years. The old man treated him kindly, even indicating that he would leave the Englishman 'something considerable at his death', but still Pitts yearned to return to his home in England.

His chance came when the Turkish Sultan asked for naval volunteers to go to Smyrna. Pitts joined them in the hope of being captured by a Christian vessel. In Smyrna he met a fellow West Countryman, Eliot, whom he had known as a boy. Dressed up by Eliot like a gentleman, complete with swinging cane, he openly walked onto a French ship whose captain had been bribed four pounds for his troubles. A year later, after almost going back to slavery when he was press-ganged into the Royal Navy on his first day back in England, Pitts returned to his native Exeter, and remained there, hardly leaving the town, for the next forty years.

Carsten Niebuhr
im 76ten Lebensjahre.

II

THE PIONEERS

Varthema's, le Blanc's and Pitts' concepts of the desert as a place to cross but never linger, and of the Bedouin as 'skulking thievish Arabs', in Pitts' words, were typical of the age. They were also a pretty accurate reflection of how most Moslems saw the desert and the Bedouin. They were the prejudices of townspeople, sophisticated enough to despise without being so sophisticated that they began to romanticize. Within a hundred years this view of Arabia was to change radically.

It was the Age of Enlightenment in Europe. Freed from the bigotry of the Inquisition and not yet corrupted by the racial arrogance of imperialism, the study of Arabic had come out of the cloisters and into the universities. In 1632 the first Professorship of Arabic was created at Cambridge. Historical texts were becoming available for the first time; and just as medieval European writers glorified in the nostalgia of knightly virtues, so medieval Arab writers glorified in the nostalgia of Bedouin virtues. George Sale – whose 1734 translation of the Koran is still one of the most beautiful renderings in English – informed his readers that the Bedouin had 'preserved their liberty . . . with little interruption, from the very Deluge'. No longer skulking and thievish, the Bedouin had become the model for all men.

The two men who, more than any others, were responsible for this never met any real Bedouin and never entered the great deserts of Arabia. Their excursion to the peninsula was confined to a tiny corner in the south-west. Yet their findings were to be of such vital importance that Palgrave was to call Niebuhr 'the intelligence and courage that first opened Arabia to Europe'.

Left: *Carsten Niebuhr in later life, parish clerk of Dithmaschen in Heligoland Bay, where he finally found the 'tranquillity of the Orient' just thirty miles from where he was born.*

Their names were Peter Forsskal and Carsten Niebuhr. They could not have been more different. Forsskal, a brilliant botanist from Sweden forced into exile for his political ideals, was lofty, haughty and learned, utterly convinced of his own righteousness. Niebuhr, a Dane who worked as a farmhand in Friesland until the age of twenty-one when he went to school and then university to study mathematics and astronomy, was unsure of himself, down-to earth and revelled in anonymity. His only cultural accomplishment was that he played the violin. Until he met Peter Forsskal he had no political views; but then, until he met Peter Forsskal he had never dreamed.

Forsskal, a year older than Niebuhr, was regarded as the rising star of the Scandinavian Enlightenment, a budding Montesquieu. He had entered the University of Uppsala at the age of thirteen, and within three years wrote essays in Hebrew. From Uppsala he studied first botany under the celebrated Linnaeus, then theology, philosophy and Oriental philology under Michaelis at Göttingen. He became a corresponding member of the German Academy of Science at twenty-four.

He returned to Uppsala the intellectual celebrity of Sweden, and wrote a powerful critique of the monarchy: *Thoughts on Civil Liberty*. Liberty, he declared, was dearer than anything else save life itself. The greatest defence against tyranny were the freedoms to complain and to withdraw your consent: two freedoms Forsskal made much exasperating use of during his short and stormy career. When the Swedish authorities forbade its publication on the grounds that it was revolutionary, Forsskal had five hundred copies secretly printed and distributed them himself, challenging the government to arrest him. Forsskal was not arrested, the incident was forgotten and the book was almost forgotten. But the ideas contained within it were to have a profound effect on Carsten Niebuhr, who took them as dogma.

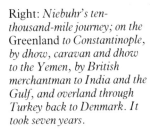

Right: *Niebuhr's ten-thousand-mile journey; on the* Greenland *to Constantinople, by dhow, caravan and dhow to the Yemen, by British merchantman to India and the Gulf, and overland through Turkey back to Denmark. It took seven years.*

Left: *Baurenfeind's engraving of the Danish man-of-war,* Greenland, *in Marseilles on its way to Constantinople, with Baurenfeind himself in the foreground sketching the scene. On his left Forsskal is examining a plant and on his right Niebuhr, surveying the landscape.*

Right: *Detail from 'A Desert Scout' painted by R. G. Talbot Kelly in 1902. By then the Bedouin of Arabia were the only uncolonized Arabs left. No longer threatening, they were already becoming mere figures in a landscape. (Mathaf Gallery, London)*

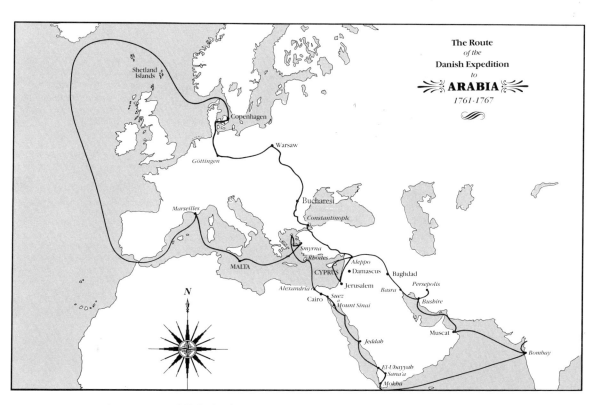

The Route
of the
Danish Expedition
to
ARABIA
1761-1767

Niebuhr lived and Forsskal died, and it was Niebuhr who came back to Europe with Forsskal's concept of the Bedouin. 'Liberty, independence and simplicity', Niebuhr wrote. They could have been Peter Forsskal's own words bout the ideal citizen, and they had such influence that within a few years Edward Gibbon was to write:

> The slaves of domestic tyranny may vainly exult in their national independence; but the Arab is personally free; and he enjoys, in some degree, the benefits of society, without forfeiting the prerogatives of nature. . . . If the Arabian princes abuse their power, they are quickly punished by the desertion of their subjects, who had been accustomed to a mild and parental jurisdiction. Their spirit is free, their steps are unconfined, the desert is open, and the tribes and families are held together by a mutual and voluntary compact.[1]

The two men came together in the office of J. H. E. Bernstorff, the Danish Foreign Minister. Bernstorff had chosen them to be part of a scientific expedition to Arabia, which he saw as a way of enhancing the reputation of the King of Denmark, Frederich V. Bernstorff's guiding light was the learned Michaelis, one of the first 'Orientalists'. The purpose of the expedition was to answer the hundreds of questions thinking men were asking about 'the Orient', which was still at that time a place which had not yet been corrupted by the Romantics into a state of mind. The list of questions Forsskal and Niebuhr took with them ran to 235 pages, ranging from whether the circumcised gained more pleasure than the uncircumcised and local proofs of virginity to details on the tides in the Red Sea, the existence of mermaids and social attitudes towards spitting.

At first Niebuhr was unimpressed with Forsskal, and regarded his insistence that all members of the expedition should be equals as pretentious and irrelevant. He considered Forsskal to be opinionated. Over the next few weeks they met the other members of the expedition. Two of them, Georg Wilhelm Baurenfeind, an artist from Nuremberg who avoided all disputes by immersing himself in his work, and Christian Carl Kramer, an unfortunately lazy Danish doctor who was to assist Forsskal, were the most easy-going of men. The third was a disaster. Supposedly a philologist, Friedrich Christian von Haven was unstable, aristocratic, argumentative and ambitious. Forsskal wanted to take a fellow Swede and student of Linnaeus as his assistant, but by this time Kramer had already been appointed. Accompanying them as servant was an old Danish trooper, Berggren.

While Forsskal, Niebuhr, Baurenfeind and Kramer spent 1760 preparing for their journey, von Haven took himself off to Paris and Rome, allegedly to study Arabic. Niebuhr, more quietly, was learning it in Germany. His modesty and commonsense impressed the Danish Foreign Minister. When Niebuhr, map-maker and surveyor, had a special astrolabe made to calculate longitudes, Bernstorff had to insist that Niebuhr claim for it on expenses. He appointed Niebuhr treasurer, in the hope that this would head off the inevitable clash between Forsskal and von Haven, and raised the status of this most self-effacing of men by commissioning him in the Danish Army with the rank of Lieutenant of Engineers.

Below: *D'Anville's 1755 map of Arabia, printed a decade before the Scandinavian expedition, was gradually corrected over the next two hundred years.*

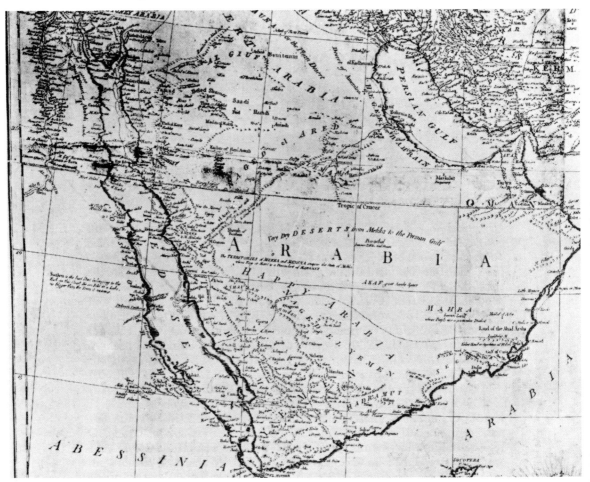

Right: *Alexandria, one of the Mediterranean's most thriving sea-ports when the Scandinavians arrived in 1761.*

Von Haven returned from Rome and was furious when he heard that Forsskal's insistence that all should be equal had been accepted. As first chosen, and the oldest Dane, he had assumed that he would be leader. When the party left Copenhagen on 4 January 1761 on the Danish man-of-war *Greenland* von Haven refused to travel with the rest and went overland to Marseilles. The others travelled as equals; all except one, the long-suffering Berggren. Forsskal's fine and noble sentiments about liberty may have applied to the Bedouin, but they did not yet apply to Swedish servants.

Beyond Marseilles relations between von Haven and the others reached such a low ebb that in Constantinople von Haven bought enough arsenic 'to serve as the last meal for a couple of regiments', in Forsskal's words. Niebuhr was convinced that von Haven was going to kill them all.

They arrived in Alexandria expecting to spend only a few months in Egypt. They were there a year. The 'natives' were very obliging, and when Baurenfeind expressed to his host in Cairo his wish to draw a circumcised girl, the host clapped his hands and summoned an eighteen-year-old slave girl for Baurenfeind to draw. Even the Bedouin were civil: when they robbed Forsskal while he was collecting botanical specimens they thoughtfully left him his underpants. Niebuhr also found the 'natives' obliging, and he would dress in Arab costume and disappear into the back streets of Cairo and Alexandria on long Orwellian journeys, integrating himself with the humble humanity with which he identified and observing the city with the freedom of the insignificant.

To pass the time they hired troupes of dancing girls, bare-faced and bare-breasted, which were drawn by Baurenfeind.

Below: *Baurenfeind's drawing of the Egyptian dancing girls.*

> At first we did not find any particular pleasure in watching them, both because the instruments and the vocal music were very poor, and because the women assumed all kinds of highly indecent postures; and although to begin with we found them all equally ugly, with their yellow hands, blood-red nails, black and blue jewellery round their ears, ankles, necks and nostrils and vile-smelling hair; and although their voices were awful, we ended up thinking they were the finest singers and dancers in all of Europe.[2]

Alas, even in their happiest moments their joy was marred by their fears of von Haven and his arsenic. 'More than once', wrote Niebuhr, 'he has been in the kitchen just before dinner and suddenly left to dine with some French businessman. You can imagine what our appetites were like after that.'

After a year in Alexandria and Cairo they left for Suez by caravan. It was August 1762, the hottest time of year. The caravan of some four hundred camels was carrying shipbuilding material, including a complete anchor hanging from a wooden beam carried by four camels. All the expedition rode horses, except Niebuhr who, significantly, took a camel. Once at night they heard a shot, and both Forsskal and Niebuhr drew their guns. There were no bandits: it was the great Haj caravan returning from Mecca.

Four days after leaving Cairo they arrived in Suez. They spent a month there, mainly for the benefit of von Haven whose main task was to study Arabic manuscripts and biblical inscriptions on Mount Sinai. He failed at every turn. He was unable even to get into the library of St Catherine's monastery on Sinai and so missed the *Codex Sinaiticus*, then unread by western eyes – because he had neglected to ask the Greek Orthodox bishop in Cairo for a letter of introduction.

They set sail for Jeddah on 8 October in a dhow. The dhow towed three more behind it, forming not so much a convoy as a floating caravan, one carrying horses, another sheep, while the third was a boatload of prostitutes, who kept up a brisk trade with the pilgrim ship throughout the voyage. The dhow on which the Scandinavians sailed held six hundred passengers, a crew of seventy-two and a captain who needed brandy to steady his nautical eye. The decks were packed with passengers, enterprising merchants setting up their stalls on the forecastle. The best cabins, including the one below the Danes and Swedes, were reserved for entire harems on their way to Mecca.

All good things come to an end. As the Arabian coast came into sight the ship's guns fired off in celebration of the safe voyage, lanterns were hoisted on the rigging and a collection was taken by the passengers for the captain. Jeddah itself had hardly changed since ibn Battuta visited it four hundred years earlier, and hardly changed one hundred and fifty years later when Lawrence wrote of the town hanging 'between the blazing sun and its reflection in the mirage which swept and rolled over the wide lagoon', and described as Elizabethan half-timbers gone mad the houses with their fantastically wrought balconies where women could see without being seen.

Above: *St Catherine's Monastery, Sinai, where von Haven failed to discover the* Codex Sinaiticus.

Right: *Detail from 'Suez', by David Roberts, where Niebuhr and Forsskal first saw the Red Sea and secured the dhow that took them to Jeddah.*

Left: *Baurenfeind's engraving of the expedition's dhow off Jeddah.*

David Roberts R.A.

Left: *The 'floating coffee hold', Baurenfeind's impression of the ship that took the members of the expedition on their last lap to the Yemen.*

They were well received, Niebuhr setting up his astrolabe in the Pasha's palace, mapping the town, visiting Eve's grave and studying the local peasant economy. When the Pasha, believing Niebuhr could foresee the future, asked him to judge which of his servants had stolen two hundred ducats, the Frieslander demurred. So the Pasha lined his servants up and gave each a piece of paper to swallow, announcing that the guilty one would be unable to do it. Sure enough there was one who could not swallow. He duly confessed.

The rest did little. Forsskal collected seeds and information on political economy which he proceeded to use against the right-wing von Haven with all the intellectual subtlety of a double-handed sword. Von Haven, isolated and depressed, did not bother to fight back. He was a broken reed. Baurenfeind passed his time drawing, while Kramer did nothing; he had not even sent any letters or reports back to Denmark during the course of the expedition. Even the animosity of Forsskal and the others for von Haven was fading away under the blazing sun. They were learning to accept each other, like cell-mates.

The boat that took them from Jeddah was the most ridiculous of vessels: not so much a ship as a tub, a floating hold for coffee beans with a mast on top, which was returning to Mokha empty to pick another cargo of coffee. The captain and his nine-man crew were clad only in loincloths and turbans. The tub regularly stopped on the coast to trade with the Bedouin, affording Peter Forsskal his first glimpse of his political ideal. On Christmas Eve 1762 the Scandinavians landed at el-Uhayyah in north Yemen.

Their first taste of Arabia Felix was happy. A merchant lent them a house and the Emir sent them a sheep and an apology for not coming in person to meet them. The Emir was no stranger to Europeans. Coffee traders had landed at the port and he was a master of that Arab virtue of long-suffering politeness to Europeans. His politeness even survived the events in the customs house next morning when Forsskal – never the most tactful of men – wanted to demonstrate his microscope and asked the good gentleman for a louse. The Emir quietly pointed out that he was not in the habit of carrying such things about his person, but found a lesser official who was able to oblige. Under the microscope the louse was so large that the lesser official remarked that it must be a European louse since Arab lice were never so big. Forsskal gave him a four *stuiver* tip. The next day a man rushed up to Forsskal with a whole handful of lice, offering them at only one *stuiver* each.

Niebuhr's telescope caused equal astonishment. He directed the telescope, which showed everything upside-down, at a woman walking across the market. The Arabs were so amazed to see the woman upside-down, with her clothes still as normal and not falling about her head, that they cried '*Allah akbar!*' (God is great).

Right: *Niebuhr's plan of Sana'a. The old part of the city has hardly changed and is still recognizable today.*

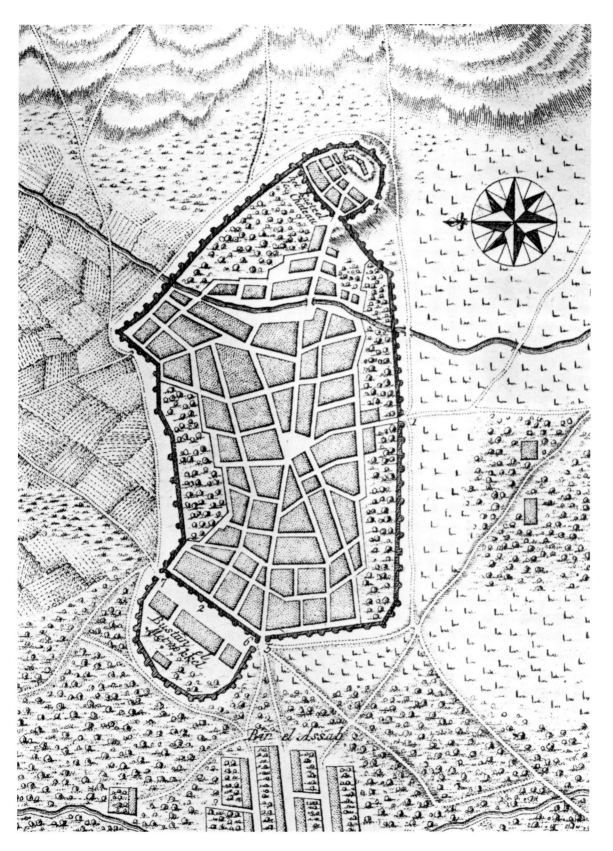

In the six weeks they spent in el-Uhayyah each immersed himself in the Yemen in his own way: Baurenfeind drawing, Kramer hiring a porter to keep away the patients, Forsskal investigating the market here, condemning the legal principle of blood vengeance there, discovering a new plant somewhere else, and Niebuhr map-making. Even von Haven became positive. 'Finally we have arrived in Arabia Felix,' he wrote. 'We found a well-ordered country and have been received most favourably.'[3]

In the evenings Niebuhr and Baurenfeind played the violins and the inhabitants sat outside listening. They liked the sad tunes most of all, observed Niebuhr.

Sadly for Kramer, who was clearly one of those men created by God to pass their lives doing absolutely nothing, his talents as a doctor were much in demand. Crowds gathered outside his house every morning and the man had to exert himself to impossible limits to avoid seeing them. One elderly man, who boasted of deflowering eighty-eight slave girls, asked Kramer for a cure for impotence. Kramer was unable to help: nor could he cure a stallion which the Emir sent to him a few days later suffering from the same problem. The day was saved by Berggren, who had served in the cavalry in the war against Prussia and knew a thing or two about horses.

It was such a happy land. They were always made welcome, never molested. By the time they left they had grown genuinely fond of the Emir, who had 'the polite dignity of the nobleman and the strict integrity and candid compassion of a true friend of the human race'.[4]

Their parting gifts were the telescope and a clock. The clock caused some concern since no Yemeni had ever handled one before, but a merchant from Cairo, who had some experience of clocks, volunteered to wind it up each day. Next morning, as they were preparing to leave, a beautiful white stallion was presented to them: a modest offering to the King of Denmark from the Emir of el-Uhayyah.

Left: *Baurenfeind's sketch of the coffee hills near Mokha in the Yemen, 1763.*

Right: *The first detailed map of the Yemen: Carsten Niebuhr's survey, with Beit el-Fakih, from where the expedition radiated like the roads, as his centre.*

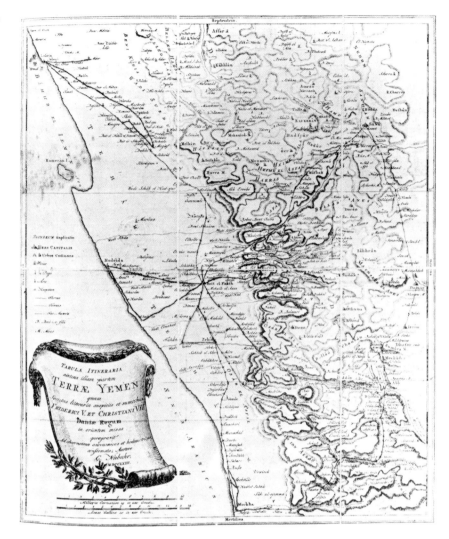

Travelling south down the Tihamah, the hot narrow plain squashed between the mountains and the sea, the Scandinavians on donkeys and their baggage on camels, they stopped after five days at Beit el-Fakih. It was the most central spot in the Tihamah, with roads radiating to Sana'a, the capital, in the east; Taizz, the Yemen's second city, to the south east; Mokha, the Red Sea port that gave its name to a coffee, to the south; el-Hudaydah to the west and el-Uhayyah to the north. The expedition radiated like the roads: Baurenfeind drawing the women in the coffee regions on the mountains, von Haven attending to social calls, Kramer avoiding his patients, Forsskal exploring the mountains for plants and political utopias, and Niebuhr mapping and watching.

Niebuhr visited most of western Yemen to make his map. These journeys were undertaken riding a donkey and dressed as a poor peasant. 'My travelling clothes consisted only of a turban, a cloak, a coat, linen trousers and a pair of slippers. . . . An old rug served me as saddle blanket in the daytime, a chair and table in the evening and a bed at night.'[5] Sometimes he passed his nights in a *mokkaia*, a coffee hut; sometimes in an inn where he slept on benches and in the morning drank milk so thick that it hung from his lips after he had taken the bowl away.

Left: *Niebuhr's view of Taizz from the north-west, with the road on the left leading to Sana'a and the one on the right to Mokha. Behind stands Mount Sabr which, the Yemenis claimed, was covered with every flower in the world.*

On one of these long expeditions, to Taizz, he took Forsskal, who in the months they had spent together had become Niebuhr's mentor. Unlike Niebuhr, Forsskal had no facility in talking to ordinary people. The two felt they needed each other. It is not difficult to picture them on their donkeys, Niebuhr always observing, Forsskal always talking. The landlady of one *mokkaia* they encountered believed them to be Holy Men and asked to be remembered in their prayers.

And so the days to Taizz passed, and the days back. We cannot be certain of the details of the political philosophy Forsskal expounded over the uncomfortable hours on the donkeys, but we can get a pretty good idea by reading Niebuhr's own description of the Bedouin political system. Their poverty was voluntary, the willing price they paid for their freedom, which is guaranteed by their right to change their allegiance from one ruler to another by voting with their feet. 'Uncomfortably lodged, indifferently fed, ill-clothed and destitute of almost all the conveniences of life', but free.

Some days out from Taizz, on their return to Beit el-Fakih, Forsskal interrupted his monologue with a shout of joy. In front of his eyes was the famed Mecca balsam tree. It had been presented to the Queen of Sheba by Solomon, Cleopatra had introduced it to Egypt, its bark had great healing qualities and Forsskal was the first western botanist to identify it. He took a cutting to send to his professor of botany, Linnaeus. The old man had told Forsskal that his one remaining ambition was to see the Mecca balsam tree before he died.

By the time the branch arrived at Uppsala it had withered. So had the man who had sent it. He was not the first to go, however. Niebuhr complained to Forsskal about headaches and shivering. When the two got back to Beit el-Fakih they found von Haven seriously ill. They thought it was just a cold and the whole group decided to go on to Mokha. What they did not know was that Niebuhr and von Haven were suffering from malaria. Nor did they know that in summer the Tihamah reaches temperatures over 110°F (45°C), and it was already late spring.

For four days they rode through the Tihamah, Forsskal and Niebuhr travelling by day, collecting plants and surveying, the rest following by night. For Niebuhr and von Haven, suffering from malaria, the journey was agony. When they reached Mokha they were firmly told that Jews and Christians were forbidden to ride in the town. The whole party had to walk. It was an inauspicious beginning.

Once inside they learnt that three English merchants were in town, but they did not introduce themselves to the merchants for fear of being taken for vagabonds. Instead they rented a house from a helpful Yemeni, Ismael Salech, whom they had met in Jeddah. Before the evening was over, but too late to alter their arrangements, they discovered that the helpful Yemeni was a confidence trickster.

The next day was worse. At the customs house the town *dola* and the customs officials insisted on examining Forsskal's collection. A bottle containing a preserved fish was opened. It had been inadequately preserved. Rotting fish and alcohol flowed all over the floor. The alcohol was bad enough, but when the customs officials found bottles containing preserved snakes they were convinced that they had uncovered an evil Christian conspiracy which was intent on killing Moslems.

Below: *Baurenfeind's sketch of Beit el-Fakih.*

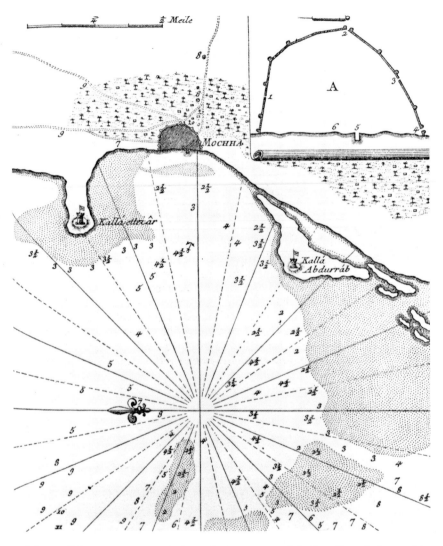

Left: *Niebuhr's map of the coffee port of Mokha, showing where von Haven was buried just to the left (north) of the town (Fig. 7).*

News of the outrage spread through the town and, before Forsskal was able to explain that the snakes were dead, Berggren raced in to tell them that their house was being ransacked by a furious mob. They rushed off, carrying the failing von Haven with them, pursued by the angry, jeering inhabitants. Finally the town's *kadi* took pity on them, stood guarantor and found them a house. Even then they had to pay four months' double rent in advance. The following day the English merchants heard of their plight – and invited them to dinner. The *dola* and the Englishmen were on friendly terms, and it was the English who advised the newcomers that, to get what they wanted, they only needed to pay the *dola* a hefty bribe. Niebuhr, who as treasurer should have undertaken the assignment, refused.

Peter Forsskal, a champion of liberty and enemy of despotic government, now took over. So fearlessly did he present himself before the *dola*, so small did he make the *dola* feel, that next morning the expedition received two sheep, a sack of rice and the polite request for Herr Kramer to attend the *dola*, who had accidentally shot himself in the foot.

When a poor unfortunate, unaware of the *dola*'s change of attitude, abused Forsskal in the street, Forsskal had to use all his influence again to get the man released from the *dola*'s prison.

The winds of change did little to help von Haven. By 25 April he was dying. 'In the course of the day he grew weaker and weaker,' wrote Niebuhr, 'and at eight o'clock his pulse appeared to have stopped. We opened a vein and he revived a little. An hour later he wrote his will. . . . He began to talk wildly and confusedly, sometimes in Arabic, sometimes French, Italian, German, Danish. Then he fell into a deep sleep, or rather faint. At about ten o'clock he died.' Forsskal, never one to mince words, added: 'His death has made the expedition incomparably easier. He had a very difficult nature.'[6]

The remaining members of the expedition, so often united against von Haven, were now divided among themselves. Some wanted to go up to Sana'a, others to go home in one of the three English ships that would be leaving in about two months' time. In the end they decided to race to Sana'a and be back before the ships left. Like so many compromises it was a disaster.

They left at sunset on 9 June, Niebuhr determining the route by astronomical observations. After two days they were in the mountains where the roads became too dangerous for travelling by night. Up in the mountains the temperature dropped, the villages were frequent and at night they slept in the security and comfort of caravanserais. After four days they reached Taizz.

The *dola* with whom they had an audience seemed uncooperative: he had heard rumours from Mokha of whole chestfuls of snakes. He was also something of a miser. When a beggar prayed at the tomb of a local saint renowned for his generosity, a hand came out of the grave with a letter asking the *dola* to pay the bearer one hundred crowns. The *dola* honoured the note, but built a high wall around the tomb to ensure it would never happen again.

Below: *'Refreshments in an Arab street' (1902), R. G. Talbot Kelly's romanticized view of the townsfolk in the Arab world. (Mathaf Gallery, London)*

The *dola* directed them to a house whose owner had been conveniently put into prison and sent them two sheep. In return Niebuhr sent him a roll of Indian linen. Berggren took it round to the *dola*, but was stopped by the porter at the gate who would not let him by without receiving a tip. The quick-witted Berggren asked if it was normal for one servant to tip another, and when this was confirmed added that then he was the one who should be getting the tip for bringing the linen. Unlike his more illustrious and better-educated masters, Berggren got by without paying. From the window of their house Forsskal stared out every day at Mount Sabr, the exotic hill above the town, reputed by Yemenis to be covered with all the flowers in the world. He applied to the *dola* for permission to visit it, but the *dola* refused. The mountain was in the territory of a hostile tribe and the *dola*'s soldiers would not venture on it. If Forsskal visited it and was killed, the *dola* would be in trouble with the Imam in Sana'a, and if he visited it and lived the *dola* would be the laughing stock of Taizz.

After constant pressure the *dola* relented and gave Forsskal permission, but as Forsskal and Niebuhr were packing they received another order from the *dola* that they were to return to Mokha. Forsskal protested. Two days passed. If they were to reach Sana'a and return before the English ships sailed, they would have to leave immediately. Then their departure was delayed: the *dola* was expecting a leaving present. Forsskal refused. Convinced of his own righteousness he went to the local judge, the *kadi*. The *kadi* took his side and wrote to the *dola*. The letter contained only one sentence. 'Do not show greed to these men, they are our guests.'

Below: *A Turkish caravanserai in the eighteenth century, far grander and more baroque than anything Niebuhr would have come across in the Yemen. The principle, however, was the same in all of them. At night the caravans came in to rest and the gates were locked until morning when the caravans departed to the next caravanserai en route.*

Right: *Niebuhr's Yerim, sketched from the window of the room where they sat for three days while Forsskal was dying.*

The next morning as the expedition packed to leave Forsskal collapsed with malaria. The others were prepared to stay but Forsskal insisted on leaving. They set out at sunset. By the next day Forsskal's pains were so intense that he could no longer sit upright on a donkey. The others were weakening too. On the fourth day they travelled no more than four miles. That night they reached the caravanserai at Mensil. After a day's rest they split into two groups: Niebuhr and Baurenfeind going ahead, and Kramer and Berggren coming behind with Forsskal. Niebuhr's condition was hardly suitable for going ahead. There was so little water available that he was unable even to rinse his mouth out between vomits. He and Baurenfeind arrived at Yerim and waited for the others to appear. They came at sunset, Forsskal lashed to a camel's hump, his face blue, his words incoherent, vomit still sticking to the camel's sides.

They tried to rest at the caravanserai but the crowds were so curious and pressing that they were forced to find a house to rent. Niebuhr went from door to door pleading. By the time they found a house the population was throwing stones.

For three days they remained cooped up in the house with the dying Forsskal. Eventually Niebuhr could take it no more. He slipped out in the clothes of a beggar and wandered the streets and the market, passed the local circumciser who doubled as surgeon and the tailors, sitting cross-legged on the pavement plying their trade. When he returned late in the evening Forsskal had gone into a coma. He died next morning. 'He was the most learned man in the whole expedition,' Niebuhr later told his son, 'and if he had lived he might have been the most learned man in Europe.'

As a botanist his death had been almost in vain. Most of his specimens had either been wrecked at the Mokha customs house, deteriorated through neglect or withered in time like the balsam branch. All that remained was a single plant, which Linnaeus described as 'tenacious, wild, obstinate and angular'. He called this *Forsskalea*; it was a species of stinging nettle.

One more tribute came to the author of *Thoughts on Civil Liberty*. It came from the *kadi* at Taizz, and was a letter of introduction that Forsskal had in his pocket to the Imam of Sana'a. Like the *kadi*'s earlier letter to the *dola* it contained only one simple sentence: 'Believe no evil in this man.'

Unable to give him a Christian burial, the others arranged for him to be carried at dead of night by six coolies, in a coffin put together by Berggren. Terrified at the thought of burying a Christian, the coolies ran after sinking him only a few feet into the ground. A week later, after the others had left, the coffin was dug up by grave-robbers, thinking it held treasure. When the *dola* ordered a local Jew to rebury the Christian, the Jew refused without payment. The *dola* told him he could have the coffin.

When the rest of the party left Yerim on 13 July they were so weak that Niebuhr was the only effective one among them. After two days on the road Berggren was so sick he had to be left behind: something that Forsskal would never have done. The monsoons had come and raging thirst gave way to perpetual dampness. Their clothes were drenched and they could hardly ride. On 16 July the rains stopped and the sun came through. They passed farms and orchards, hamlets and villages. By afternoon the hamlets and villages seemed to merge together. They had reached Seijan, the suburbs of Sana'a.

Above: *Sana'a in the early twentieth century, unchanged since Niebuhr's day. Many of the buildings are still there.*

They were welcomed by the Imam's chief scribe. He told them that they had been long expected, and although the Imam was unable to receive them for two days (he was having a little difficulty paying his mercenaries), a house was at their disposal and they could stay as long as they liked.

For the next two days Niebuhr, Baurenfeind and Kramer ate and slept. The house had its own garden, an Arab garden overflowing with fruit and fountains, a place for shade rather than a place for walking. But they were frustrated by the delay (etiquette prevented them going out into the streets until they had been received by the Imam) and depressed by their double standards over Berggren. Suddenly at the end of the second day there was a commotion outside. They rushed out. It was Berggren. Refusing to die he had followed the others, stumbling along the road from one mountain village to another. The very sight of him terrified the villagers who, frightened that he would die in their village, sent him on. In one village he had been given a donkey to hasten him on his way.

Next morning the chief scribe took them on to the palace. The audience hall was a vast courtyard with an arched roof. The floor was covered in carpets and packed with courtiers. In the middle was a fountain and behind the fountain the Imam sat crosslegged on a throne of three silk cushions. Close by him, as always, was a small silver casket of amulets, which was believed to have the power to make him invisible. On his right sat his sons, on his left his brothers, and in front of him stood the Grand Vizier. One by one the Europeans were led up to the Imam to kiss the palm of his hand.

The dialect of the Yemeni aristocracy was markedly different from that of the Tihamah peasants and Niebuhr had to hire an interpreter. He told the Imam that they were on their way to the Danish East Indies, and hearing of the 'rich and ordered government of the Imam of Yemen' decided to visit the country on the way. The Imam was pleased. There followed what had become a travelling road show and the Imam's court was treated to such spectacles as people enlarged and walking upside down, needles that pointed perpetually at the North Star and gigantic lice.

Right: *Carsten Niebuhr in the
costume given to him by the
Imam of Yemen.*

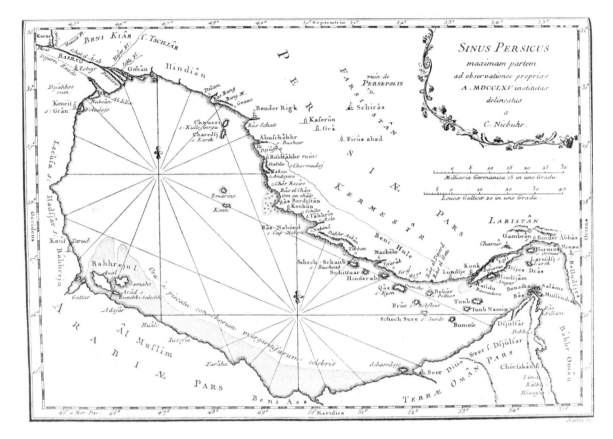

The audience over, Niebuhr moved freely about the city, visiting the market, the streets of Jewish craftsmen (each one devoted to a different trade) and the smiths, tailors, scribes, goldsmiths, shoemakers and saddlers who sat out on the pavement working while the crowds walked around them. No one threw stones at him, no one harrassed him. This, once again, was Arabia Felix. But when the Imam invited them to stay a whole year they refused. They feared that the English ships would leave without them and, wracked with malaria, they feared for themselves. At their last audience with the Imam Niebuhr was forced to ask the Imam's permission to go outside to be sick.

To get from Sana'a to Mokha they had a choice of two routes: the route via Taizz and Yerim which they already knew, and a harder one via Beit el-Fakih. They had no intention of repeating their experiences with the *dolas* of Taizz and Yarim, and Niebuhr was anxious to fill in his map, so they opted for the harder road.

They left on 26 July after ten days in Sana'a. Within a day the four sick men realized that this was the worst road they had so far encountered. They forced themselves through the 12,000-foot (3,600 m) mountain ranges; up valleys, down precipices, and across streams. It was a race against time.

After four days they reached the village of Halesi where the rains had washed the road away. Niebuhr ordered the porters to collect stones to fill it in, but Niebuhr did not have the natural authority of Forsskal. The porters refused. Patiently the sick men collected the stones themselves. All day they filled in the road and it was not until early evening when it was nearly complete that the porters offered to help. The following day, after Niebuhr lost his compass, they crossed the River Sehan twelve times, and by 1 August they were still only one third of the way. Niebuhr forced the pace.

Above: *Niebuhr's map of the Arabian Gulf, leaving out the Qatar Peninsula and placing Bahrain too far to the west, but surprisingly accurate on the Iranian side of the coast, and positioning Basra and Persepolis.*

Next day they marched double the distance and descended from the mountains into the Tihamah. Heat replaced rain. After one day in the Tihamah they reached Beit el-Fakih. From here the route was familiar to Niebuhr, but still he could not reduce the pressure if they were to reach Mokha on time. They arrived at Mokha on the morning of the fifth. They looked down at the harbour. It was empty.

Fortunately, because of a default in payment, one of the English merchants had remained. A fourth English ship, on the coffee run from Jeddah, was to pick him up in a fortnight and take him to India. When the ship arrived on 21 August 1763 Niebuhr was the only one who could walk. It was a sad voyage. Berggren and Baurenfeind succumbed within a day of each other, while Kramer – lazy to the last – waited till he got to India to die.

Carsten Niebuhr, the sole survivor of the Danish expedition, spent over a year in India. He could have returned in comfort by sea, but decided on a longer journey. He left Bombay on 8 December 1764 and sailed first for Muscat on the coast of Oman, where he saw French renegades manning the dhows, then on to Bushire in Persia, and Persepolis, the ancient city sacked by Alexander the Great. In August 1765 he was in Basra. Here he disappeared, discarding the European clothes he had bought in India, on the longest of all his Orwellian journeys, dressed in poor clothes which he believed would make him invisible. He travelled by riverboat up the Tigris to Baghdad, and by caravan across the Syrian desert to Aleppo and Jerusalem. By the time he reached Denmark he had been away for seven years.

Though honours were offered to him he refused them, declining even the post of head of a new geographical survey of Norway. Instead he devoted himself to his book and editing the diaries and notes of his hero Forsskal. He remained unsatisfied. 'He yearned for the tranquillity of the Orient,' his son wrote. The nearest he got to it was the post of parish clerk in the village of Dithmaschen in Heligoland Bay just thirty miles from where he was born. He stayed there, contented, until he died aged eighty-two in 1815.

Below: *Niebuhr's plan of Jerusalem, taken from the Mount of Olives, which he visited on his return journey to Europe.*

III

THE FIRST ROMANTICS

When Niebuhr returned to Europe he brought with him news of 'the new religion of a part of Nejd', providing Europe with its first hearsay information on the revivalist Wahhabi movement, whose desert zealots were sweeping across the Peninsula and had 'already caused a revolution in the government of Arabia'.

It had begun in 1745 when Mohammed ibn Saud, a date palm potentate of a cluster of hamlets around Diriyyah (about seven miles from the present city of Riyadh), gave political asylum to a holy man, Mohammed ibn Wahhab. Born in the Nejd in 1696 and educated in theology at Basra and Damascus, el-Wahhab was a rigid fundamentalist, opposed to every pleasure, innovation and belief not specified in the Koran, including coffee, tobacco and saint-worship, advocating in its place a stark and abstract submission to God. He rapidly gathered followers, first from the oasis dwellers of Diriyyah and then from the nearby Bedouin clans. They were formed into military communities, agriculturalists in peace and fanatics in war, and called themselves the *Ikhwan* or Brotherhood.

They swept all before them. By 1800 they had reached Aleppo to the north, the Shiite shrine of Kerbala (which they sacked) to the east and the fontiers of Oman to the south. One witness described them as 'a torrent of naked men in nothing but loin-cloths, armed with rifles and daggers'; another told the Sherif of Mecca they 'came like locusts, or a stream out of the hills after rain'.

In the spring of 1803 they besieged Mecca, the defenders laying primitive landmines at the approaches to the city and the Wahhabis retaliating by cutting off the sweet water supply from Arafat, reducing the population to drinking Zem-Zem water (see page 9). The siege lasted two months, with the population forced to eat dogs and cats. When the Wahhabis eventually entered the city victorious, they tore silk dresses, smashed water pipes and burnt a mountain of coffee beans. The siege at Mecca had given time for both Jeddah and Medina to prepare their defences, and both withstood the Wahhabi army when it arrived outside their walls. Three years later the Wahhabi armies came back unexpectedly; all three cities were sacked.

Left: *Detail from 'Ascent of the lower range of Mount Sinai' by David Roberts.*

The clash of swords and the chants of the half-naked Faithful – clad, like Macaulay's Puritans, in 'ostentatious simplicity of dress' – reverberated through a Europe engulfed by war. Lying at the crossroads of three continents, Asia, Africa and Europe, and on the route to India, Arabia's political influence stretched from the Atlantic to the Pacific. Three of the warring powers in particular – France, Russia and Britain – wanted information on the new forces that were now masters of the Peninsula; and each was to send its chosen agent to uncover that information. Thus it was that Domingo Badia-y-Leblich, born in Biscay in 1766 and secret agent of Napoleon Bonaparte, arrived in Tangiers on 29 June 1803, on his way to Alexandria and, eventually, Mecca.

Like most spies, Badia-y-Leblich, or Ali Bey el-Abbassi as he called himself, is remarkably reticent about himself. All he says is that:

> After passing many years in Christian states and studying their arts and sciences most useful to man. . . I resolved to visit the Moslem world and perform the Pilgrimage; observing the manners, customs and geography of the countries I passed through, in order to make the laborious journey some use to the country I will finally adopt as my home.[1]

Left: *The Bedouin, all things to all travellers: men saw in them what they wanted to see, and that was usually themselves.*

Above: *Mohammed Ali,*
founder of modern Egypt,
whose 'dark and designing
countenance and penetrating
eyes' saw through the disguises
of every European traveller
and spy to visit Mecca from
Badia-y-Leblich to Léon
Roches.

That country was Republican France.

Assuming the character of a prince of the Abbasids (descendants of the Prophet via Harun el-Rashid), he travelled through Morocco in such style that he was presented to the sultan. Badia gave him twenty muskets and bayonets, a barrel of gunpowder and an umbrella. The sultan gave him in return a couple of black loaves baked by the sultan himself and two women from his harem; a double sign of friendship.

Badia stayed in Morocco two years, sending his employers a report just before he left about forty British ships-of-the-line on their way to the Cape of Tarf al-Gharb, later corrupted to Trafalgar. His entourage leaving Morocco on the Haj was the most spectacular that year. In Tripoli the Pasha begged him to stay. In Alexandria Chateaubriand acknowledged him the most learned Turk in the world and a 'worthy descendant of Saladin'. In Cairo he was received by Mohammed Ali.

The Spaniard says little about Mohammed Ali (no doubt he said more in his reports), except that he had plenty of nous but lacked finesse. There are, however, no lack of other descriptions of the enigmatic Albanian who, by first destroying the power of the Mamelukes, and then keeping Britain and France at bay, made the modern state of Egypt. William Turner, who travelled for a while with Burckhardt in the Levant and Egypt, describes Ali's 'dark and designing countenance and penetrating eyes' which reminded Turner of Richard III's power to 'smile and smile and murder while he smiles'.[2] Mohammed Ali certainly realized that 'Ali Bey' was no Abbasid, but allowed the spy to continue since it suited his purpose of playing the Great Powers off against each other – a policy he later followed when he allowed Burckhardt and Roches to continue. Badia, too, noted his 'deep distrustful eyes'.

On 15 December 1806 Badia left Cairo for Mecca with a five-hundred-camel caravan. 'My part in the caravan was a mere fourteen camels and three horses, since I had left most of my possessions and servants in Egypt.' Impatient at the speed of the caravan he used to ride on ahead with two servants who would lay out a carpet and cushion in the sand and serve him a picnic. As soon as the caravan had passed by they remounted and repeated the manoeuvre.

Badia left the caravan at Suez and embarked on a dhow so high at stem and stern that it reminded him of a Trojan galley. The method of sailing – four men stationed in the bow to look out for rocks, anchoring off the coast at night and rarely loosing sight of land – inspired little confidence in him; and since the ship struck a rock and the captain had hysterics, this apprehension would seem perfectly reasonable. Badia and his entourage took to the lifeboat, leaving the others behind. They were somewhat shamefaced in the morning to find themselves picked up by the very dhow they thought had sunk. The episode ended with everyone weeping on each other's shoulders.

They arrived safely in Jeddah, where Badia's extravagent display of wealth provoked such jealousy in the local governor that he deliberately set out to insult Badia at public prayers by placing his prayer mat so that it overlapped Badia's. He then instructed his servant to tell Badia, the Abbasid prince, to move. The 'prince' complied, and the governor took over his carpet. With faultless charm Badia waited till the end of prayers then loudly presented his carpet to the governor, announcing that since the governor had knelt on it he could never use it again.

In Jeddah he contracted malaria, and when he left for Mecca he had to ride in a litter. The next day, about mid-afternoon, he put on the *ihram* (pilgrim's dress) and, passing around volcanic mountains and through deep and dark gorges, saw in front of him through the gathering dusk the Holy City. 'Behold the forbidden house of God,' Badia's guide announced melodramatically.

The vast courtyard of the Temple, the house of God covered from top to bottom in a black cloth and enveloped in a circle of lights, the strange hour and the silence of night, the guide speaking like one inspired: all made up a picture that I will carry with me forever.[3]

There were two centres of power in the city: the Sherif, responsible to Mohammed Ali, and the Wahhabis, responsible to God. Badia gave his paymaster, Napoleon – and eventually the rest of the world – the first detailed eye-witness account of the puritan Wahhabi revolutionaries.

They do not rob except when they are certain the object belongs to an enemy or an infidel. They pay in cash for goods and services. Rigorously disciplined, they endure hardships in silence, marching to the ends of the earth if so ordered.[4]

It was the Sherif of Mecca, the other centre of power, who was to be the greater threat. Informed of Badia's arrival by the astute Mohammed Ali, the Sherif summoned him to an audience. The Sherif asked Badia about himself. Where did he come from? Aleppo, the spy replied. The gentle interrogation went on. The Sherif sounded him out on the wars in Europe, and French designs on Arabia. Finally he complimented Badia on his Arabic. Badia spoke it just like an Arab, the Sherif added with an edge. He would even give Badia his own guide, chosen from among his most trusted servants. Such honours. Badia thanked him. Who was that guide to be? The guardian of the holy Well of Zem-Zem. This was the post of the Poisoner-in-Chief (for who can refuse a glass of holy water when offered?). Badia took to carrying an antidote all the time.

Above: *'The Jeddah Caravan', by Etienne Dinet, the way in which Pitts, Badia-y-Leblich, Seetzen, Burckhardt, von Maltzan and hundreds of thousands of others travelled to Mecca. (Mathaf Gallery, London)*

In spite of the Sherif and the Wahhabis, Badia still found time to determine the exact position of Mecca by astronomical observations. Later he lost the hair from his instrument and could not find a replacement. Men's hairs were non-existent since every man in Mecca shaved his head, and women's head hair was forbidden him on religious grounds. He also gave Europe its first description of the Haj since Joseph Pitts.

> Only at Arafat can you form a proper idea of the great spectacle presented by the Haj; the countless thousands from all nations and of all colours, coming through a thousand dangers and hardships from the furthest corners of the earth to worship the same God; the Caucasian giving a helping hand to the African, Indians and Persians fraternizing with Algerians and Moroccans: all members of one family, all equal before their Creator.[5]

His description of the city is less lyrical. Since the Wahhabi occupation the population had shrunk from a hundred thousand to sixty thousand; the houses were crumbling because Mecca lacked the skilled labour that came from Egypt to repair them, and the schools were as decayed as the houses. Only during the Haj did the city show any sign of life, when half the population became hoteliers and guides, and the other half servants in the Temple. On 26 February, the Haj season over, the Wahhabis ordered all pilgrims and foreigners out of the city. Four days later Badia, still spending liberally, left for Jeddah and from there took a dhow to Yanbu, the port of Medina. He set out from Yanbu with his entourage for Medina but was intercepted by Wahhabis – who condemned the pilgrimage to Medina as saint-worship – and turned back to Yanbu. There the Wahhabis, lacking the subtleties of Mohammed Ali, expelled him from Arabia.

After being shipwrecked in the Red Sea he arrived at Suez and crossed the Eastern Desert with an escort of ten Turkish soldiers and fifty Bedouin; returning to France via Cairo, Jerusalem, Damascus and Aleppo. In Europe he joined the staff of Joseph Bonaparte in Spain, retreating with him into France ahead of the advancing British troops. He supported Napoleon again after the latter's return from Elba, but after the restoration of the Bourbons felt increasingly out of sympathy with the times. In 1818 he returned to the Middle East (though it is not certain in what role) but got no further than the castle of Balka on the Pilgrim Road outside Damascus. There he died; of dysentery according to the English, and of poison administered by the English according to the French. It is the last mystery of this most mysterious of men.

In the same month, December 1806, as that in which Badia left Cairo for Mecca, another agent of a foreign power was approaching the Egyptian capital on the same quest, Ulrich Jasper Seetzen. Thirty-nine years old and in the service of the Tsar of Russia, he was probably the most academically qualified of all the Europeans who went to Mecca. He had studied medicine, botany, mineralogy and engineering as well as Arabic. He called himself an 'Orientalist' but was really a spy. His task was to report on the military state of the central Asian khanates which stood in the way of Russia's expansion towards India. It was to gain credibility for this mission that he came to Arabia to make the Haj. Yet there was a very unscientific, positively unstable strain about this intellectually well-equipped man. Travelling along the Danube, he was convinced that his Serbian escort planned to murder him, but a few days later those same Serbians had to plunge into the river to rescue him after he had thrown himself in during a fit of Wertherian melancholy.

Above: *Detail from 'The Sermon on Mount Arafat' by Etienne Dinet. (Mathaf Gallery, London)*

He had come to Cairo from Constantinople via Damascus and Aleppo, unsuccessfully looking for the ruins of Petra and, disguised as a beggar, drawing the first map of the Dead Sea. In Cairo he disappeared into the anonymous swell of humanity (unlike many, Seetzen took his disguise seriously), re-emerging three years later as Musa, a physician.

Seetzen travelled by caravan to Suez in Badia's footsteps, and then by dhow to Yanbu; but Yanbu was in the hands of the Wahhabis who forbade entry by pilgrims to Medina, so he sailed on to Jeddah and completed the final lap to Mecca by camel. On 16 October 1809 he entered the Great Mosque.

> Imagine a rectangle, 300 paces long by 200 wide, sur-
> rounded by three or four rows of marble columns; picture
> within it half a dozen or so not very large buildings, and you
> will have an accurate idea of the sacred Mosque. All around
> it the buildings of the city rise up in tiers on the slopes of the
> hills, so you get the feeling of being in a magnificent
> amphitheatre with the great square of the Mosque as the
> arena.[6]

After a month in Mecca he made a secret journey, in spite of Wahhabi

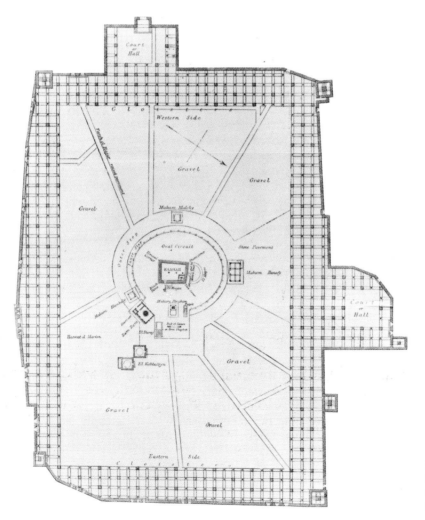

Left: *Badia-y-Leblich's plan of the Great Mosque at Mecca, with the Kaaba in the centre.*

Above: *Ulrich Jaspar Seetzen, one of the first 'Orientalists' to speak for the 'Oriental'.*

prohibitions, to Medina. There he was arrested and taken before the Emir. The Wahhabis rightly suspected him of being a spy, but mistook him for a Turk. He persuaded the Emir that he was a recent convert to Islam and not a spy, but was still ordered to leave the city. He returned to Mecca in time for the Haj and remained there for two months mapping the streets, collecting information on the political undercurrents in Islam and eating locusts – which he claimed to be delicious when fried in butter.

At the end of March 1810 Seetzen left Mecca for Jeddah. There he persuaded a Muslim scholar, Sheikh Harriza, to accompany him on a journey to the Yemen. At one moment on the voyage the curious, academic Seetzen persuaded Sheikh Harriza to keep a diary of the journey in Arabic, so the two men could compare their journals, and thus the different perspectives of the two cultures. The Sheikh had never read a travel journal and did not know what to write, so Seetzen dictated to him. Thus the 'Orientalist' was speaking for the 'Orient', and the 'Orientalist' was a spy.

The two were never able to peruse each other's journals. After landing at el-Hudaydah, their large caravan of seventeen camels excited suspicion. On the way to Sana'a Seetzen became ill with malaria, and rumours that they were magicians followed them to Aden and Mokha. On 17 November 1810 Seetzen and Sheikh Harriza set out from Mokha to cross the Hadramaut, bound for Muscat. Two days later Seetzen was murdered, poisoned on the orders of the Imam of Yemen as a suspected spy.

Mecca and Medina were the Holy Cities of Islam. Officially under the Ottoman Caliphate, the Caliph of Islam could not tolerate their occupation by a revolutionary sect. Unable to attack the Wahhabis from the north because of the great deserts that separated Turkey and Syria from Arabia, the Turks instructed Mohammed Ali to attack the Wahhabis from the Red Sea. On the eve of the departure of his army, the Machiavellian ruler used the march-past of his troops as bait for an ambush whereby he crushed the Mamelukes. With Cairo at peace Mohammed Ali felt confident to send his army to Jeddah.

Choice of commander could have gone to either of Mohammed Ali's sons, Ibrahim the elder, dishonest but competent, or Touson the younger, honest but incompetent. It went first to the younger, then to the father, and then to the elder. The results were inevitable. Under Touson half the army was lost within a few miles of where it disembarked, and the other plague-ridden half took two years to recapture Mecca and Medina. Under Mohammed Ali the Egyptian army gained victories, and under Ibrahim the population was massacred, the Wahhabi capital of Diriyyah razed to the ground (see page 69) and the Wahhabi leader, Abdallah ibn Saud, was taken to Constantinople where his head was crushed in a mortar.

Nearly a dozen European renegades accompanied the Egyptian army to the Hejaz. One was Thomas Keith, a Scottish drummer-boy from Edinburgh, of the 78th Foot Queen's Own Highlanders (Seaforth and Camerons). Taken prisoner at Rosetta and given the choice between conversion or death, Keith was converted, changing his name to Ibrahim Agha. Taken on as a slave by Touson, he attracted his master's notice by his ability to stick up for himself, joined the Egyptian army and ended his career as Governor of Medina. His governorship lasted only two months, and he was killed leading a cavalry charge in 1815. Another, Atkins (to whom posterity has given no first name), was an Englishman in charge of a Congreve rocket battery. A third, Maurice Tamisier, an Italian doctor in Egyptian service who came on a later expedition, arrived in the Hejaz in the company of an amateur conjuror and an Italian opera singer.

Alas, none of these three wrote a record of their adventures. Fortunately,

Left: *Cairo in the nineteenth century, with the minarets at Bab Zuweyleh and grand entrance of the Mosque of the Metalwis, by David Roberts.*

however, one did; Giovanni Finatti, an Italian from the Papal States whose respectable middle-class family were preparing the unlikely boy for the priesthood. He was saved from the Church by conscription into Napoleon's armies, which he anxiously set about avoiding. First he paid a substitute, but when the substitute deserted and Finatti's father and brother were arrested as hostages, the boy reluctantly enrolled. He deserted in the Tyrol but was captured when he came home and only saved from execution by an act of grace to mark Napoleon's visit to Venice. Sent to Scutari, he deserted again, in the company of fifteen other Italians and the sergeant's wife, and took refuge with the Turks.

Refusing to change their religion, they were sent to work in the quarries. Finatti rapidly tired of the quarries, was converted, and became pipe-bearer to a Turkish general whose wife he seduced. A third time he deserted, escaping this time to Egypt with the help of an Albanian trader, and enlisted as an Albanian soldier. Thanks to his earlier drilling he became a *balik bash* (corporal) in charge of six soldiers of Mohammed Ali's bodyguard. He fought in Mohammed Ali's campaign against the Mamelukes in Upper Egypt and in the massacre of the Mamelukes in the Cairo citadel, where he grabbed a slave girl as booty and married her.

He crossed the Red Sea with the Egyptian army in 1811 and was nearly killed outside Yanbu, where the heat and thirst were so desperate that when the Egyptian order to advance came, Finatti recounts, the soldiers received it with joy, even though they knew they were going to be slaughtered. Invalided out of the army with rheumatism, he returned to Egypt where he heard that his Turkish general's wife had born him a son. He immediately divorced his own wife for 'levity of conduct'.

With the arrival of Mohammed Ali in Arabia, and the change of fortune for the Egyptians, Giovanni Finatti, always ready to be on the winning side, re-enlisted. Regrettably for him he was sent to Confuta near Jeddah, where the garrison was besieged by the Wahhabis. Overwhelmed, the Egyptians fled, only to be cut off from their line of retreat and besieged again at the small coastal village of Lid. For the fourth time in his military career Finatti deserted. Travelling alone across the desert he was eventually found by some Bedouin, who gave him food and water and took him to Mecca.

Mecca, the Italian found, was 'neither large nor beautiful in itself, but there is something in it that is calculated to inspire a sort of awe'. He sat outside Mohammed Ali's house holding aloft a poster written in Turkish demanding an interview. On the sixth day he got what he wanted. He told Ali of the incompetence of his officers and their reversals at Confuta and Lid. In the 'greatest rage imaginable', because his officers had withheld the news from him, Mohammed Ali gave Finatti five hundred piastres and ordered him to rejoin the army at Taif and not to speak of the reversals to anybody.

Giovanni Finatti's story ends happily. He stayed with the Egyptian army till the end of the campaign without deserting, caught the plague and was evacuated to Egypt. There he met the wealthy English traveller Sir William Bankes who employed Finatti as his dragoman through Egypt, Palestine and Syria. Finatti returned with Bankes to Wales where, pleased with the simple manners of the Welsh villagers, he remained happily for the rest of his days.

Into this tumult in the Hejaz came a bearded holy man, Sheikh Ibrahim, alias Johann Ludwig Burckhardt. Like Badia-y-Leblich he served a nation other than his own, like Seetzen he was on his way to somewhere else, and like both of them he was a collector of intelligence. He was not an 'official' spy, on the payroll of the British Secret Service, he was an employee of the African Association, paid to get to Timbuktu. But the leading lights in the African Association and the leading lights in the British Foreign Office were one and the same, as were the opinions of the African Association and the policies of the British government. Johann Burckhardt did as much to provide the British government with information on the desert peninsula that lay between Europe and India, as Badia and Seetzen had provided for the French and Russian governments; in fact, he provided far more.

He was born in Basle in 1784. His father, a colonel in the Swiss army, was an enlightened liberal. A friend of Gibbon and Goethe, he hated the excesses of the French Revolution and was imprisoned for a time by the puppet Helvetic Directory. He sent his son to exile in England. Like so many political exiles, Burckhardt soon adopted England as his spiritual home. 'One can in our time breath freely only in this country.' He resolved to serve his adopted homeland in one way or another, and after spending months living

Below: *Abdallah ibn Saud, the Wahhabi leader, captured by Ibrahim Pasha and taken to Constantinople where his head was crushed in a mortar.*

on bread and cheese while vainly trying to get into either the Civil Service or the army, he was taken on by the African Association.

After twelve months at Cambridge learning Arabic, medicine and astronomy, Burckhardt left England in 1809 for Malta. There he spent two more months becoming accustomed to Eastern dress and practising his Arabic. He told the Maltese he was an Indian Moslem and, asked to utter some words in Hindustani, he rattled off a few phrases in Swiss German. Everyone agreed it was a barbaric language.

Leaving Malta on 9 June in a caique with three Tripoli merchants and their slaves, he sailed first to Rhodes and then to Suedieh on the Levantine coast. There he had his first shock. His Cambridge Arabic and pretentions of being an Arab were laughed at. It was worse in Antioch where crowds besieged his vermin-infested room chanting 'Infidel' at him. He took a caravan to Aleppo to escape. Pronounced '*haram*' (unclean) he had to eat by himself, sleep by himself and walk by himself.

Realizing he had much to learn before he could even think of passing as an Arab, he abandoned his disguise in Aleppo. He remained in the city for two and a half years perfecting his Arabic, and even made a translation of *Robinson Crusoe*, which he called *Dur el Bahr*, Pearl of the Sea. After a year he began to make excursions out of the city to Turkoman nomads, Kurdish shepherds and Syrian peasants. After two years he felt confident enough to resume his Arabic disguise, this time as a physician in search of medical herbs. Once he was captured by a group of Syrian nomads who stripped him. Finding no money they assumed that he had swallowed it and imprisoned him for two days while they waited for the result. Nothing happened, and Burckhardt was reluctantly released.

It was on these excursions that he first encountered the Bedouin. Imbued with the liberalism of the Enlightenment and memories of Gibbon, he was a perfect candidate for the idealization of the Bedouin in the wake of Forsskal.

> It may be said, without exaggeration, that the poorest Bedouin of an independent tribe smiles at the pomp of a Turkish pasha; and without any philosophical principles, but guided merely by the general feeling of his nation, infinitely prefers his miserable tent to the palace of a despot.[5]

He never, however, lived for long periods with the Bedouin; he accompanied them on no great desert crossing and, like Niebuhr and Forsskal, his

Below: *Cairo as it was during Burckhardt's stay, with the Nile in the foreground.*

information on them was culled from coffee shops and caravanserais on the periphery of their lands.

What he did do, like Niebuhr, was to become more and more like a young poor scholar, sleeping in the dirtiest caravanserais with his coat as a blanket, eating with camel drivers in the cheapest of cafés. His favourite dishes were lentils with yoghurt, and cucumbers stuffed with rice and mincemeat. After two and a half years in Aleppo the transformation seemed complete. In June 1812 he left for Syria, Palestine and Egypt. Johann Ludwig Burckhardt had become Sheikh Ibrahim.

He left the city alone, dressed as a poor traveller on an unremarkable mare so as not to excite greed among the Bedouin. He picked up his guide from a nearby village and on the third day was skirting the western shores of Galilee. At Tiberias he returned to his lodgings after climbing Mount Tabor to find they had been taken over by an Englishman, Michael Bruce, the lover of Lady Hester Stanhope. After recovering from the shock of what seemed to be a Syrian peasant addressing him in flawless English, Bruce took Burckhardt to the Spanish monastery at Nazareth to meet the extraordinary Englishwoman described by one French resident as 'the most interesting ruin in the Lebanon'. The niece of Pitt and once the brightest star in Regency London, Lady Stanhope lived in a world of fantasy. She was in Nazareth preparing for her triumphal progress to Palmyra with forty camels where her entourage of generously-bribed Bedouin would crown her 'Queen of the Desert'.

The two took an instant dislike to each other. Their ways were so different, and each was jealous of the other. He called her 'that evil woman', while she – who could give as good as she got – wrote to a friend: 'Sheikh Ibrahim the traveller after leaving me at Nazareth went God knows where into the desert and has discovered a second Palmyra.'

The second Palmyra was the ruins of Petra, which Seetzen had searched for unsuccessfully three years earlier. Burckhardt first heard of it near Shobak, the Crusader castle where the locals spoke of a dead city in the Wadi Musa. He recalled a passage from Eusebius, which stated that the tomb of Aaron was near Petra. The Wadi Musa lay off the main route, so on the excuse of sacrificing a goat at the tomb of Aaron, he got his guide to lead him to the Wadi Musa, 'unknown to ancient as well as modern geographers'.

After walking though an awesome canyon, the Siq, he came upon the city built of stone by the Nabataean kings in Hellenistic times; the temples, theatres and houses carved out of the rockface. 'The situation and beauty . . . are calculated to make an extraordinary impression upon the traveller, after having traversed . . . such a gloomy and almost subterranean passage.' But when Burckhardt tried to explore the dead city he was halted by his guide, who said: 'I see now that you are an infidel, who has some particular business amongst the ruins of the city of our forefathers; but depend on it we shall not suffer you to take out a single part of the treasures hidden therein.'[4]

On 1 September 1812 Burckhardt arrived in Cairo in search of a caravan to Timbuktu. He soon found out that there would not be a caravan for at least a year, so he spent the time living like a poor student, talking to the scholars in the el-Azhar Mosque and making long journeys up the Nile beyond Aswan into unexplored Nubia, discovering the half-buried Temple of Abu Simbel on the way.

Above: *Lady Hester Stanhope, an extremely flattering portrait of her by Sir David Wilkie when she was in her fifties. 'Now that her earthly kingdom had passed away,' wrote Kinglake, 'she strove for spiritual power, and impiously dared, as it was said, to boast some mystic union with the very God of very God.'*

Coming back from Upper Egypt, Burckhardt met the English adventurer and confidence-trickster James Silk Buckingham, who later became a founder of the *Athenaeum* journal. Buckingham wrote of their meeting:

> He was dressed in the commonest garments as an Arab peasant or small trader, with a blue cotton blouse covering a coarse shirt, loose white trousers, and a common calico turban . . . he had a full dark beard, was without stockings, wearing only the slip-shod slippers of the country, and looked so completely like an Arab of the north – a Syrian having a fairer complexion and lighter eyes than the Egyptians – that few would have suspected him to be a Swiss, as he really was, but have taken him to be a native of Antioch or Aleppo.[6]

Learning back in Cairo that there were to be further delays before a caravan left for Timbuktu, Burckhardt resolved to visit Mecca. The title of Haji would act as a passport and greatly improve his chances of getting to Timbuktu.

With his sights set on Mecca, Burckhardt joined a caravan at the village of Assiut, an important slave-trading post where, as he put it, the 'manufacture' of eunuchs took place. The operation was performed by two Coptic monks reputed to 'excell all their predecessors in dexterity'. The thought of the severing must have concentrated the Swiss's mind.

> I have received a letter from Mr Fiott from Messina. . . he most seriously advises me to undergo a certain operation . . . To engage me still further he adds in his last letter the expression: *'I think it would do you no harm'.*[7]

The caravan took him to Shendy, one of the biggest slave markets on the Nile, with five thousand slaves passing through it each year. One interesting line in the trade was the *muk-haeyt*, the sewn-up ones. 'Girls in this state are worth more than others, they are usually given to the favourite mistress or slave of the purchaser, and are often suffered to remain in this state during the whole of their lives.' Most of the unsewn-up ones made their living from prostitution and selling *bouza*, a beer made from fermented *durra* (similar to wheat), originally from Ethiopia. Burckhardt describes it as 'a pleasant prickly taste something like champagne turned sour'. The girls were skilled at massage, rubbing a mixture of sheep's fat, musk, sandalwood and an assortment of scents into their client's back. Four of them worked the caravanserai Burckhardt was staying at, and were not in the least disconcerted

Above: *'Petra' by David Roberts, 1839.*

by the presence of others trying to sleep as they worked through the night.

Burckhardt bought a slave for sixteen dollars and joined a caravan for Suakin. It was made up of some hundred pilgrims, three hundred slaves, two hundred camels with thirty horses bound for the Yemen. Many of the slave owners used their female slaves for profit, selling their services for two measures of *durra*; one for the master, the other for the slave.

At Suakin, where he was arrested by the Emir and only released after showing his *firman* from Mohammed Ali, Burckhardt embarked on a *say* for Jeddah. The *say* was only nine feet across and thirty-five feet long, with a ballast of *durra*. Most of the ninety pilgrims, merchants, slaves and crew were seasick, but Burckhardt found entertainment in a fellow-passenger, a Greek sea-captain who amused Burckhardt with 'the account of his travels in Europe and the palpable falsehoods and absurdities which he uttered respecting what he had seen in England and the manner of its s inhabants'. Dropped off onto the shore 'a gunshot' distance from Jeddah to avoid paying duty on his slave, he arrived in the port to discover that his eighteen-month-old letter of credit made out in Cairo was invalid; so he sold his slave for forty-eight Spanish dollars, three times the price he had paid.

With the forty-eight dollars he bought a new set of clothes and, dressed as 'a reduced Egyptian gentleman', set out to investigate Jeddah. It was not only the entrepôt of Arabia, but of Egypt and India too, with ships paying four hundred thousand dollars per year in customs duties. The hub of Jeddah was the thirty tobacco shops and coffee houses, one of which sold hashish, or *bast* (cheerfulness). The market was crowded with money dealers, copper sellers, scent merchants, sandal makers, tailors, barbers, sweetmeat vendors and beggars. The two richest merchants were worth between one and four hundred thousand pounds each, yet they still worked as shopkeepers, haggling with their customers over a quarter of a dollar. Within a week Burckhardt's investigations were cut short by malaria. He was cured by a local barber who bled him.

Above: *Johann Ludwig Burckhardt, from a sketch made by the British consul in Cairo just before Burckhardt's death.*

Recovering from his illness, his luck began to change. He wrote to Bosari, Mohammed Ali's doctor whom he had met in Cairo, asking him if the Pasha would accept his out-of-date letter of credit. Before he received a reply Yahiya Effendi, Touson's doctor, hearing of Sheikh Ibrahim's plight, advanced him three thousand piastres against a bill of exchange payable in Cairo. Then a suit of clothes, five hundred piastres for travelling expenses and a summons to Taif came from Mohammed Ali. Burckhardt was getting rich. He changed the three thousand piastres into gold, and hid it in his girdle before setting out for Taif. He had been in Jeddah for one month.

Mohammed Ali, who suspected Sheikh Ibrahim's identity, ordered him to by-pass Mecca, but Burckhardt's guide, unaware of his master's suspicions, took his charge right up to Mecca, giving him a fine view of the city. In Taif, where the figs, peaches, apples, apricots, vines and pomegranates diffused a fragrance 'as delicious to the smell as was the landscape to the eye', Burckhardt stayed with Bosari, who suspected him of being an English spy and questioned him closely. The suspicions were shared by Mohammed Ali, who 'knew perfectly well in the Hejaz that I was no Muslim,' but took no action.

He found Mohammed Ali at his headquarters, the ruined castle of Sheikh Ghaleb, seated in a large salon with the *kadi* of Mecca on one side and Hassan Pasha, the Albanian general, on the other. In the middle of a half-circle of staff officers sat some Bedouin chiefs. After concluding his other business, Mohammed Ali dismissed everyone except the *kadi*, Bosari and Burckhardt. The Allies had entered Paris and Napoleon had gone into exile on Elba, to 'expose himself in a cage to the laughter of the universe', as Mohammed Ali contemptuously put it. The Egyptian ruler's fears were that now Britain would turn her attention to the Middle East and he studied the English spy closely. At one time Burckhardt was somewhat confused by the news that the Swedes had occupied Genoa, but on further questioning discovered that it was the Swiss who had occupied Geneva. The subject of Sheikh Ibrahim's identity and his projected trip to Mecca never came up.

That evening Burckhardt expressed surprise to the *kadi* that Mohammed Ali should doubt he was a Muslim. The *kadi* replied that it had been left to him to decide. When prayer time came Burckhardt made a point of chanting the longest chapter of the Koran he knew. Nothing was resolved and soon he realized that he was in 'a sort of polite imprisonment'. He resolved to escape from it by annoying his host Bosari as much as possible, appropriating the best room in the house and calling for meals at the most inconvenient times.

As a Moslem Bosari could never refuse a guest's request, but he could use his influence to speed the guest on his way. On his tenth day in Taif Sheikh Ibrahim got permission to visit Mecca.

To avoid travelling with the *kadi*, who was also going to Mecca, he rode with three Albanian soldiers who had pooled their resources of a thousand dollars for some currency speculation. (In Jeddah the Spanish dollar was worth eleven piastres, in Taif thirteen.) They had sewn up their money in bags, neglecting to leave anything out for the journey; so Burckhardt ended up picking up the bill at every coffee house on the way. He did not mind, and found the soldiers good company. Close to Mecca he encounted the *kadi*'s party in a violent thunderstorm, with torrents of water separating the Ottoman judge from his travelling harem. Burckhardt watched with satisfaction as the *kadi* manfully forded the torrents to rescue his wailing entourage.

The next day, 9 September 1814, Burckhardt entered Mecca. It became a second England to him. 'During all my journeys in the East, I never enjoyed such perfect ease as at Mecca and I shall always retain a pleasing recollection of my residence there.' Six days later, after a brief impression, he returned to Jeddah to buy a new slave and stock up with flour, biscuits and butter, which were three times as expensive in Mecca; because of the Wahhabi guerrillas he was forced to stay three months before returning. There he encountered James Silk Buckingham again, who had avoided the heat by crossing the Red Sea half-submerged in a net. It was while dining with Buckingham on an English merchantman from Bombay that Burckhardt met Donald Donald, who had been captured with Thomas Keith (that unlikely governor of Medina) at Rosetta, and had changed his name to Othman. Donald and Burckhardt became fast friends. During the meal Buckingham persuaded the two Moslems, one genuine, the other fake, to drink some wine. Burckhardt drank a glass and joined Buckingham in encouraging Donald, who drank half a glass and was promptly sick (which he put down to Divine Wrath). One wonders just how seriously Burckhardt took his disguise. The captain of the merchantman had no doubt of his origins and presented him with a pocket volume of Milton.

Right: *A desert caravan, like the one Burckhardt joined from Mecca to Medina after Mohammed Ali's defeat of the Wahhabis outside Mecca.*

Left: *Mecca as seen through European eyes. The acres of imaginary open space suggest that it was through the eyes of someone who had never actually been to the Holy City.*

Back in Mecca Burckhardt rented a room in a quiet quarter of the town where he could write up his notes and read Milton in peace, and began his explorations of the Holy City. Soon the days took on a pattern: walking the streets in the cool of early morning, stopping at the coffee shops at midday, returning to his room in the afternoon to write up his notes and wandering the streets again in the evening.

The streets were wide (to facilitate the thousands of pilgrims who flocked there each year) and the grey stone houses were high and parapeted, so the women in the harems could look down into the street without being observed. The main thoroughfare was the Messai, lined with cafés selling *raki*, disguised by cinnamon and sugar and sold as 'cinnamon water'. It was also the street of public execution and while Burckhardt was there a man was beheaded for robbing a Turkish pilgrim. This appears to have been a relatively enlightened punishment. Previously, thieves had been flayed alive.

Running off the Messai was the market where rugs, perfumes, sandalwood, coral stones and slaves were sold. The market became a favourite spot for Burckhardt: lounging in the shade under the vaulted stone roof drinking coffee and smoking his narghile while collecting material for the hundreds of pages of *Travels in Arabia* and *Notes on the Bedouin and Wahhabi*, and this in spite of recurrent attacks of malaria. 'The worse effect of ill-health upon a traveller, is the pusillanimity which accompanies it, and the apprehension with which it fills the mind.' And all the time there were the city sounds: the rising and falling tones of the call to prayer from the minarets, the whispers of prostitutes, the cries of street traders, the chanting of boys in the Koranic schools and the haunting melody of the water-carrier's song ('Paradise and forgiveness be the lot of him who gave you this water').

Burckhardt was disappointed to find no great centre of knowledge in Mecca – 'learning and science cannot be expected to flourish in a place where every mind is occupied in the search of gain or of Paradise' – but he liked the hybrid people, counting forty different languages spoken in the city.

> In every Haj some of the pilgrims remain behind . . . hence most of the Meccawis are descendants of foreigners from distant parts of the globe, who have adopted Arabian manners, and by intermarrying have produced a race which can no longer be distinguished from the indigenous Arabian.[8]

His landlord was of Uzbek Tartar descent, from Bokhara in southern Russia.

Burckhardt stayed for the Haj and saw amongst the pilgrims one of Mohammed Ali's wives, whose encampment, 'enclosed by a wall of linen cloth, 800 paces in circuit, the single entrance to which was guarded by eunuchs in splendid dress', was inhabited only by women. It reminded Burckhardt of *One Thousand and One Nights*.

He wanted to leave at the end of the Haj but the Wahhabi threat forced him to stay. The town was almost deserted after the exodus of pilgrims. There was uncollected rubbish everywhere. The outskirts of Mecca stank with the smell of dead camels. After a while the smell was so bad that the populace took to stuffing pieces of cotton up their nostrils.

Outside the ring of mountains defending the city the Wahhabis held the country and lines of communication. It was a standard guerrilla siege. Once when it appeared that there was about to be an assault on the city the population panicked. Burckhardt and his slave took refuge in the Great Mosque. But Mohammed Ali, who was now in charge, had a far more astute understanding of the limits of guerrilla war than either the Meccans or the Wahhabis. By tempting the lightly-armed guerrillas to besiege Mecca he was forcing them to adopt a positional war for which they were least suited, to hold 'ground' (the cardinal sin of a guerrilla), and to denude the interior of troops to maintain a thin shell around the city (as the Bedouin did around Medina in 1916 until Lawrence arrived). It worked exactly as Mohammed Ali had planned. A feint outside the town brought the Wahhabi cavalry into the open. The Egyptians wheeled round while others attacked from the flanks and in five hours five thousand Wahhabis had been slaughtered. Unfortunately for Mohammed Ali the victory did not have the strategic effects he intended, since his army did not follow it up by sweeping through the troop-denuded interior. His military machine did not match his military mind; the instrument was unequal to the intention.

The three hundred prisoners taken were impaled on stakes along the road from Mecca to Jeddah. It was the biggest defeat the Wahhabis had suffered in their half-century of existence. The way to Medina was now open.

The fifty camels in Burckhardt's caravan travelled along the coastal road, riding endless nights through valleys of shifting sand and chains of stony hills. Once he fell asleep and rode for eleven hours before waking. Another time, riding in front of the caravan, he got too far ahead and stopped to wait. When the camels failed to appear he retraced his steps. All fifty were standing still in lines, every man asleep. 'When the camel hears no voices about it, and it is not urged on by the leader, it slackens its pace and at last stands still to rest; and if the leading camel once stops, all the rest do the same.'

Most of the caravan was made up of Malays. One day an almost destitute Malay was separated from the caravan and lost. Found by some Bedouin he offered them twenty piastres if they would lead him back to the caravan. When he got back, his fellow Malays disclaimed all knowledge of him and refused to pay. The Bedouin decided to strip the Malay and hold him to ransom. Burckhardt was furious. He seized the lead camel's halter, made it crouch so all the other camels followed suit, and refused to let the caravan proceed until the Malays had paid out twenty piastres. Then, appealing to the Bedouins' honour, he persuaded them to keep only ten piastres for themselves and give the other ten piastres to the Malay.

In Medina he found lodgings near the mosque and on his first day in the city he bumped into Yahiya Effendi, who had advanced him the money in Jeddah the previous July. Yahiya noticed that Burckhardt had a supply of quinine and asked Burckhardt for it since several of Touson's staff were down with 'fever'. Burckhardt could hardly refuse.

Below: *Medina as seen through Moslem eyes: the first photograph of the Great Mosque, taken by a Turkish officer about 1880.*

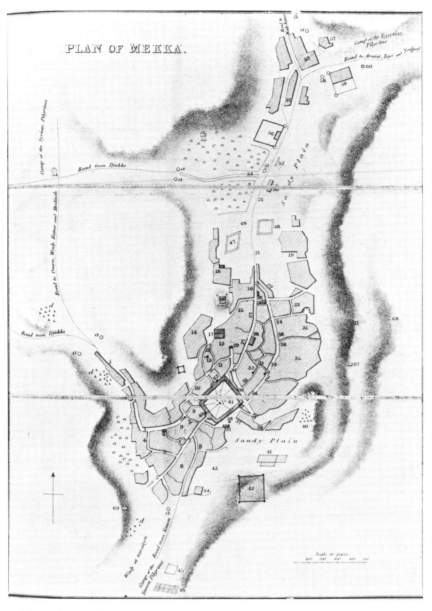

PLAN OF MEKKA.

Not only was Touson in Medina, but Touson's mother too, returning from the pilgrimage and bearing Touson gifts 'to the value of about £25,000 sterling, among which were twelve complete suits . . . a diamond ring worth £5,000; and two beautiful Georgian slaves.' Touson, according to Burckhardt, was the only member of the family 'whose breast harboured any noble feeling . . . and even his enemies cannot deny his valour, generosity, filial love and good nature.' At night Touson slept on a carpet in the street outside his mother's house, 'offering a testimony of respect and humility which does as much honour to the son, as to the character of the mother who could inspire him with such sentiments.'

Two days after giving Yahiya his quinine, Burckhardt bitterly regretted his generosity. The 'fever' that Yahiya spoke of was the plague and Burckhardt himself was down with it, sweating profusely and vomiting daily, while outside he could hear the mourning of the funeral crowds taking the corpses of victims to a nearby mosque. His slave, 'a poor fellow who by habit and inclination was more fitted to take care of a camel than to nurse his drooping master', was little help. To make matters worse he discovered that his slave had taken to washing the corpses lying in the mosque as a pious act. His only consolation was his copy of Milton and a nice old landlady who chatted to him from the upper storey of the split-level interior without being seen by him.

By the middle of April the plague had abated. Weak and dejected, Burckhardt abandoned his projected return to Egypt overland, and left for Yanbu to sail by dhow to Suez. He passed the fifteen-hour marches sweating and vomiting.

At Yanbu, he discovered the plague was already there. The death rate reached fifty a day and the streets resounded with 'those heart-rendering cries which all over the Levant accompany the parting breath of a friend or relative'. Many fled the city to camp outside, but the plague followed them. Two people were buried alive by mistake. 'One of them gave signs of life at the moment they were depositing him in the grave, and was saved; the body of the other, when his tomb was reopened several days after his burial to admit the corpse of a near relation, was found with bloody hands and face, and the winding sheet torn by the unavailing efforts he had made to rise.'

It was eighteen days before he got a ship. The ship took the plague with it and several passengers died at sea, but the plague did not spread, which Burckhardt puts down to the continual sea-sickness of the passengers. At Suez he joined Mohammed Ali's wife's caravan and arrived in Cairo on 24 June 1815 after an absence of two and a half years.

Burckhardt never fully recovered from the plague and he lingered two more years in Cairo awaiting the caravan to Timbuktu that never came. He died on 15 October 1817, Donald Donald the Scottish renegade at his bedside, and was buried as Sheikh Ibrahim, in accordance with his status as Haji and scholar, in the great Moslem cemetery outside Bab el-Nasr, the Gate of Victory. 'Men's lives are predestined,' he wrote; 'we all obey our fates.'

In the year that followed their victory over the Wahhabis, the Egyptian army was completely reformed by Mohammed Ali. The inhabitants were treated well, goods were paid for, customs dues diminished, grain distributed, and in any dispute with the army, the population was always favoured. As the Egyptians grew stronger so the Wahhabis became weaker; the leadership was disputed, southern Wahhabis received no support from northern Wahhabis, and southerners gave none in return. From his headquarters at Tabara, Mohammed Ali decided to take the war into the Wahhabi heartland; but following the defeat of Napoleon at Waterloo and fearing British designs on Egypt, Mohammed Ali went home, leaving command to his elder son, Ibrahim, who possessed all the cruelty of his father, without any of his cunning and magnanimity.

Moving slowly but surely, never venturing on ground he had not first made his own, Ibrahim advanced steadily across Arabia, forgetting the efforts his father made to win the hearts and minds of the people, but killing and laying waste to all he encountered. By April 1818 he razed the Wahhabi capital Diriyyah to the ground.

It was not Ibrahim's intention to occupy the Nejd; the last thing he wanted was to be tied down by a guerrilla war in an inhospitable land. His aim was to destroy, something that he unhappily excelled at.

Unfortunately, this point was not fully appreciated by the British government in India who were plagued by pirates operating from the Gulf and who viewed the Wahhabis as dangerous upsetters of the status quo. They imagined the Nejd happily settling down to tranquil administration and, supremely secure in this world of administrative make-believe, despatched to the Nejd a British officer 'to congratulate Ibrahim on the reduction of Deriah' and coordinate Anglo-Egyptian operations on the Pirate Coast.

His name was Captain George Sadlier of His Majesty's 47th Foot. Rarely have the laurels of geographic exploration dropped on the head of one more reluctant and less suited. He left Bombay on the East India Company's cruiser *Thetis* on 14 April 1819, and after an unsuccessful attempt to get the Sultan of Oman to join in the alliance, landed at Hasa on 28 June. Hasa, he discovered, was not only empty of Ibrahim, but was about to be evacuated by the Egyptians.

Below: 'Cairene Interior', by Frank Dillon (1823-1909), which romanticized Arab life. (Mathaf Gallery, London)

Right: *The Mamelukes charging the British at Rosetta, where Thomas Keith and Donald Donald were captured.*

Hearing that Ibrahim was at Manfuhuh (now a suburb of Riyadh) he rode east with the evacuating Egyptians. Sadlier must have been a difficult man to travel with: his ideas on the relative stations of sahibs and natives never endeared him to his Bedouin escort.

> The procrastinations, duplicity, falsity, deception, and fraudulence of the Bedouin cannot be described by one to a European in language which would present to his mind the real character of these hordes of robbers. To attempt to argue with them on the principles of justice, right or equity is ridiculous; and to attempt to insist on their adhering to promises or agreements is equally fruitless.[9]

Poor man. Poor Bedouin.

Finding that Ibrahim was not at Manfuhuh but had gone to Diriyyah, Sadlier followed. At Diriyyah there was no Ibrahim, but evidence of his work all around. 'Every beam and stick in the town was burnt, and every tree in the plantations and gardens cut down.' At Diriyyah, realizing the futility of his mission, Sadlier wanted to go back. But so bitter were the feelings of the population against the Egyptians that 'the whole country was in arms' and it was impossible to retrace his steps. There was nowhere for him to go but forward to Rass, where Ibrahim was reported to have set up his camp. At Rass he discovered that Ibrahim had packed and gone only two days previously.

By the time Sadlier caught up with Ibrahim he was in the suburbs of Medina which, to Sadlier's intense fury, he was forbidden to enter lest he be 'displeased' by some of the remarks made by the Faithful. He had to camp out with the harem three miles away. On 9 September he finally met his elusive goal, 'who received me with affability and courteousness; and . . . seemed gratified that the news of his victory had reached as far as Calcutta', but who showed no interest whatsoever in an alliance against the pirates. Then he was sent off to Yanbu with the harem, a most painful indignity. Of course he was ridiculous in his boots, breeches and stiff-necked collar, consigned from one side of the Peninsula to the other 'like a bale of goods', as the Arabs put it; but there was genuine humanity in his disgust at Ibrahim's excess, and he was the first European since the sixteenth century to cross the sub-continent. It would be another hundred years before Harry St John Philby repeated the feat.

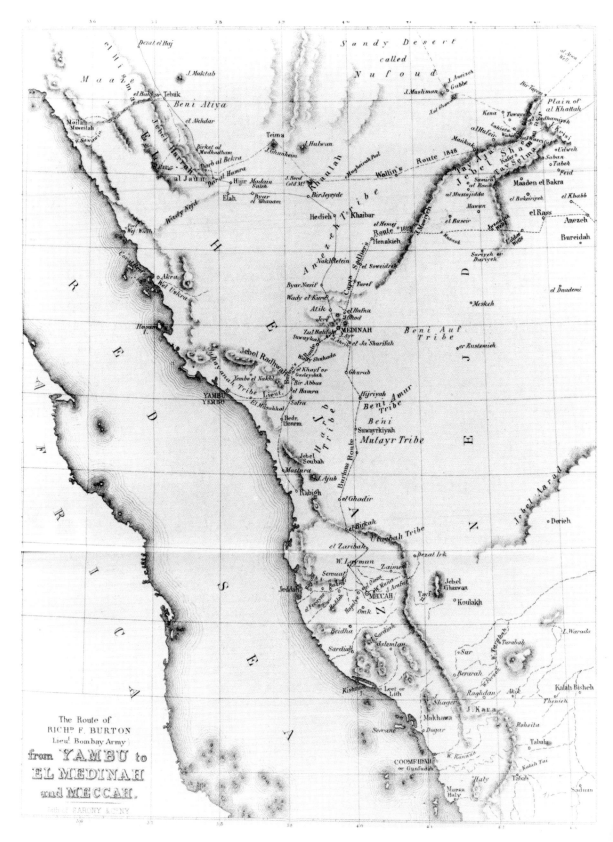

The Route of
RICHᴰ F. BURTON
Lieuᵗ Bombay Army
from YAMBU to
EL MEDINAH
and MECCAH.

Lith J SARONY & CᵒNY

IV

THE OPPORTUNISTS

In the years that followed Captain Sadlier's most reluctant of journeys, the coastal districts of Arabia were being systematically surveyed and explored. Though Ibrahim chose to ignore the power that the exasperating Sadlier represented, the coastal sheikhdoms from Kuwait to the Yemen were steadily coming under British influence. A sign of the times was the appointment in 1838 of the first British consular official in Jeddah; while along the coast the captain and crew of the British survey ship *Palinarus* – Haines, Wellsted and Whitelock – exerted a profound influence from Oman, which Wellsted and Whitelock explored in 1836, to Aden which Haines occupied in 1839.

In the sixteenth century the coast had been dominated by the Portuguese, who occupied Socotra and Muscat. In 1649 the Portuguese were evicted from Muscat: the local Omani tribe waited until a Sunday when they knew the garrison would be drunk, then crept in and slaughtered the lot. In 1747 a garrison of newly-arrived Persians suffered the same gruesome fate: the Persians were invited to a banquet in Baika, but when they sat down to eat their throats were cut. Oman assumed a precarious independence, its flourishing trade with India regularly threatened by Wahhabi pirates. The British supported the Omanis, providing naval patrols in the Gulf. On one of them, the frigate *Seahorse*, came a young midshipman, Horatio Nelson, in 1775. A quarter of a century later the first British Political Agent established himself at Muscat and promptly died of heatstroke.

Opinions of the Omanis from western outsiders varied. Lieutenant Whitelock of HMS *Palinarus* wrote that 'quarrels are seldom heard; old age is always respected; hospitality is proverbial'. An American naval mission under Edmund Roberts, on the other hand, thought the country had possibilities but was unhygienic. In particular Roberts could not bring himself to eat the local halva, stirred 'with the naked feet of sweating niggers'.

Left: *Burton's route to Mecca, showing both Sadlier's and Wallin's journeys.*

73

Left: *J. Struys' sketch of Muscat in about 1665, after the eviction of the Portuguese.*

Lieutenant James Wellsted, who landed in Oman with Whitelock in 1836, wrote of 'verdant fields of grain and sugar-cane,' and the women as the most 'frolicsome, laughter-loving dames' he had ever beheld. He traded opium pills, which the people regarded as an aphrodisiac, in exchange for the local wine. Two months later he looked west from Jebal Akhdar at the Empty Quarter stretched out below him.

> Vast plains of loose drift-sand, across which even the hardy Bedouin scarcely dares to venture, spread out as far as the eye could reach. Not a hill or even a change of colouring in the plains occurs to break the unvarying and desolate appearance of the scene.[1]

The following year he set out again with Whitelock into the interior but was turned back by a Wahhabi raiding party at Buraimi. He returned to Muscat, wrote a book, and was accused of monopolizing the credit that should have been shared with Whitelock. In the grip of a delirious fever, he shot himself twice in the mouth and lingered on for another three years before dying in India aged thirty-seven.

Though Aden was occupied, the Yemen unveiled, Oman explored and the southern coasts surveyed, the mountains and fertile interior, the Hadramaut, was still unknown. It was penetrated by Adolph von Wrede, a Bavarian soldier of fortune who had seen service with King Otho of Greece and settled in Egypt. He arrived at Mukalla, some three hundred miles east of Aden, on 26 June 1843 under the name of Abd el-Hud, a pilgrim on the way to the tomb of his namesake, Hud, a Hadramaut saint. After marching nine days north through a series of valleys, he passed through an immense ravine that opened up into the settlements and date palms of Wadi Doan.

Left: *Aden in about 1848, when its population was a mere five hundred. In spite of ten years of British occupation there was still little evidence of British influence. It was not until two decades later with the opening of the Suez Canal that the port began to develop a European look.*

Unlike his contemporaries, von Wrede had no illusions about the Bedouin being taken in by his disguise and answered their questions about how many eunuchs were in the court of Queen Victoria as best he could. At Khoraibe he was received by the chief of the Beni Issa, and after a fruitless trek to the south-west, which ended with him being turned back at the coast, he pushed on to Wadi Amd. There the sheikh, who had been to India and spoke English, lent him a copy of Scott's *Life of Napoleon Bonaparte*. From Wadi Amd he marched to Sawa on the very edge of the Empty Quarter, as awe-inspiring to von Wrede, the first European to see it from the west, as it had been to Wellsted, the first to see it from the east.

> Conceive an immense sandy plain strewed with numberless undulating hills, which gave it an impression of a moving sea. Not a single trace of vegetation, be it so scanty, appeared to animate the vast expanse. Not a single bird interrupts with its note the calm of death.[2]

He returned to Khoraibe to make the journey to Hud's tomb, but never got nearer than the village of Sif. Realizing he was a European, the population 'raised a horrible cry' and, taken for an English spy (the memory of the occupation of Aden was still fresh), he was beaten by the mob and fled, leaving behind both baggage and notes.

He got back to Europe but, without proof of his journey, his account was dismissed as make-believe. Disillusioned with Europe he emigrated to Texas where he committed suicide in 1870.

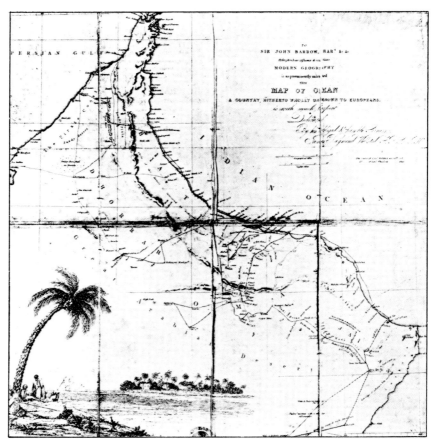

Right: *Wellsted's map of Oman (1838), the Empty Quarter filled in by an idyllic fantasy of the Romantic imagination.*

Two years before von Wrede's arrival in Arabia a very different type of traveller arrived in Mecca. Léon Roches was a spy, an idealist and the first of the opportunists. He had been born in Grenoble in 1809, brought up by an aunt after his mother died and his father emigrated to Algeria. At the age of twenty-three he abandoned his legal studies and joined his father in north Africa as an officer in the National Guard. An incurable romantic, he became infatuated by a fourteen-year-old Algerian aristocrat, Khadidja; but her parents refused to allow her to marry a Christian and she was forced into an arranged marriage.

Roches learnt Arabic, kept up a secret liason with Khadidja through her Negro nurse, and became an interpreter in the French campaign against the Algerian nationalist leader Abd el-Kader. Like many liberal and Republican Frenchmen he admired el-Kader as another Mohammed Ali, but with Roches this turned into an obsession almost as strong as that for Khadidja.

Taking on the role of a French convert to Islam he proposed to seek out Abd el-Kader in an attempt to bring Moslem Algeria and Christian France into a new accord, but how far his motives were those of a spy and how far those of an idealist is hard to say. He rode for days through the Algerian interior, passed on from one guerrilla chieftain to another, uncertain of his own future and loyalties, before reaching Abd el-Kader's camp of fifteen thousand men, twelve thousand horses and ten thousand camels, the cone-shaped tents forming a great circle. El-Kader was campaigning against

Left: *Abd el-Kader, the Algerian leader who fought the French for a quarter of a century, and whose magnetic personality and military skills were the catalyst that sent Roches to Mecca.*

Right: *Nomad tents in north Africa. Tents like these would have made up the city of tents surrounding el-Kader's headquarters, which Roches visited in his search for the Algerian leader.*

the Goulouglis, a half-Turkish half-Algerian tribe fighting on the side of the French. Khadidja's husband was a Goulouglis chief.

Abd el-Kader was so struck by Roches' sincerity that he not only personally undertook Roches' religious education, but also engaged him as his private secretary. Increasingly under the influence of el-Kader, Roches found that the outer religious conversion was matched by an inner one, the beauty and simplicity of Islam reawaking a chord within himself and bringing him back to Christianity. Once Roches' father found his way to Abd el-Kader's camp and begged his son to return. El-Kader offered Roches the opportunity to leave if he swore to keep up his Moslem faith. Roches refused. This had a profound effect on el-Kader who – although only a year older than Roches – now treated him like an adopted son.

After the Goulouglis Abd el-Kader turned his army on Ain Madhi, stronghold of the pro-French marabout Sidi Mohammed el-Tedjini. It was to Ain Madhi that Khadidja and her husband had fled after the demise of the Goulouglis. The walled town was besieged for four months. Roches discovered after the assault was over that Khadidja had died during the siege. In the great tradition of nineteenth-century romantics, he wanted only to join her.

Abd el-Kader's next campaign was against the French. Roches was faced with a stark choice; whether a French spy or a French idealist his position was impossible. He announced to el-Kader that he could not bring himself to bear arms against his own countrymen. El-Kader rebuked him.

'The day you took up our religion you broke all ties that bind you to the infidels.'

'Then I am no Moslem.'

Abd el-Kader turned to him. The punishment for apostasy from Islam was death.

'Go. I leave your punishment to God. Get out of my sight and never repeat to another Moslem what you have said to me, for I could not guarantee your life. Go.'

Roches returned to Paris where 'Orientalism' was in vogue. He met Thiers and the Duke of Orleans, was invited to salons and was lionized as the famous Abd el-Kader's confidant. Ill-at-ease and gnawed by the guilt of betrayal, he returned to Algeria in 1840.

Now he had a new plan, and the plan was taken up with enthusiasm by the French Secret Service. Roches was convinced that the war could be ended if the Algerians were persuaded that eternal damnation did not await those who lived under infidel rule, and if the French would respect the Moslem faith.

He drew up a *fettoua* or religious edict, and with financial backing from the French went to the University of Cyrene in Libya to have it accepted by the *Ulema*. In Cyrene the *Ulema* said it should be passed on to the University of el-Azhar in Cairo, where the *Ulema* said it should be passed on to the supreme body of *Ulemas* meeting in Mecca.

While in Cairo Roches was presented to Mohammed Ali. The contrast between the world-wise, leonine and heavy Mohammed Ali and the ascetic, bird-like and tiny Abd el-Kader could not have been more apparent. The Egyptian ruler expressed his admiration for the Algerians in their struggle against the French and compared it to the speedy pacification of Egypt by Napoleon. It was nothing to do with race, Roches replied, but geography. Algeria was a country of mountains and deserts, inaccessible except by sea from the north; Egypt was flat, its sedentary population concentrated in the delta and without any natural protection. Mohammed Ali admired Roches' honesty but was not taken in by the Frenchman's cover of being a Moslem convert. Roches writes of seeing reflected in the monarch's eyes the cold-blooded cruelty with which he ordered the massacre of the Mamelukes.

Roches left Cairo and journeyed by sea from Suez to Yanbu, where he was shocked by the treatment of Algerian pilgrims, two hundred of whom were packed in boats meant only for fifty, and took time off from espionage and deception to complain of their lot to the Sherif of Mecca, the European consuls in Jeddah and – through French diplomatic agents – Mohammed Ali and the Sublime Porte.

From Yanbu he took a camel to Medina, catching his first sight of the city through the palm trees in its suburbs. Thirteen days later he was in Mecca, where he stayed for a fortnight, renting a room at eight francs a day in a house built into the eastern wall of the Great Mosque from where he could compare the pious pilgrims with the life of the market stalls and coffee shops around. It was impossible for him to separate the searchers for material and spiritual gain. Like many well-heeled pilgrims he went inside the Kaaba. 'You pay when you mount the steps guarded by eunuchs, you pay when you enter, pay when you leave, pay when you kiss the key of the door which the *Agha* gives you, pay when you descend the steps – always pay.'

On 8 January 1842 he left Mecca for Taif, residence of the Sherif of Mecca, where the *Ulemas* of Mecca, Medina, Baghdad and Damascus were assembled. In spite of the uncompromising opposition of one member, Roches' *fettoua* was given the seal of approval. For Abd el-Kader, deprived of his most powerful weapon, it was the beginning of the end.

His mission over, Roches returned to Mecca to complete the pilgrimage, still disguised as a Moslem. But at Arafat he was recognized by two Algerians as a French official. As the sermon came to an end the cry went up: 'Seize the Christian', and the crowd surged towards him. Suddenly he was grabbed by six powerful Negroes, gagged, and carried off. He thought his end had come, but instead he was tied on a racing camel and rushed to Jeddah (in a mere eight hours) and put on a dhow to Egypt. It turned out that Mohammed Ali had communicated his suspicion that Roches was a French spy to the Sherif of Mecca, who had discreetly provided him with a bodyguard. Roches had remained completely unaware of his protectors until they emerged from the angry crowd and carried him off.

Three months after spending Christmas in Mecca, Roches spent Easter in Rome, where in a crisis of guilt he resolved to escape from the French Secret Service by becoming a Jesuit. But the French did not accept his resignation and persuaded the Pope, Gregory XVI, to convince Roches that his vocation was in more secular society. He returned to Algeria to take part in Abd el-Kader's final defeat and ended his career as France's ambassador to Japan.

Right: *The Orient of the Paris salons. 'A Coppersmith, Cairo', painted in 1884 by Charles Wilda.*

CH. WILDA PARIS 1884

Ten years later another equally unconventional opportunist, Lieutenant Richard Burton, adventurer, egotist and imperialist, made his way to Mecca. He called himself an Elizabethan out of his time, but he would perhaps better be described as a fascist out of his time, obsessed by 'blood', the relative shapes of brains of different races and the difference in size between the Arab and Negro penis. Yet in spite of his vileness he had his saving graces, and unlike most of the liberals who abhorred him, he could actually speak the languages (forty-one by the time he died) of the people whom he bullied. He was mean with money but never in spirit, and though he treated blacks badly, he treated everyone badly. He was a glittering star in a grey and bourgeois sky. The world would have been a duller place without him.

Burton was born in 1821, the son of a mother who claimed descent from an illegitimate son of Louis XIV and a father whose military career had been ruined the previous year by refusing to testify against Queen Caroline during her trial for adultery, and who had gone into self-imposed exile. Burton's education was spent in half the cafés, brothels and hotels of Europe. He was sent to read Arabic at Oxford in spite of pleas to his father to study at the University of Toulouse, but within an hour of his arrival became the laughing stock of the University when he challenged a fellow undergraduate, who had ridiculed his moustache, to a duel. When he was eventually rusticated he left blowing a trumpet and riding his carriage over the college flowerbeds; but on arriving in London told his parents he had been given a vacation for getting a double first.

Commissioned in the 18th Bombay Light Infantry at the age of twenty-one, he was garrisoned in the Sind, the centre of Islamic India. It was there that he first got the idea of visiting the Holy Cities. In the Sind his linguistic accomplishments and intimacy with Moslem life got him the job of intelligence officer under Napier. But disguised as Mirza Abdullah, a half-Arab half-Persian from Bushire, his reports on the different methods of buggery practised in male homosexual brothels went into such detail that his conventional army career was as ruined as his father's. 'Disappointment is the salt of life', he wrote.

He returned to Europe, living out 'four years of European effeminacy' on half-pay until sponsored by the Royal Geographical Society 'for the purpose of removing that opprobium of modern adventure, the huge white blot which in our maps still notes the Eastern and Central regions of Arabia'. His employers, the East India Company, granted him a year's leave to 'pursue his Arabic studies in lands where the language is best learnt', but – to Burton's fury – refused him the three years needed to cross the 'huge white blot' and return overland from Mecca to India.

He left London on 3 April 1853, arriving in Cairo disguised as a Persian, Bismillah Shah (King, by the Grace of God). Discovering that Persians were looked down on as heretics, he quickly transformed himself into a Dervish. Dervishes, he found out, attracted too much attention, so he changed again into Sheikh Abdullah (God's Servant), an Afghan doctor brought up in India. It was quite a climb down from King, by the Grace of God.

Like the earlier Mirza Abdullah – and all of Burton's other personae – Sheikh Abdullah was a marginal, a cosmopolitan, belonging nowhere like Burton himself; and as with all his characters Burton wanted to *be* Sheikh Abdullah, rather than just act him. He even took to practising Sheikh Abdullah's profession, and greatly increased the value of two Ethiopian slave girls by curing them of snoring.

Here in Cairo, with a little help from opium, Burton rediscovered the inner peace and contentment of the East: 'the savouring of animal existence, the passive enjoyment of mere sense, the pleasant langour, the dreamy

Above: *Isabel Burton. 'If I were a man, I would be Richard Burton; but, being only a woman, I would be Richard Burton's wife,' she wrote. She first set eyes on him in Boulogne before his pilgrimage to Mecca, and married him ten years later. 'Isabel acted towards Burton very much as England was then acting towards the East. She colonized him.' (Lesley Blanche,* The Wilder Shores of Love*)*

Above: *Richard Burton by Louis Desanges, presented to him, with his wife's portrait (see above left), as a gift on his wedding day.*

tranquillity, the airy castle-building'. The castles were in Mecca and Burton was to be Don Quixote. For Sancho Panza he found an eighteen-year-old Meccan boy, Mohammed, who would accompany him to the Holy City. To get there he took fifty pounds in Maria Theresa dollars (the local currency) and thirty pounds in English and Turkish currency hidden in his leather belt; and for the journey he equipped himself with toothpick, goatskin water bag, needle, thread, dagger, stash of opium, gigantic yellow umbrella and a notebook concealed inside a copy of the Koran.

Left: *Arabia, with the Turkish-controlled coastal regions clearly marked in green, the independent interior in orange.*

After crossing Sinai the two men boarded a *sambuk*, the fifty-ton *Golden Wire*, designed to carry sixty pilgrims and bulging with ninety-seven. Like bilge water, Burton found his own level; a gang of Egyptian thugs who had commandeered the poop throwing out all who had been installed already. When some of the passengers objected, Burton earned the acclaim of the thugs by picking up an earthenware water jug weighing a hundred pounds and throwing it down on the protesting swarm of humanity below. It was the action of a very frustrated man: he had just discovered that his opium was packed in the bottom of the hold and was unobtainable until the *Golden Wire* reached Wajh a week later where 'a druggist sold me an ounce of opium at a Chinese price.'

They sailed by day and anchored off the coast at night. Mornings were the most pleasant time. By noon 'all colour melts away with the candescence above' and the sun beat down ceaselessly until dusk when 'the enemy sinks . . . under a canopy of gigantic rainbow.' At night, when the ship was still, 'the horizon is all darkness, and the sea reflects the white visage of the night'.

From the poop he got his first glimpse of Arabia. 'Verdure there was none, but under the violet and orange tints of the sky the chalky rocks became heaps of topazes, and the brown-burnt ridge masses of amethysts.'

At Wajh the Egyptian thugs picked a quarrel with a café owner, 'an ill-looking, squint-eyed, low-browed, broad-shouldered fellow', and smashed up his café. In spite of the opium Burton had new worries: an Afghani who had also settled in India and was intensely suspicious of 'Sheikh Abdullah'. He had travelled over much of central Asia and spoke five or six languages. Burton was as suspicious of him as he was of Burton. 'These fellows are always good detectors of the incognito.' Fortunately Burton had known the Afghani's uncle, 'a gallant old man who had been civil to me in Cairo', which saved him.

Twelve days out of Suez the *Golden Wire* slowly beat its way up-wind into Yanbu harbour, to the town of white-washed buildings with domes and minarets, framed by the sunburnt plain beyond. Here, amid the 'over-armed and over-dressed population', Burton and his Egyptian friends set about procuring camels to Medina. They got them at three dollars a beast, half in advance and half on arrival. They passed the time in the cafés, eating, drinking coffee and smoking their pipes. One evening Amm Jamal, the most senior of the Egyptians, quietly took Burton aside and told him that if he was to avoid paying the tax on infidels (the *Jizyat*), he must be careful always to talk and dress like an Arab. So much for 'Sheikh Abdullah'.

Coming ashore at Yanbu Burton had stepped on a poisonous sea urchin. Hardly able to walk he was forced into the indignity of renting a litter, normally reserved for women. 'My reason for choosing a litter was that notes are more easily taken in it than on a dromedary's back, and the excuse of lameness prevented it detracting from my manhood.'

They left Yanbu on 19 July 1853, threading their way through the narrow dusty streets past white-washed walls and piles of rubbish, emerging into a desert that dazzled under the brightness of the moon. As usual on a caravan, somebody started to sing. They rode through the night until 3 a.m. Six hours later he was woken by his companions and given a breakfast of biscuit, rice and tea. He fell asleep again till 2 p.m. when he was served a lunch of biscuit, rice, stale bread and sour milk. Then everyone loaded and set off.

'All was sun-parched, the furious heat was drying up the sap and juice of the land.' Burton was in his element. He was also the first European in Arabia to try to express the 'Inner Journey', which the very monotony of the landscape provokes. 'Desert views are eminently suggestive; they appeal to the future, not the past; they arouse because they are by no means memorial.' Later, on the way to Mecca, he was to describe a vista so desolate that there was nothing but Allah. Sadly though, such metaphysical speculations did not make him a better man. His cameleer, 'like the lowest orders of Orientals, requires to be ill-treated; gentleness and condescension he seems to consider proof of cowardice and imbecility'.

He was surprised when a Bedouin interrupted his thoughts to ask him for *baksheesh*, especially since the Bedouin came from the Beni-Harb, 'which has kept its blood pure for the last thirteen centuries'; but he reassured himself that 'they had been corrupted by intercourse with pilgrims'. He then went on to describe the Bedouin in his usual offensive manner.

> The outer ring of these Fighting-Sons was contemptible; small chocolate-coloured beings, stunted and thin, with mops of coarse bushy hair, burnt brown by the sun, straggling beards, vicious eyes, frowning brows, screaming voices, and well-made, but attentuated, limbs.[3]

Below: *'Haji Abdullah'. 'There is something indescribably revolting to our feelings, in the position of an English officer, even though it may be in the pursuit of very interesting and desirable information, crawling among a crowd of unbelievers, around the objects of their wretched superstition; sharing and, perhaps, exaggerating their miserable exhibitions of reverence.' (Edinburgh Review)*

Burton's small caravan now joined up with a larger one of some two hundred camels, looking like 'contrabandistas of the Pyrenees'. The column of camels wound their way, 'not without a kind of barbaric pomp', through a dull khaki landscape beneath a steel blue sky touched by purple, until they ascended through a desolate and broken valley into the Hejaz.

There, to Burton's delight, the caravan was attacked by bandits. But to his chagrin the escort did nothing about it, not wanting to start a blood-feud with the tribe that was shooting at them. Instead, they discharged their guns to create a smoke screen and the whole caravan raced through the danger spot, losing a mere twelve men.

They made their approach to Medina on 25 July, riding through a valley covered in lava.

> I now understood the full value of a phrase in the Moslem ritual, 'And when his eyes shall fall upon the trees of al-Meinah let them raise their voice and bless the Apostle with the choicest of Blessings.' In all the fair view before us nothing was more striking, after the desolation through which we had passed, than the gardens and orchards about the town.[4]

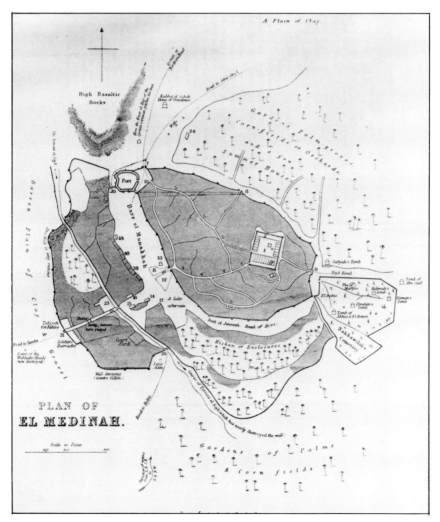

Left: *Burton's plan of Medina, with its outlying palm groves and the Great Mosque (Fig. 1) facing south-south-west towards Mecca.*

Above: Burton's first view of Medina, coming out of the valley of lava and looking down on the city in the plain below.

After pontificating on military tactics, female circumcision, linguistics, Islamic history, horticulture and haemorrhoids ('The patient looks with horror at the scissors and the knife, so they seldom succeed in obtaining a radical cure'), Burton found time to describe the town. Medina was walled with four gates, the tall minarets of the Great Mosque and its five lesser mosques (which seemed to bear the same relationship to it that Wren's City churches bear to St Paul's in London) piercing the sky. Inside the walls it was cramped and dirty; outside there was a fountain among palm trees, a white-washed fort and the cemetery of el-Bakia. For Burton the outside was far preferable to the inside, where he was constantly besieged by beggars – the only 'natives' in the world that Burton feared.

> Some were wild beggars and picturesque, who sat upon the ground immersed in the contemplation of their napkins; others, angry beggars who cursed if they were gratified, and others noisy and petulant beggars, especially the feminine party near the *Kadi*'s tomb, who captured me by the skirt of my garment, compelling me to ransom myself. There were, besides, pretty beggar boys who held out the right hand on the score of good looks; ugly beggars, emaciated rascals whose long hair, dirt, and leanness entitled them to charity; and lastly, the blind, the halt, and diseased, who, as sons of the Holy City, demanded from the Faithful that support which they could not provide themselves.[5]

He saw the seven thousand-strong Damascus caravan arrive in the city, 'the main stream that carries off all the small currents that, at this season of general movement, flow from Central Asia towards the great centre of the Islamic world.' In one night a suburb of tents sprang up outside the walls, of every size, shape and colour, ranging from the gilt-topped marquee of the Pasha to the ragged prism of the tobacco seller. They were pitched in order with thoroughfares running to the four points of the compass. Burton and his Egyptians were impressed. They decided to join the Damascus caravan.

Left: 'A Grandee's Litter', like the one Burton used: 'a vehicle appropriate to women and children, fathers of families, married men, 'Shelebis' (Exquisites), and generally to those who are too effeminate to ride.'

A few days later, towards nightfall, the suburb of tents became the scene of confusion. Tents lay on the ground, camels roared as they were loaded. Horses galloped about, men rushed wildly in all directions, women and children sat confused and lost on the ground. In the middle of all of this Burton was having a screaming match with his cameleer who refused to load his wooden trunk on the justifiable grounds that the camel was already overloaded. Every now and then a shot was fired and the whole caravan thought it was about to move off. It was not until the following morning that the caravan finally set off, with Burton and his friends pushing their way to the front.

The desert they were travelling through was a succession of table-top plains on different levels, separated by abrupt ridges of volcanic rock ribbed with furrows and fissures. 'Nowhere have I seen a land in which Earth's anatomy lies so barren.'

Five days out of Medina Burton's party were trapped by Ali bin Ya Sin, a garrulous minor religious official and Meccan guide. The toothless old miser – who had the annoying habit of mumbling verses of the Koran not quite quietly enough – had been sharing his litter with an Egyptian. After a row over a copper coin Ali bin Ya Sin had thrown him out. A little apprehensive of the consequences of his action, he ingratiated himself in Burton's party, seeing them as an effective protection from the furious Egyptian. Burton assigned one of his own Egyptians, Sheikh Nur, to Ali's litter.

> Sheikh Nur, elated by the sight of old Ali's luxuries, promised himself some joyous hours; but next morning he owned with a sigh that he had purchased splendour at an extravagant price of happiness – the senior's tongue never rested throughout the livelong night.[6]

Next morning Burton watched a dispute between a Turkish pilgrim who could not speak Arabic and a Bedouin who could not speak Turkish. In exasperation the Turk struck the Bedouin. That night the Turk had his stomach ripped open by a knife. He was comfortably wrapped up in his shroud and left in a half-dug grave to die peacefully.

The caravan continued to Sufaynah, about half way between Medina and

Mecca, where the Medina road and the Baghdad road converge. There the Damascus caravan met the caravan from Baghdad; an explosive mixture of two thousand Wahhabis, Shiites, Kurds, Persians and Arabs. 'I never saw a more pugnacious assembly: one look sufficed for a quarrel.' There was little love lost between them; neither yielded precedence to the other and from then on it became a race for Mecca. With his usual total disregard for the feelings of others, Burton calmly sat watching the Wahhabis while puffing on his pipe. One Wahhabi, feeling increasingly provoked, took out his dagger. He quickly sheathed it when Burton's Egyptians went for their pistols.

Resting that night, Sheikh Abdullah was approached by his namesake, a tall thin man of about forty, who asked him for medicines. Burton, on investigation, found that he was suffering from the effects of opium withdrawal, and generously prepared a pipe for him, inviting him to join their party.

> I never met amongst the Arab citizens a better bred or a better informed man. At Constantinople he had learnt a little French, Italian and Greek; and from the properties of a shrub to the varieties of honey, he was full of useful knowledge and openable as a dictionary.[7]

They continued south-east, sometimes ahead of the Baghdad caravan, sometimes racing to catch it up. They ascended a forbidding ridge onto a broad gravel tableland, 'a desert peopled only by echoes.' The desolation continued through the night when the gravel plain broke up amid jet-black volcanic rocks. Camels stumbled, their shadows accentuated by the glow of burning torches. The air was thick with the smell of incense from the cressets that the slaves of notables swung ahead of their masters. All sense of order was lost. Burton, making his way through the human and volcanic chaos became entangled with a party of Syrians. He drew his sword, but the wiser Sheikh Abdullah stayed his hand.

Below: *The Caravan to Mecca. 'Jebel Nour' by Etienne Dinet. (Mathaf Gallery, London)*

Two night-marches later they were at el-Zaribah, the frontier of the holy land, where they washed, shaved and donned the *ihram*.

> Then Sheikh Abdullah, who acted as our director of consciences, bade us be good pilgrims, avoiding quarrels, immorality, bad language, and light conversation. We must so reverence life that we should avoid killing game, causing an animal to fly, or even pointing it out for destruction, nor should we scratch ourselves, save with the open palm, lest vermin be destroyed, or a hair uprooted by the nail. We were to respect the sanctuary by sparing the trees, and not to pluck a single blade of grass. As regards personal considerations, we were to abstain from all oils, perfumes, and unguents; from washing the head with mallow or with lote leaves; from dyeing, shaving, cutting, or vellicating a single pile or hair; and though we might take advantage of shade, and even form it with upraised hands, we must by no means cover our sconces. For each infraction of these ordinances we must sacrifice a sheep.[8]

Above: *The Pass of Death, where Burton's caravan was attacked by Bedouin.*

Coming out of el-Zaribah the two caravans were running neck-and-neck. They continued like that until dusk when they were attacked by Bedouin snipers. The first shot, marked by a small curl of smoke from high in the rocks, brought down a dromedary, and the mass of pilgrims and camels, packed in the pass, panicked. While the Pasha and his officers of the Damascus escort spread out a carpet to debate what to do, the Baghdad caravan's Wahhabi escort charged up the hill and dispersed the snipers. Unable to take part in the charge, Burton calmly called for his supper while the caravans were under fire.

Burton made no secret of his admiration for the Bedouin's militarist hierarchical society 'in which the fiercest, the strongest and the craftiest obtains complete mastery over his fellows'. They are hardly the words of Peter Forsskal, the lover of liberty, but Forsskal's eulogy on the Bedouin way of life had taken on a momentum of its own. Men saw in the Bedouin what they wanted to see, and that was usually themselves.

Left: *Burton's picture of 'The Sermon on Mount Arafat', sketched on the ninth day of the pilgrimage.*

Above: *'The Stoning on Mount Arafat', by Richard Burton.*

The two caravans marched on through the night, their way lit by the flames of aslepias bushes, set on fire by the escort to clear the path of snipers. The camels, exhausted and half-blinded by the flames, slipped and stumbled on the 'livid red' embers that carpeted the sand. Ali bin Ya Sin's litter, with the other Sheikh Abdullah in it, turned completely over, somersaulting the occupants out onto the ground.

A day from Mecca they passed troops of Bedouin girls, looking over orchard walls and laughing while children offered the pilgrims fresh water. At 4 p.m. they came upon a steep and rocky pass. They rode through it until after midnight. At 1 a.m. the pass opened up and the night resounded with cries of 'Mecca!' and 'The Sanctuary!'. Before them were the outlines of the Holy City.

The caravans made their way into the city through the northern suburbs, past the trees around the Sherif's palace with its elaborate wooden balconies and overlays, and past the cemetery of Jannat el-Ma'da, through the narrow lanes of the Afghan quarter, the dark streets crowded with sleeping figures, to Mohammed's house. Mohammed invited Burton to be his guest and the Englishman promptly took advantage of his position to insist that the store room be cleared for his personal use, hogging the best part of the communal drawing room until it was ready. A group of Turkish pilgrims who had rented rooms from Mohammed's mother, and included a nice old retired colonel, regarded the manners of the Englishman dressed as an Afghan as utterly appalling and decided to ignore him until he became more civilized. Later the retired colonel and the British officer became quite friendly. 'As the charming Mrs Malaprop observes, intercourse is all the better by beginning with a little aversion.

The next day Burton saw the Kaaba for the first time.

> I may truly say that of all the worshippers who clung weeping to the curtain, or who pressed their beating hearts to the stone, none felt for the moment a deeper emotion that did the Haji from the far-north.[9]

Left: *A square in Jeddah, drawn by Burton on his return from Mecca. 'In the square opposite us was an unhappy idiot, who afforded us a melancholy spectacle. He delighted to wander about in a primitive state of toilette, as all such wretches do; but the people of Jeddah, far too civilized to retain Moslem respect for madness, forced him, despite shrieks and struggles, into a shirt, and when he tore it off they beat him.'*

The streets around the Kaaba were packed with pilgrims from all corners of Islam, each national grouping following its own guide. Many stayed all day and night, praying around lanterns and haggling around market stalls. It was not until 2 a.m. that Burton and Mohammed returned to Mohammed's house. The streets were completely safe, there were no night watchmen, and the population slept on their beds on the pavement outside their houses.

Burton performed the rest of the Haj in company with the other fifty thousand pilgrims. At Arafat he met again the dreaded Ali bin Ya Sin, who was in search of his camel. Burton forgot about the man during the Sermon, being more interested in an eighteen-year-old girl with soft citron-coloured skin. He was rewarded by 'a partial removal of the *yashmak*', showing a dimpled mouth and rounded chin. 'The pilgrim was in ecstacy.'

Later, when he tried to sketch her, Ali bin Ya Sin – doubtlessly aware that 'Sheikh Abdullah' was a *farrangi*, a European – stopped him, crying: 'Effendi, sit quiet, there is danger here.' When Burton ignored him he became more insistent. 'What art thou doing? Thou wilt be the death of us.' Burton was furious. Intent on revenge he 'seized the pot full of savoury meat which the old man had previously stored for supper and, without further preamble, began to eat it greedily, at the same time ready to shout with laughter at the mumbling and grumbling'. Somewhat ungrateful to the man who had just saved his life.

The pilgrimage over, Burton explored the city and its people. Most Meccans, he observed, had Negro concubines; the men were flabby; the women were attractive; and the language of the Meccans was the filthiest in the Moslem world. In the slave market he naturally identified more with the slavemasters than the slaves. As for the slaves they appeared perfectly happy, 'laughing loudly, talking unknown tongues and quizzing purchasers, even during the delicate operation of purchasing'.

One day he was invited to dine by the ubiquitous Ali bin Ya Sin, for whom the laws of hospitality must have been very trying at times. Burton agreed with Mohammed that Ya Sin had only made the invitation 'for the simple purpose of exalting his own dignity'. Burton condescended, expecting to be the guest of honour. He arrived in Ali's house and made himself at home on the divan, settling down with the other guests to pipes when suddenly there was a commotion and everyone rose. The guest of honour was not Burton, but a eunuch.

He was a person of some importance, being the guardian of some domes of high degree at Cairo and Constantinople: the highest place and the best pipe were unhesitatingly offered to and accepted by him. . . . It was a fair lesson of humility for a man to find himself ranked beneath this high-shouldered, spindle-backed, beardless bit of neutrality; and as such I took it duly to heart.[10]

The Pilgrimage over, the conqueror – just a little humbled – hired two camels for thirty-five piastres, bid farewell to his friends, and left the city with Mohammed for Jeddah. The Jeddah road was crowded with departing pilgrims. Before they had even left Mecca they had found themselves entangled in the Damascus caravan.

At one coffee shop Burton and Mohammed met a Turk who could speak Hindustani, Pushtu, Armenian, English, French and Italian. He had been a dragoman to English travellers and had visited France, Italy, South Africa, India and England. He realized immediately that Burton was English and kept sending him up: 'Then who the damn are you?'; 'By God, you must budge, you'll catch it here.' Later it was said that Burton silenced him with a dagger: perfectly probable from a man who, when asked by a doctor at a wedding breakfast how he felt about killing a man, replied, 'Quite jolly, doctor, how do you?' Burton arrived in Jeddah, 'not having more than tenpence of borrowed coin', went to see the British vice-consul, Mr Cole, bullied him into giving him his passage fare to Egypt and bought a ticket on a steamship. The town had all 'the licence of a seaport': drinking houses and whorehouses overflowed in the white-washed labyrinth packed with returning pilgrims. After several thoroughly enjoyable days, Burton's ship was ready to sail. Only then, so Burton claims, did Sancho Panza realize his Don Quixote was 'a sahib from India'.

Looking back a few months later and balancing the risk, Captain Burton advised his readers against attempting the pilgrimage themselves.

Below: *The Bedouin girl Burton sketched on Mount Arafat.*

The first Badawi who caught sight of the Frank's hat would not deem himself a man if he did not drive a bullet through the wearer's head. At the pilgrimage season disguise is easy on account of the vast and varied multitudes. . . . But woe to the unfortunate who happens to be recognized in public as an Infidel. [Readers should not] attempt Mecca without disguise, until the day comes when such steps can be taken in the certainty of not causing a mishap; an accident would not redound to our reputation, as we could not in justice revenge it.[11]

On his return from Jeddah, while still in disguise, Burton met a thirty-four-year-old German, Heinrich von Maltzan, in Shepheard's Hotel. Unlike Burton, von Maltzan realized that if he was to penetrate Arabia in disguise he would require years of preparation. It turned out to be seven years, most of them spent among Moslems in Algeria and Morocco. After seven years he met a hashish smoker in Algiers who lent the German his name and passport in return for six months' supply of smoke.

In 1860 von Maltzan arrived in Cairo and met the ageing Sheikh Mustapha, also bound for Mecca, where it was his ambition to be buried. The two, plus Mustapha's Ethiopian slave, left Cairo on 23 April for Quseir, where they took a dhow to Jeddah. In Jeddah von Maltzan congratulated himself on finding a cheap hotel, only to be woken by screams at three in the morning. His neighbours were howling dervishes. His first sight of Mecca was at dawn.

There was not a single man who did not cry out *Labbayk* (Here I am) with all the strength of his lungs, the strong and healthy roaring it out, the sick and weak uttering it with conclusive exertion using their last feeble breath in that holy moment. . . . At such moments the Moslem forgets the whole world. He thinks only of the holy things, seen and unseen, which lie before him.[12]

Above: *The Kaaba in Mecca, the simple stone altar built by Abraham, which Mohammed Asad, the European convert, called 'a parable of man's humility before God'.* (*Mathaf Gallery, London*)

Since Burckhardt and Badia, Mecca had become a place for tourists, and von Maltzan's reactions – in spite of that initial insight – were those of a tourist. He compared the city with a lunatic asylum, full of half-naked groaners covered in sweat and dust.

He stayed for twenty days in the Afghan quarter where he was unlikely to meet any Algerians who might see through his disguise. At Arafat, where Sheikh Mustapha died, von Maltzan was bored. But when he went to the Turkish baths after his return to Mecca to wash off the filth of fifty thousand pilgrims he met some Algerians who recognized him as a Christian. Fourteen hours later he was in Jeddah, without even his clothes. He did, however, have his Algerian friend's passport, which he duly returned. The hashish-smoker happily adopted the title Haji and took to carrying his passport with him everywhere so that, should anything happen to him in his cloud of smoke, he could show it duly stamped to the Almighty, and be let into Paradise. Von Maltzan's end was less happy. He committed suicide in 1874.

Strangely enough, von Maltzan makes no reference to that most extraordinary of Meccan residents, the redoubtable Miss Macintosh. She was the daughter of a Devon doctor, sent to India as a governess and taken prisoner at Lucknow aged twenty. She married one of the Indian Mutiny leaders, who gave her the name 'Lady Venus' and converted her to Islam. He took her to Mecca where he died and she remained there for nearly twenty years, making a precarious living embroidering skull-caps.

The English traveller John Keane, who used to see her shopping and taking tea in the arcades around the Great Mosque described her as having the appearance of a reduced gentlewoman; and although references to her past life pained her and she seemed lonely at times, she was content. When the British discovered her and offered her the opportunity to be 'rescued', she refused, and spent the rest of her life in Mecca and Moslem India, where she lived entirely with her co-religionists, as if she had never had any other life.

Two years after von Maltzan and still during Miss Macintosh's residence in the city, a pedestrian tourist arrived. This was Herman Bicknell, the most suburban of pilgrims, who not only was the only one to proclaim his nationality (with the exception of Philby who is an exception to everything), but the only one who managed to reduce the most sacred shrine of Islam to the dimensions of his home suburb of Norwood. Bicknell arrived from Norwood via Jeddah on the steamer *Sacred Carpet* in May 1862. The very banality of the man makes him astonishing. The Great Mosque is a 'quadrangle', the Kaaba is, well, 'cubical'.

Not sorry to leave a shade temperature of 110°F (45°C) he returned to Norwood where he wrote a letter to *The Times*, 'to encourage other Englishmen, especially those from India, to perform the Pilgrimage, without being deterred by exaggerated reports concerning the perils of the enterprise'. Then he recommended his guide, Sheikh Mohammed 'Umr Faneir-Jizadah, an excellent fellow who 'is extremely courteous and obliging, and has promised to show to other Englishmen the same politeness which I experienced with him myself'.

Burton never forgave him.

Below: *With Mecca laid bare, the explorers moved towards the interior.*

V

AGENTS OF FOREIGN POWERS

By the mid-nineteenth century, Mecca had been invaded by tourists, but there were still 'huge white blots' on the map of Arabia. The Prussian geographer, Karl Ritter, drew a map of Arabia in 1852. This was reasonably accurate along the coasts and in the Hejaz, but what he placed in the interior was still very much guesswork. Sadlier's journey helped, but the oases of Hail and Riyadh were as elusive as Tibet or Timbuktu.

Geographical ignorance was matched by political ignorance. Since the Egyptian withdrawal, no foreigner had been allowed into the Wahhabi-controlled interior except the Persian pilgrims who raced through and never lingered, milked by the Wahhabis on the way. Yet the strategic importance of the Peninsula had not lessened since Napoleon's time. Indeed, steamships, railways, canals and empires had increased its importance, and questions began to be asked. Who ruled in Riyadh? Were they Wahhabi or not? How powerful was the Prince of Hail? What forces did these rulers command? What territories did they hold? Four men penetrated into the interior to find the answers: an 'Orientalist', a Jesuit, a horse-dealer and an eccentric English diplomat. All were players in a greater game, and all saw something different, though they looked at the same things.

After the Egyptian withdrawal, so reluctantly witnessed by Sadlier, the Wahhabi empire had steadily reasserted itself. The change in Saudi fortunes came when Turki ibn Abdallah, a Saudi prince taken hostage by Ibrahim, escaped from captivity, raised a Wahhabi army and re-occupied Riyadh. Within a decade central and northern Arabia was under his sway. Turki was murdered in 1834 and a usurper ruled for forty days before Turki's son Faisal overthrew him with the help of a Hail warlord, Abdallah ibn Rashid, who led the assault party through an unguarded window in the castle.

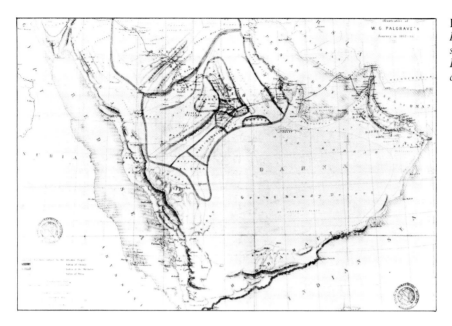

Left: *Palgrave's route through Hail and Riyadh to the Gulf, showing the extent of both the Rashidi and the Saudi domains.*

For a second time, with the Wahhabi empire threatening them, the Egyptians took the offensive. Faisal was captured and imprisoned but escaped again and with Abdallah ibn Rashid's help retook his throne.

Faisal ruled his Wahhabi state according to the Koran, with only a short interruption when Egypt tried to reassert herself, for a total of thirty-one years. He became totally blind and not a little mad for the last few years of his reign. He was admired but not liked, according to the English diplomat Lewis Pelly, British Resident in the Gulf, and was 'spoken of with a sort of dread in which respect and hatred were curiously mixed'.

Abdallah the Kingmaker was rewarded with the governship of Hail, and became Emir of Jebal Shammar, on the northern marches of Arabia. He maintained his loyalty to Faisal throughout his life, but his son, Talal, so astutely played off Turks, Egyptians, Wahhabis, and later the European powers, that he was able to transform the province into a virtually independent state, protecting northern Arabia from the excesses of Wahhabism, and maintaining a secular and infinitely more tolerant society. The two capitals, Hail and Riyadh, could not have contrasted more.

The first to bring news of these developments back to Europe was the 'Orientalist'. George Augustus Wallin was born in 1811 on an island in the Gulf of Bothnia and, although he was expelled from school, could speak nine languages by his early twenties. He attended the Oriental Institute in St Petersburg for two years, then completed his education with a study of medicine.

He arrived in Cairo in April 1845, where he lived for over a year as a Moslem, playing the Arab flute and attending courses in theology at el-Azhar, where Roches had presented his *fettoua* four years earlier. There he was taken on by the Egyptian Foreign Office who financed his journey into the Arabian interior. In return, he was to report back to them on the political developments there. For a cover he adopted the role of horse-dealer.

He left Cairo in April 1845, accompanied by two Bedouin. After crossing Sinai and spending two months in Maan near the Dead Sea, he rode due east across the Syrian Desert to the Wells of Weisat, and then on to Jawf, gateway to the Nafud, the red desert that guards Arabia in the north.

On 1 September he started across the Nafud. By day their route was marked by two pyramids of stones and rocks, the peaks of Aalem. At night they followed a guide who kept 'the polar star on his left shoulder-blade.' On the tenth day, almost dehydrated, they reached the waters of Jubbah. A few days beyond lay Hail, surrounded by cornfields and vegetable gardens, and protected by the encircling Jebal Shammar mountains. It was a thriving, prosperous and secure area, and its ruler, Abdallah ibn Rashid, was widely respected.

> Power and wealth alone did not procure Abdallah this charismatic authority among the Arabs; rather it was his unique personal qualities, his intrepidity, his manliness, his sense of justice, his unflinching adherence to his word, his unsurpassed hospitality and his benevolence to the poor who never left his door hungry. These virtues, the highest a Bedouin can be endowed with, Abdallah was graced with to a high degree.[1]

Wallin passed two months in Hail and came to regard the Jebal Shammar as an ideal state. Of course it was not an ideal state but, like Forsskal's myth a century earlier, it took on a momentum of its own. Men saw in the Hail townsmen what they saw in the desert Bedouin, a mirage. Wallin was wrong in one respect – which the next visitor to Hail, Palgrave, was also to get wrong. He assumed that the Jebal Shammar was a kingdom controlled by townsfolk and that the Rashidis came from the towns. Reality proved even more romantic to nineteenth-century eyes than myth. Rashidi power was Bedouin power; the Bedouin had taken the towns and the towns had civilized the Bedouin. It was nearly forty years before the Blunts – English aristocrats with a natural predisposition to Bedouin princes – arrived in Hail and spotted the difference.

Wallin wanted to go on to Riyadh and the Gulf but was forced to abandon the project because of tribal wars and lack of money. Instead, he joined a caravan of Persian Shiite pilgrims on their way to Mecca. He found them 'awkward and tiresome', and he was glad to part company in Mecca. He arrived in Jeddah with only a shilling in his pocket.

Right: *The Jebal Shammar: Wallin's, Palgrave's and later the Blunts' ideal state.*

Wallin returned to Cairo but was back in Arabia three years later. He landed at the Red Sea port of Muwaylih in February 1848 and crossed the Hejaz Mountains to Tabuk in the north-west corner of the sub-continent. Still in his disguise of horse-dealer, he went on to Taima on the edge of Wahhabi territory, the first European to set foot in it.

There he joined some half-dozen other horse-dealers on their way to Hail. When he got there he discovered that Abdallah ibn Rashid had died and been replaced by his son Talal. Wallin stayed a month. Again he wanted to get to Riyadh; but Talal, who realized that he was a Christian, persuaded him that he would be killed if he tried to enter the Wahhabi heartlands. Instead Wallin rode east and north-east, to Meshed Ali and Baghdad, eventually arriving in Basra penniless.

He returned to Finland in 1850 and was appointed Professor of Oriental Languages at Helsinki University, but could not settle. Two years later he died, while preparing for a third attempt to reach Riyadh.

Egypt was not the only power interested in Arabia. The excavation of the Suez Canal, begun by Ferdinand de Lesseps (the French Emperor Napoleon III's cousin-in-law), had started in 1859. Both France and England had their eyes on the Peninsula. Ironically, the first of their agents to get there was an Englishman in the service of the French, William Gifford Palgrave.

His background was the most bourgeois and urbane of all nineteenth-century English explorers. He was, quite literally, a class apart. His father, Sir Francis Palgrave, changed his name from Cohen, and was the founder of the Public Record Office. Speaking almost of himself, Sir Francis wrote in his tome *The Rise and Progress of the English Commonwealth*, published in 1832 (the year of the First Reform Act), that the genius of the British lay in the openness of their ruling class, never frightened, like so many aristocracies, to recruit new members from the aspiring classes, 'thus increasing the energy of the state without endangering its stability.'

Gifford was the only one of Sir Francis' sons to get close to endangering the stability of the state, and even he ended up in the Foreign Office, a very pillar of stability. Of his other brothers, Francis became Professor of Poetry at Oxford and compiler of *Palgrave's Golden Treasury*, Inglis became editor of *The Economist*, and Reginald became Clerk of the House of Commons.

'Giffy's' career was more eccentric. After a conventional Church of England education at Charterhouse, he came under the influence of Newman and the Anglo-Catholics at Oxford. In spite of a First in Greats and a Second in Mathematics he threw up a career in the Church and, deliberately abandoning his intellectual background, joined the Indian Army as a subaltern; the first of many revolts and false starts which ensured that 'Giffy' never achieved the success of his more illustrious brothers.

It was 1847. In January he left England, in February he caught his first sight of Arabia from a steamer in the Red Sea and in March he arrived in India. He was commissioned in the 8th Bombay Native Infantry. Two years later he was converted to catholicism, threw up his military career and joined the Society of Jesus. After four years at the Jesuit College of Madras and three years in Rome he was sent to the Lebanon. He adopted his father's original name of Cohen, which means priest in Hebrew.

From the Lebanon he wrote to his brother Inglis: 'with so frequent changes of abode, companions, languages, etc., I feel equally at home, or, if you wish, equally a stranger and a sojourner, as all my fathers were.' Later he changed his name again, to Father Michael Sohail. Like Burton he was uncertain of his identity; but unlike Burton he had a far more attractive psyche, uncertain of his loyalties, his beliefs and himself.

Above: *William Gifford Palgrave, from a photograph taken in 1880, by which time he had renounced catholicism, the priesthood and Napoleon III: the face of a deeply troubled man.*

Right: *David Roberts' view of Lebanon from Mount Sidon, where Palgrave served as a Jesuit and was almost killed in 1860 by the Druses when they massacred many Christian communities, in far less happy circumstances than Roberts' idyllic scene suggests.*

Father Michael Sohail's first political involvement in Lebanon came during the Christian-Druse massacres of 1860. He was almost killed at Sidon, and although he never took up arms, is reported to have used his military training to help organize the Christian defence of Zahla. Like so many Lebanese Christians who survived the communal attacks, he saw the French peacekeeping force sent by Napoleon III as a deliverance. After a lecture tour of Ireland to raise money for the Christians he went to Paris where – with the assent of the Vatican – he became an agent for Napoleon III.

His first mission was to Egypt to sound out Halim Pasha, grandson of Mohammed Ali, on the Emperor's project of making him Viceroy of Egypt under French suzerainty. The mission was a failure but he was still able to bring back to France a carefully prepared plan for a French invasion of Syria from Egypt. At the time his enthusiasm for Napoleon, like his earlier enthusiasm for Newman, knew no bounds. Later he was to denounce Napoleon as 'that colossal imposture overthrown at Sedan', as he was to denounce Newman and catholicism. His sincerity, however, in all his turns, cannot be doubted.

In 1862, he was sent on a second mission to report on the Arabian kingdoms of Hail and Riyadh. It was irresistible to a man like Palgrave. Hail had only been penetrated once, by Wallin seventeen years earlier, while Riyadh had yet to be unveiled.

To make the journey he changed his name again, to Saleem Abou Mahmoud el-Eys, a Syrian Christian who practised medicine. For a companion (Jesuits are not allowed to travel alone) he took a newly-ordained Greek priest, Geraigiri, who adopted the name of Barakat.

Following roughly the same route as Wallin, they set out from Maan on 16 June 1862, 'dressed like ordinary middle-class travellers of Inner Syria'. They took enough medicines to 'kill or cure half the sickmen of Arabia', and were escorted by three Bedouin. After seven days of hard riding, setting off before dawn and concealing themselves in the dips and hollows on the desert surface at night, they reached Wadi Sirham. They were now in the territory of Talal ibn Rashid.

Above: *Jawf from the north, the spot where Palgrave first saw the city, coming out of the steep valley of red sandstone onto the open plain.*

> Much did our Bedouins talk of Talal, and much extol his vigour, his equity, his active vigilance, his military prowess, though at the same time they repined at his unwarrantable repression of Bedouin liberty, and the restraints he imposed on the innate right of nomads to plunder, rob, and murder at their own free discretion – complaints which, contrary to the intention of our informants, rather raised than diminished our esteem for this ruler.[2]

From Wadi Sirham, safe in the security of ibn Rashid's territory, they rode south-east to Jawf. Their first sight of the oasis came while descending a steep valley formed by shelves upon shelves of red rock, the town below half hidden by the foliage of surrounding palm-groves and fruit trees. The first sight of the inhabitants (Palgrave was always more interested in human nature than nature) was two prancing horsemen, fully dressed and fully armed, who galloped up to them with dates and sweet water, pronouncing a hearty *Mahaba* ('Welcome'). The *Mahaba* was important. The Wahhabis insisted on a long and drawn-out formal greeting in which the 'peace', 'mercy' and 'blessings' of God were frequently invoked. In the semi-independent and liberal-minded Shammar the inhabitants preferred the more secular *Mahaba*.

The elder of the horsemen, tall, about forty, with a silver-hilted sword proclaiming his importance, was called Ghafil el-Habub, head of one of the leading Jawf families. He led them through groves and gardens, streets and lanes, until they reached a small courtyard surrounded on three sides by apartments. It was Ghafil's house. The party dismounted and Ghafil led them into the coffee room, a large rectangular chamber, about fifty feet long and twenty feet high. It was covered in carpets.

Right: *A romantic Victorian view of Arab horsemen.*

Palgrave and Geraigiri sat on the best cushions while Ghafil's slave Soweylim made coffee. Palgrave, who like most Jesuits combined courage and intellectual rigour with an appreciation of the better things in life, watched every move. First Soweylim warmed the coffee pot, about two-thirds full of water. Next he selected the coffee beans, three or four handfuls, warming them on the fire but never burning them 'after the erroneous fashion of Turkey and Europe'. Then he put on the water to boil while grinding the beans in a mortar 'to a sort of coarse reddish grit, very unlike the fine charcoal dust which passes in some countries for coffee, and out of which every particle of real aroma has long since been burnt or ground'. The coffee beans ready, Soweylim mixed them with boiling water in a small pot, putting it back on the fire to boil and slowly stirring it with a small stick. The second it began to boil he took it off and added *heyl* (an Indian spice) and saffron. The coffee was ready. The whole ceremony had taken over half an hour.

> When all had been thus served, a second round is poured out, but in inverse order, for the last this time drinks first, and the guests last. On special occasions, a first reception, for instance, the muddy liquor is a third time handed round; nay, a fourth cup is sometimes added. But all this put together do not come up to one-fourth of what a European imbibes in a single draught at breakfast.[3]

Ghafil's coffee room became Palgrave's base for the next fortnight. He liked the town and its people. They were 'tall, well-proportioned, of a tolerably fair complexion, set off by long curling locks of jet-black hair, with features for the most part regular and intelligent'. And he liked the hospitality. 'Nowhere else, even in Arabia, is the guest, so at least he be not murdered before admittance, better treated, or more cordially invited to become in every way one of themselves.'

The most important meal among such hospitable people was supper: coarsely ground wheat in a vast dish overflowing with butter, meat and vegetables, served scalding hot and eaten communally with the fingers of the right hand. After the meal the guests washed their hands and sat on the flat roofs talking, smoking or just staring out at the cool colours of the evening.

> Neither dust nor vapour, much less a cloud, appears; the moon dips down in silvery whiteness to the very verge of the palm-tree tops, and the last rays of daylight are almost as sharp and clear as the dawn itself. Chat and society continue for an hour or two, and then everyone goes home, most to bed.[4]

He stayed for two weeks and enjoyed it. True to his bourgeois and cosmopolitan background he had infinitely more sympathy for the towns-people than the Bedouin. 'The Bedouin does not fight for his home, he has none; nor for his country, that is anywhere; nor for his honour, he has never heard of it; he aims and cares for none. His only object in war is plunder', and grazing space. Unlike Palgrave's liberal-minded and relatively enlightened townsfolk, the Bedouin were simply not the raw material of civilization.

After about twelve days, and beginning to get restless, he met a dozen minor chiefs of the Sherarat who were on their way to Hail to give their allegiance to Talal ibn Rashid. Palgrave and Geraigiri joined them. They left on 18 July. It meant crossing the Nafud in the height of summer.

Left: 'A coffee shop in Cairo', by David Roberts. Such coffee shops were a common meeting-place for men throughout the Arab world.

Right: *Jubbah, two-thirds of the way across the Nafud. Lady Anne Blunt called it 'one of the most curious places in the world'.*

Like Wallin, Palgrave found himself in an ocean of rolling reddish sand dunes, running in endless burning ridges, some three hundred feet high, stretching from north to south. Climbing one after another at an oblique angle, 'it proved worse than aught imagined'. Sometimes a track appeared, more often there was none; the dessicated wind-swept surface had long since lost the tracks of those who had been there before. It reminded Palgrave of the Inferno from Dante's *Divina Commedia*.

It was not just a test of courage and endurance; it was a test of nerves. Some of the Sherarat in the party planned to kill and plunder the two Syrian strangers. Palgrave took this in his stride and after a few days the others in the caravan persuaded the Sherarat to abandon their plan. After about sixty miles they spotted the two lonely pyramids of rock that Wallin had followed – the peaks of Aalem. 'They stand out like islands. . . . Their roots must be in the rocky base over which this upper layer of sand is strewn like the sea-water over its bed.'

The further they penetrated into the Nafud the more barren it became; horizon after horizon of sun-soaked dried-up waves of desert. When they finally arrived at the oasis of Jubbah, two-thirds of the way across, they knew that the worst was over. Three days later they found themselves on the verge of a large plain 'girt on every side by a high mountain rampart'. In front of them lay the oasis city of Hail. 'The town walls and buildings shone yellow in the evening sun, and the whole prospect was one of thriving security, delightful to view.'

They made their way through the city gate to ibn Rashid's palace. Crossing the courtyard they passed through a second gate into a smaller enclosure crowded with courtiers, petitioners and officials, where they were met by Seyf, the Court Chamberlain. Then, to both Palgrave's and Geraigiri's horror, they were accosted by two men who claimed to have known them in Syria. Fortunately a third announced that he recognized Palgrave from Cairo. By concentrating on the contradictions between their stories and adopting a 'fixed and vacant stare', they extricated themselves from the situation. 'Never mind them,' Seyf said, 'they are talkative liars, mere gossips.' He swept them through another courtyard containing the Rashidi artillery (including one gun marked '1810', with 'GR' stamped on it), into a high and pillared reception room. He sat down and offered them coffee. They told him they were physicians. He gave them leave to stay as long as they liked.

After coffee they returned to the outer courtyard just before Talal came in. Zamil, Talal's treasurer and chief minister, was on one side of him, and Abdul Mahsin, his political advisor, on the other. Mahsin was a refugee from the Wahhabi south and was to become an 'intimate acquaintance and steady friend'. Talal himself looked about forty (he was thirty-seven), short and swarthy with long black hair and dark piercing eyes. 'His glance never rested for a moment; sometimes it turned on his near companions, sometimes on the crowd; I have seldom seen so truly an "eagle eye" in rapidity and in brilliance.' Everyone stood up as he came into the enclosure. He acknowledged the two physicians and told Seyf he would grant a private audience with them the next day; then he swept out of the palace courtyard, leaving the crowd to amuse themselves with two tame ostriches.

The next day Palgrave was presented to Talal.

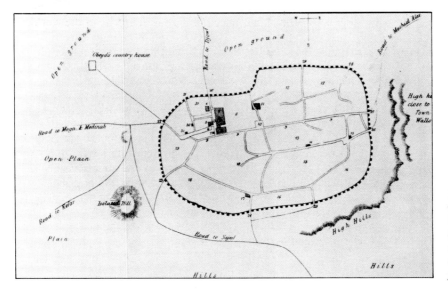

> The young sovereign possessed, in fact, all that Arab ideas require to ensure good government and lasting popularity. Affable towards the common people, reserved and haughty with the aristocracy, courageous and skilful in war, a lover of commerce and building in time of peace, liberal even to profusion, yet always careful to maintain and augment the state revenue, neither over-strict nor yet scandalously lax in religion, secret in his designs, but never known to break a promise once given, or violate a plighted faith; severe in administration, yet averse to bloodshed, he offered the very type of what an Arab prince should be. I might add, that among all rulers or governors, European or Asiatic, with whose acquaintance I have ever chanced to be honoured, I know few equal in the true art of government of Talal.[5]

Above: *Travellers in the Nafud, with the twin conical peaks of Aalem, Wallin's, Palgrave's and the Blunts' landmark, behind them.*

Palgrave's and Geraigiri's medical practice opened up the following morning in the house provided for them by Talal. It consisted of two rooms, about eight feet by sixteen, separated by a courtyard with a flat roof for sleeping on. The courtyard served as waiting room, with empty saddle bags and carpet ends for seats. In one of the rooms, on a floor covered in carpets, Palgrave sat cross-legged. Around him were a pair of scales, two mortars, some fifty boxes

Left: *Palgrave's plan of Hail, with Talal's palace (shaded) in the north-west quarter. His own house, facing it on the main square, is marked directly to the west of the palace.*

Right: *Drowned in a sandstorm. According to Palgrave the only difference between sandstorms and Hell was that sandstorms were not eternal.*

of drugs, a line of bottles and two medical treatises in Arabic. Discreetly concealed behind a cushion were two other medical books, one in French the other in English, 'to be consulted in secret if necessary.' He was never short of patients. Once Talal sent over his two sons as a mark of his esteem. They were perfectly healthy so Palgrave prescribed them cinnamon water and sugar and sent them home, 'the small boys thinking that if this be medicine, they will do their best to be ill for it every day.'

A time-table developed. They rose from their roof mattresses an hour before dawn and in the still half-light made their way to the city gate. They continued beyond the city for about a mile to a cluster of rocks. There they sat and talked, watching the city and its surrounding mountains take on colour under the rising sun.

By the time they had returned to the town, bought a breakfast of water-melon in the market and eaten it, there was already a queue of patients in their courtyard. Surgery, which gave Palgrave an excellent entrance into the Hail society, continued until early afternoon, and was followed by a two-hour siesta. The cool of the evening was given over to social visits and the day ended with a meal of rice and meat followed by the single obligatory cup of coffee and a pipe.

The streets and the people of the streets were what interested Palgrave most. They had a democracy that he had found nowhere else in the world.

> Mixed with the city crowd, swordsmen and gaily-dressed Negroes, for the Negro is always a dandy when he can afford it, belonging mostly to the palace, are now going about their affairs; the well-dressed chieftain and noble jostles on amid the plebian crowd on terms of astounding familiarity, and elbows or is elbowed by the artisan and the porter; while the court officers themselves meet with that degree of respect alone which indicates deference rather than inferiority in those who pay it. . . . The morning air in the streets yet retains just sufficient coolness to render tolerable the bright rays of the sun, and everywhere is that atmosphere of peace, security, and thriving known to the visitor of Arabia, but less familiar to the Syrian or Anatolian traveller. Should you listen to the hum of discourse around, you will seldom hear a curse, an imprecation, or a quarrel, but much business, repartee, and laughter.[6]

Left: *A mirage, as nineteenth-century artists who had never left Europe imagined it to be. If the artist had ever seen a mirage, the camels would be across the horizon, where the shimmering marriage of sand and sky merge in waves of rising heat creating a watery lake-like image.*

Though Mahsin and Talal were friendly to the two travellers, the pro-Wahhabi faction at court, lead by Talal's uncle Obied, treated him with xenophobic distrust. Talal had taken to neutralizing Obied by giving him command of long-distant and protracted military operations. The day before Palgrave's departure Obied was going out on one of them. Palgrave watched Talal inspect Obied's column before it left. At the end of the march past, Obied galloped up to Palgrave and, wishing him well, gave him a letter of introduction to Faisal ibn Saud, the Wahhabi ruler in Riyadh. Later Palgrave, distrusting Obied, opened the letter. It warned the Wahhabis that Palgrave was a magician, a capital offence. Palgrave destroyed it.

In spite of this danger Palgrave still decided to go on. 'We had already got so far that to turn back from what we had yet to traverse, be it what it might, would have been an unpardonable want of heart.'

Accompanied by Geraigiri, he left with a small caravan, leaving Hail in the early morning. All but two were good companions, mostly small businessmen with wives 'wrapped up from head to foot in their large indigo blue dresses . . . like inanimate bundles to be taken to market somewhere'. The exceptions were a couple of Egyptian confidence tricksters, Mohammed and Ibrahim. One was a cook and the other a bankrupt shopkeeper. They had spent a few months in Mecca and learnt enough of the place to claim that they came from the Holy City and had been cheated out of their merchandise. They were sour, bad-tempered and quarrelsome: and they were out to exploit the hospitality of everyone in Arabia who would listen to them.

The caravan worked its way first over steppeland and then over sand. Once they were attacked by Bedouin. Of the fifteen matchlocks that the caravan could muster, one had no firing pin, a second was jammed and a third was so rusty it presented a greater danger to the person firing than the fired upon. To add to the comedy the two 'Meccans', both riding one camel for economy's sake, tried to gallop off abandoning their fellow travellers, only to find to their fury that their camel refused to leave her fellow beasts. 'A few shots guiltless of bloodshed were fired for form's sake on either side, till at last our assailants disappeared in the remote valley.'

After six days they came out of ibn Rashid's territory and reached the Wells of Uyan. There Palgrave saw his first Wahhabis. He had crossed a frontier, and he was the first European since Sadlier to have done so.

Right: *Detail from 'The Caravan', painted by Talbot Kelly in 1899. (Mathaf Gallery, London)*

The central provinces of Nejd, the genuine Wahhabi country, is to the rest of Arabia a sort of lion's den, on which few venture and fewer return . . . . Its mountains, once the fastness of robbers and assassins, are at the present day equally or even more formidable as the strongholds of fanatics who consider everyone save themselves an infidel or a heretic, and who regard the slaughter of an infidel or a heretic as a duty, at least a merit.[7]

Inevitably such a rigorous system produced a sub-culture of secret tobacco-smokers, closet silk-wearers and drug-takers. The Jesuit found the use of the local narcotic widespread, producing 'effects much like those ascribed to Sir Humphrey Davy's laughing gas; the patient dances, sings, and performs a thousand extravagances ، . . till after an hour of great excitement to himself and amazement to the by-standers, he falls asleep, and on awakening has lost all memory. To put a pinch of this powder into the coffee of some unsuspecting individual is not an uncommon joke, nor did I hear that it was ever followed by serious consequences'. Palgrave tried it twice on others and reported it as harmless.

The plant that bears these berries hardly attains in Kaseem the height of six inches above the ground, but in Oman I have seen bushes of it three or four feet in growth, and wide-spreading. The stems are woody, and of a yellow tinge when barked; the leaf of a dark green colour and pinnated, with about twenty leaflets on either side; the stalks smooth and shining; the flowers are yellow, and grow in tufts, the anthers numerous; the fruit is a capsule, stuffed with a greenish padding, in which lie embedded two or three black seeds, in size and shape much like French beans; their taste sweetish, but with a peculiar opiate flavour; the smell heavy and almost sickly.[8]

The party continued to Buraydah, where the great Persian Haj caravan was camped outside the town walls. Its arrival gave the harsh and grasping Wahhabi governor Muhanna the opportunity to fleece the Shiite heretics of one hundred and eighty gold tomans. This proved a double blessing for Palgrave, since it meant that Muhanna had little time to bring 'his cunning and rapacity' to bear on the two Syrian physicians. It meant also that they were able to secure the services of Abu Isa, the caravan guide, who was going to Riyadh with the Persian Naib responsible for the caravan to complain about Muhanna's greed. Abu Isa agreed to take Palgrave and Geraigiri along.

The man hailed from Aleppo. 'His education, the circumstances of his early youth, had rendered him equally conversant with townsmen and herdsman, with citizens and Bedouin, with Arabs and Europeans.' A revolutionary in his twenties, he had fled from Syria after the unsuccessful 1852 insurrection against Turkey, taking to a 'mercantile career' as he wandered from place to place, unable to return home.

> Certainly a roving life is no good school for probity in dealings, nor for delicate morality in private conduct. Yet Abu Isa possessed both these qualities in a degree that drew on him the admiration of many, the derision of some, and the notice of all. No one had ever heard from his lips any of the coarse jests and *double entendres* so common even among the better sort of Arabs in their freer hours, and his life was of a no less exemplary correctness than his language. Not a suspicion of libertinism had ever attached itself to him; at home or on his journeys he was and always had been a faithful and (though wealthy) a monogamous husband. Equally known for unblemished honour in money transactions, he never contested or delayed the payment of a debt, and his partners in business bore unanimous witness of his scrupulous fidelity.[9]

This very honesty proved Abu Isa's downfall. Three times he lost his fortune and had now ended up a caravan guide, keeping as far away from his Wahhabi employers, 'whose straight-laced exclusiveness he disliked and ridiculed', as he could. To Palgrave he became more than just a caravan guide; he became his 'inner' guide, on a deeper and far harder journey that was to end in Palgrave replacing his faith in catholicism with faith in humanity. It was Abu Isa who taught him that faith.

Left: *Detail from 'An Encampment of Pilgrims at Night, Mina' by Etienne Dinet. Such cities of tents sprang up outside all the cities where the Haj caravan stopped. (Mathaf Gallery, London)*

Right: *'European Travellers in the Orient', by Horace Vernet. Despite the journeys of Wallin, Palgrave, Guarmani and Pelly, the interior of Arabia remained closed for the most part to western eyes until the Blunts' visit in 1879.*

The party assembled outside the eastern gate on Friday 3 October. They were not sorry to leave. The town had the aura of genteel decline. Resentment against the Wahhabis had brought Buraydah to the edge of revolt. Her sister town of Unayzah was already in revolt and a Wahhabi army was camped outside Buraydah on its way to put down the insurrection.

Abu Isa's caravan was made up of Palgrave, Geraigiri, the Naib and his three companions, a Basra merchant and the two Egyptians who, 'weary of ill luck at Buraydah, had determined to try the doubtful generosity of Faisal'. 'Formerly there were fifty robbers,' Mohammed Ali, the Naib, remarked after they had left the town. 'Now there is only one. But that one is the equivalent of the other fifty.'

> He was a thorough Persian, and full sixty years old or even more, but in full vigour of body, and, had he not been a habitual opium-chewer, of mind too; his beard and whiskers were so carefully dyed with henna and black, that at a little distance he might almost have pased for a man of forty. He spoke Arabic badly, Turkish somewhat better, and Hindustani remarkably well, for he had been many years agent of the Persian government at Hyderabad in the Deccan; very witty and enjoying a joke, verbal or practical, shrewd from long conversance with affairs, though, like most Persians too, not difficult to dupe; talkative and gay, but occasionally yielding to violent and most indecorous fits of passion; a devout Shiite and adorer of Ali and Mahdi, at the mention of whose name I have seen him prostrate himself full length on the ground; in a word, he was a 'character', and the circumstances of the journey brought him out in every light and every point of view.[10]

They left beneath moonlight at a brisk trot, with the two 'Meccans' on their overloaded camel, trying desperately to keep up.

Above: *Persian Shiites enjoying tobacco. Such luxurious and ungodly practices, coming from foreigners and heretics, only confirmed the Wahhabi's prejudice against them.*

> The night soon cooled into a chill; our party was not at first a cheerful one. The Naib had parted from Muhanna in a fit of extreme ill-humour; his attendants were sulky to keep in tune with their master; the two Meccans could not decide between them which should ride their single camel and which should walk, . . . Abu Isa was making ineffectual attempts to enliven the party . . . . The Nejdians kept aloof, looking on us conjointly as a pack of reprobates, whom they would more gladly plunder than escort. Lastly Barakat and myself were not without anxiety touching what might lie before us at Riyadh.[11]

They travelled by night, on a roundabout route to avoid the fighting between the Wahhabis and the Unayzah rebels. Their route took them over ranges of dunes where camels sank up to their knees and riders had to dismount and gently coax them through. Beyond the dunes was a plateau and on the plateau were oases. At one of them, Az Zilfi, they came upon an encampment of Solibah Bedouins. Their nomadic existence had protected them from the worst excesses of Wahhabism.

The women were unveiled, and quite as forward as the men, or forwarder. A very pretty girl of the tribe played off this morning a trick too characeristic for omission. Its victim was the old Naib . . . . The young lady, accompanied by two of her relatives, contrived to come and go backwards and forwards before the Persian group, till her glances had fairly wounded Mohammed Ali's heart. He engaged her in a long and endearing conversation, and ended by a proposal for marriage. The family with well-affected joy gave a seeming assent, and accordingly when at last we climbed our dromedaries to pursue our journey, behold the dark-eyed gipsy-featured nymph with an elderly Solibah relation, perhaps her father, both mounted on scraggy camels, alongside of the Naib, who with looks of unutterable tenderness was making the handsomest offers to his future bride. These she received with becoming bashfulness, and half an hour of the way bantered her enamoured Strephon to her heart's content; till on our making a brief halt for breakfast at the verge of the town-gardens, she pretended to recollect I know not what valuable left behind in the Solibah camp, and went back with her kinsman to fetch it; after giving a woman's promise of a speedy return. The deluded swain tarried in hope, and made us all tarry with impatience for nearly two hours; but neither bride nor bridesman reappeared.[12]

There was another minor crisis with the Naib a few days later at Mazahimiyah when the old man ran out of his illicit stock of tobacco. The Naib asked high and low but everyone professed ignorance. Fortunately the more resourceful and discreet Abu Isa got him two pounds of the 'Satanic leaf' and all was well.

After eight days they reached the ruins of Diriyyah, birthplace of Wahhabism: a ruin surrounded by palm trees, untouched since Sadlier's day. Seven hours later they looked out over Riyadh.

Right: *The universal Bedouin tent. A basic triangle, the tent emerged from Mesopotamia, where it was made from the skin of domesticated sheep, goat and camel, and spread as far as the Atlantic in the west and China in the east. Wherever it went the tent adapted itself to its environment. In the mountains its steep sloping roof gave it protection from snow and rain, the sides held down by rocks to keep out the wind. In deserts the roof was spread out, to provide protection from the sun, while the sides were open for ventilation.*

Before us stretched a wide open valley, and in its foreground, immediately below the pebbly slope on whose summit we stood, lay the capital, large and square, crowned by high towers and strong walls for defence, a mass of roofs and terraces, where overtopping all frowned the huge but irregular pile of Faisal's royal castle, and hard by it rose the scarce less conspicuous palace, built and inhabited by his eldest son, Abdallah. Other edifices too of remarkable appearance broke here and there through the maze of grey roof-tops, but their object and indwellers we were yet to learn. All around for full three miles over the surrounding plain, but more especially to the west and south, waved a sea of palm-trees above green fields and well-watered gardens; while the singing droning sound of the water-wheels reached us even where we had halted, at a quarter of a mile or more from the nearest town-walls.[13]

They were challenged at the city gate. Abu Isa answered, and they were allowed to enter. They found themselves in a broad street flanked by two-storey houses and different sized mosques. The street led into a large square, on the other side of the square was Faisal's palace. By the entrance to the square a group of Negroes sat and stared. The palace was a sprawl of interconnected rooms and passages, deliberately built as a labyrinth to confuse potential assassins. Inside was a palace-within-a-palace, Faisal's own private apartments, an even more confusing labyrinth to protect the blind old despot from violent death. A clumsy colonnade crossed the square from the palace to the central mosque, giving Faisal a private and protected passage from his place of government to his place of prayer. Both his father and his uncle had been assassinated while visiting the mosque. The palace gate, protected by so many guards that they almost choked the dark passage, seemed more like the gates of a prison than a palace. Long benches hewn out of the earthen wall lined the adjoining passage.

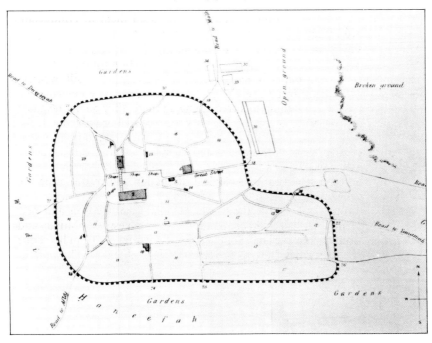

Left: *Palgrave's view of Riyadh, surrounded by gardens. In the centre is the great square and market, with Faisal's palace on its southern side, while the road on which Palgrave came into the city runs from the north-west (top left) into the city.*

Right: *Palgrave's plan of Faisal's labyrinthine palace. His private appartments and harem opened on to the Harem Court, marked in white, top centre.*

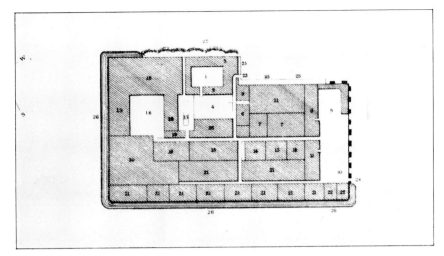

Abu Isa went straight into the palace to announce the arrival of the Naib. Palgrave and Geraigiri sat down and waited. They waited half an hour. No one came up to them. Finally their existence was reluctantly recognized by the Foreign Minister, Abdul Aziz. He invited them into the palace and gave them coffee. Palgrave disliked him from the very beginning. 'A reserved and equable exterior, smooth tongue, a courteous though grave manner; and beneath this, hatred, envy, rapacity and licentiousness enough to make his intimacy dangerous, his enmity mortal, and his friendship suspected.'

Abdul Aziz provided them with rooms. The two Jesuits waited until they were alone then relaxed with the forbidden weed. There was a knock at the door. They hastily put out their pipes, flapped the smoke out of the open window and guiltily opened the door. Before them stood an Indian Moslem dressed as an Afghani. He introduced himself as Abdul Hamid, an Afghan prince studying religion. Palgrave disliked him too. He turned out to be a murderer on the run from Peshawar, and the first of several spies sent by the Wahhabis to test him. 'Throwing out hints like angling hooks, in hopes to fish up truths from the bottom of the well,' he tried them in Hindustani, Persian and even English, but the two would not be caught out.

Hardly had he gone before there was another knock at the door. It was one of the *Meddeyyi*, the hated religious constabulary or Inquisition, who had absolute power to root out heretics, infidels, tobacco-smokers, silk-wearers and adulterers. 'Pacing from street to street, or unexpectedly entering the house to see if there is anything incorrect going on there, they do not hestitate to inflict at once and without any preliminary form of trial or judgement, the penalty of stripes on the detected culprit.' Just as Abdul Hamid had tested them on nationality, so the *Meddeyyi* tested them on religion. But for every citation of the Koran that he made, the Jesuits replied with two. Soon they were indulging themselves in a theological discussion and by the time the *Meddeyyi* departed he had become 'half a friend'.

More dangerous than any of these was Abdallah, Faisal's son and heir apparent. He hated his half-brother, Saud, he was ruthlessly ambitious and he had successfully taken over most of the reins of government from his senile father. Palgrave describes him as a Henry VIII look-alike. Throughout Palgrave's stay in Riyadh Abdallah cultivated him, regularly inviting him to his palace, supposedly seeking medical advice. In spite of his suspicions, Palgrave accepted these calls and was quite pleased when he cured one of Abdallah's prize mares. Only later did the real reason for Abdallah's cultivation of Palgrave emerge.

Faisal meanwhile was nowhere to be seen. The doddery old man, convinced that the Persian Naib and the two Syrian doctors were planning to murder him, had hidden in the date-palm trees outside the city, protected by his bodyguard of black slaves. In spite of Palgrave's efforts to get an interview Faisal remained there until the foreigners had left, only once emerging from the foliage to review the Wahhabi troops on their way to suppress the revolt at Unayzah. 'There sat the blind old tyrant, corpulent, decrepit, yet imposing, with his large broad forehead, white beard, and thoughtful air, clad in all the simplicity of a Wahhabi.' It was clear that the foreigners were not welcome and it took a long time before the two physicians got permission from Abdul Aziz to practise medicine. Even then they were so hemmed in by restrictions that they could hardly work.

Matters came to a head in the fifth week. Abdallah summoned Palgrave to his palace and asked him for some of the strychnine that he heard the doctor had. To Palgrave there was no doubt he intended to use it against either his father or half-brother. Palgrave refused. The next day Abdallah asked again. After he had tried a third time Palgrave went up to him and whispered in his ear. 'Abdallah, I know well what you want the poison for, and I have no mind to be an accomplice in your crimes, nor to answer before God's judgement-seat for what you have to answer for. You shall *never* have it.' Abdallah went black with rage.

That same evening, 21 November, Palgrave was again summoned to the palace. He entered a long and gloomy chamber, lit only by the flicker of a fire in the hearth.

> After an interval of silence, Abdallah turned round towards me, and with his blackest look and a deep voice said, 'I know perfectly well what you are; you are no doctors, you are Christians, spies and revolutionaries come hither to ruin our religion and state on behalf of those who sent you. The penalty for such as you is death, that you know, and I am determined to inflict it without delay.[14]

Palgrave turned to him. 'Ask pardon of God.'

There was another silence. Abdallah clapped his hands. A slave appeared. He was carrying one cup of coffee. To accept it might mean death, but to refuse it and offend the laws of hospitality also meant death. But Abdallah did not have poison, Palgrave quickly reasoned, otherwise he would not be so anxious for the strychnine. Palgrave picked up the cup and drained it, uttering the name of God (*Bismillah*). 'Abdallah's face announced defeat.'

By the time Palgrave returned to his lodgings it was past midnight. With a 'feeling of lonely dread' he told Geraigiri and Abu Isa what had happened and prepared for a hasty departure. Two days later the three slipped out while the population was at prayers. Abu Isa led them to the Hufuf road where he left them and returned to Riyadh to establish a good alibi, after agreeing to meet them by the Hufuf road three days later.

> After winding here and there, we reached the spot assigned by Abu Isa for our hiding place. It was a small sandy depth, lying some way off the beaten track, amid hillocks and brushwood, and without water: of this latter article we had taken enough in the goatskins to last us for three days. Here we halted, and made up our minds to patience and expectation.
>
> Two days passed drearily enough. We could not but long for our guide's arrival, nor be wholly without fear on more than one score. Once or twice a stray peasant stumbled on us, and was much surprised at our encampment in so droughty a locality . . . . So the hours went by, till the third day brought closer expectation and anxiety, still increasing while the sun declined, and at last went down; yet nobody appeared. But just as darkness closed in, and we were sitting in a dispirited group beside our little fire, for the night air blew chill, Abu Isa came suddenly up, and all was changed for question and answer, for cheerfulness and laughter.[15]

Next morning they set out for the Gulf. They had one more desert ahead of them, the Dahna; another 'red' desert. Guided by Abu Isa they spent five days crossing it, joining up after a few days with a small caravan of about half a dozen camels. In the small hours of the fifth day, not far from Hufuf, they disturbed a swarm of locusts. Locusts are an Arabian delicacy. Palgrave's fellow travellers went wild with joy.

> The swarm now before us was a thorough godsend to our Arabs, on no account to be neglected. Thirst, weariness, all was forgotten, and down the riders leapt from their sad starting camels; this one spread out a cloak, that a saddlebag, a third his shirt, over the unlucky creatures destined for the morrow's meal. Some flew away whirring across our feet, others were caught and tied up in cloths and sacks.[16]

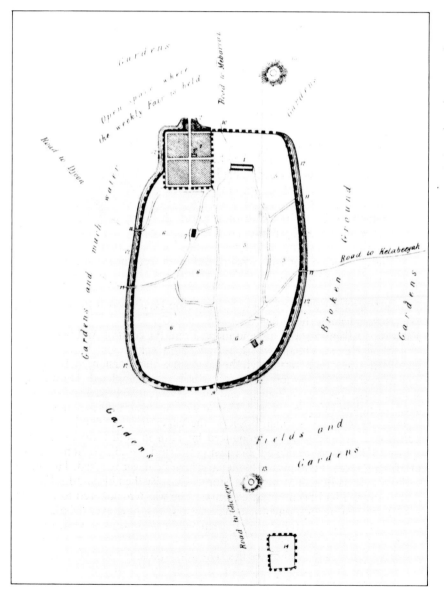

Left: *Palgrave's plan of Hufuf, a town of some twenty-four thousand in Palgrave's day, dominated by the citadel (top left) with its thirty towers and moat, which could be filled up from the town's springs in times of danger, and from where the Wahhabis tried to impose their puritanism on the reluctant populace.*

Geraigiri had tried one and pronounced it to be oily and disgusting; Palgrave could not even bring himself to try one. He was anxious to get on to Hufuf. 'Luckily Abu Isa still retained enough of his North Syrian education to be of our mind also. Accordingly we left our associates hard at work, turned our startled and still unruly dromedaries in the direction of Hufuf, and set off at full speed over the plain.'

Next day they were in Hufuf. It was a relief after Riyadh. The town was rich, tobacco was plentiful and the girls were pretty.

> Wahhabism exists indeed, but only among the few who form the dominant and hated class; while its presence serves by natural reaction to render the main bulk of the inhabitants yet more averse to a system whose evil they know not only by theory, but more by frequent and bitter experience.[17]

Palgrave doctored in the day and was received by families and friends at night. For the first time since leaving the Lebanon he ate fresh fish. Once he was invited on a picnic. Palgrave, Geraigiri and ten others rode eight miles out of Hufuf to a hot spring out of which seven streams flowed in different directions. It was called the Mother of Seven.

> The breeze was delightful; we examined the fountain-head in all its bearings, then bathed, swam, wrestled, drank coffee, chatted, dined, smoked, slept, and bathed again. All went merry as a marriage-bell till we discovered that, by one of those omissions inseparable from a picnic, no coffee cups had been brought, a circumstance which had remained unnoticed till the coffee itself was ready, and nothing remained for us but to drink it out of the sooty coffee pot wherein it had been prepared. Luckily one of the party, cleverer than the rest, rode over at a venture to a neighbouring village, whence he soon returned with a donkey-load of cups.[18]

Three weeks later Palgrave, Geraigiri and Abu Isa arrived at the Gulf. The sea was 'like a leaden sheet, half ooze and half sedge.'

Palgrave's adventures did not end there. From the coast of Arabia he went on to Qatar, Persia, Oman (where he was shipwrecked) and Basra, before returning to Europe on very much the same route that Carsten Niebuhr had taken a hunded years earlier. A great feat had been completed. He was the first man to cross Arabia diagonally, and the first to visit both Hail and Riyadh.

He returned to Europe in March 1864 to write up his travels in a monastery in Germany, but like so many others, the experience of Arabia left him unfulfilled. The next year he renounced his faith in both Catholicism and Napoleon III, joined the British Foreign Office and was almost immediately sent off on a secret mission to Abyssinia, which he never reached. He ended his life in 1888 as British Minister in Montevideo. By then his youthful follies with the French had been forgotten. Instead he was remembered for 'one of the most interesting and romantic books of travel that have ever delighted the public.' (*The Times*). Rarely has a spy remained true to himself while serving so many conflicting masters.

Palgrave was not the only traveller sent into Arabia by Napoleon III. No spy is ever trusted. Every spy's report must be verified by an independent source. The man Napoleon sent in to verify Palgrave's report was an Italian,

Below: The desert locust, essentially the common grasshopper, multiplied in its desert breeding grounds in the Empty Quarter, forming clouds of insects which stripped bare all vegetation in their path. Gregorio da Quadra, one of the earliest Arabian travellers, pronounced them edible, Wallin found them excellent fried, while Wilfrid Blunt enthused that they were best boiled and dipped in salt with the legs taken off. Palgrave, normally the most courageous of men, did not dare to try one.

Carlo Guarmani. He could not have been more different than 'Giffy' Palgrave. He had spent fourteen years in the Levant, working as horse-dealer, Prussian consul and French Postal Agent. Brought to the attention of the French Foreign Office by their Levantine Service he was summoned to Paris to meet Napoleon III. Provided with the commission to buy Arab stallions for the royal studs of Paris and Turin, he was sent to Arabia to confirm or deny the Jesuit's reports. He had little interest in this second commission, indeed he was little interested in politics, but he saw it as a way of financing an expedition into Arabia to find what he regarded as the most wonderful horses in the world. Unlike so many of the English travellers of the nineteenth century, he had no private income to support himself with. He was a wheeler-dealer who lived on his wits and loved horses; and Arab horses were his greatest love of all.

'Releasing myself from the embraces of my sorrowful family . . . who thought I was on my way to a voluntary execution,' he set out from Jerusalem on 26 January 1864 under the name of Khalil Aga of Damascus, Master of the Pasha's Horse. He crossed the River Jordan with an old family retainer, Mohammed el-Jazzawi, and four Taamri Palestinians in freezing weather.

After five days he arrived at Qualaita where the Taamri passed him on to the Bani Hamida, who in turn passed him on to the Bani Sakhr. Completely lacking in the racism so common among English and French travellers, he describes his leavetaking from them with dignity and delicacy. The Taamri 'kissed every inch of my face without actually touching me' and 'whispered the sound of a kiss in my ear', the Bani Hamida 'gave repeated kisses on my mouth, the first quickly without moving the lips, the later ones longer, each lasting about two or three seconds', while the Bani Sakhr 'imprinted a kiss on my face'. Only a man confident of his place in the world and his sexuality could have written those words.

Even more moving is his description of the fifty Arab mares that the Bani Sakhr kept near their encampment. They were tough, hardy and the fastest animals Guarmani had ever seen. They grazed in the open in daytime and were called in at night by their owners, each horse recognizing her master's voice. The most sensitive of animals, they never needed a bridle except in battle. Their owners prized the mares more than their own wives.

That night there was a cloudburst. The wind built up and the rain deluged down. Guarmani watched the women rush out to secure the tent, while their men sat motionless inside. From the corner of his eye he saw his servant Mohammed get up to help the women. He stayed him with a motion of his hand. It was unbecoming for men to do women's work.

Next day he saw the quality of the Bani Sakhr riding when the males of the encampment raced off on a leopard hunt. Mounting their horses by placing one hand on the horse's mane, the other on their upright spear, and vaulting onto the horse, they galloped through the desert after the leopard until they had run it down and surrounded it. Provoking the leopard, they waited until it became confused and tried to break out. As it charged through the circle of horsemen the nearest rider sprinted up to it, brought his horse to a perfect halt just out of range of the leopard's leap and transfixed it with a spear through the neck.

After three days with the Bani Sakhr, Guarmani set out due south for Taima with his faithful servant and a quick-witted and intelligent Bani Sakhr lad called el-Draibi. It was 3 February.

It rained steadily for five days, Guarmani protecting himself by putting his fur coat over his head. It gave him good cover to write his notes and make compass bearings. On the second day of the rainstorm they saw a party of Sherarat Bedouin in the valley coming towards them. Fearing it might be a raiding party they galloped up one of the slopes only to look back and see that the 'raiding party', equally frightened, had galloped up the other. It all ended with Guarmani and his party being invited to supper by the Sherarat. Supper, Guarmani discovered, was a meagre meal of flour and vegetable roots that the Sherarat, one of the poorest tribes in Arabia, had to forego in order for their guests to eat. Mindful of the Bedouin code and of the Sherarat's self-respect Guarmani ate gratefully while an old tribesman improvised a poem which he sung to the accompaniment of his *rababa* (a single-stringed violin) 'the final word of each verse repeated like a refrain by the empty mouths of his family'.

After five hard days, averaging forty miles a day, the rain ceased and they came to Fajr where they were welcomed by Salim el-Khawi, the Sherarat chief. His people were so poor that they wore nothing but a leather loin cloth. Two days later they reached Taima, which Varthema had passed through, an oasis of some two thousand people, surrounded by a fortified wall. Unfortunately Guarmani's camels were so terrified of the fortifications that they refused to go through the town gate. It was not until some of the inhabitants brought out a herd of their own camels to lead them in that they consented to enter the town. Its oddest feature was a gigantic municipal well, 'some forty metres in circumference with forty-eight camels drawing water all the time'.

The Emir, 'small, about sixty, with a red face and a fat unBedouin-like stomach', welcomed him and gave him a letter of introduction to Talal ibn Rashid. Leaving Mohammed and the Palestinians in Taima to look after his valuables he travelled on alone, save for a single guide of the Walad Ali.

Three days later he had his second close encounter with Arab horses, at the

Below: The Arab thoroughbred. Carlo Guarmani thought it was the most beautiful horse in the world. 'Two Arab Horsemen' by John Frederick Lewis.

encampment of Sheikh Rajjia of his guide's tribe, the Walad Ali. The Sheikh suspected him of being a Turkish agent and proceeded to subject him to an endless stream of complaints about Wahhabi injustice and oppression. It was some time before Guarmani was able to bring the subject round to horses. Rajjia proudly boasted of the speed and stamina of his herd, but when Guarmani asked to see them Rajjia said that they were out grazing and could not be brought in.

A few days later, riding on towards Khaybar, Guarmani came upon Rajjia's horses. The grooms were friendly so Guarmani and his guide stayed with them for three nights. Each day he marvelled at the horses he saw around him; but though he loved them as a connoisseur he had no intention of buying any of them. 'Their small size would not have been appreciated in Europe, whose people do not have faith in the regenerative power of the thorough-bred.'

After a day's march over black petrified larva ridges Guarmani reached the oasis of Khaybar, the first European to visit it since Varthema and Le Blanc (if indeed he had ever got there). As they approached the town the Negro governor came out to greet them. In Varthema's day the town had been populated by Jews, whose ruined fort – the Qasr al Yahud – still dominated the town. Since then the Jews had fled or been massacred, replaced by a colony of Negroes.

Here Guarmani changed his lone guide for two from the Hutaim tribe, 'thieves by profession', but well-known and well-liked in the deserts they were passing through. After three days they encountered thousands of Ataiba Bedouin on the move. They were northerners, refugees from the Wahhabi army of Abdallah, Palgrave's old enemy. He had driven them from Qasim and lined up his forces to the south, to prevent them linking up with the southern Ataiba. It was an unforgettable sight: a thousand tents, a people in motion, spread out over the drylands as far as the eye could see.

On 8 March Guarmani arrived at the tent of Maflak ibn Sfuk, the Ataiba chief. At first Maflak tried to dissuade him from staying. The Wahhabi army was about to attack. Their position was precarious to say the least. But Guarmani, with an admirable display of human solidarity, insisted on remaining. Maflak, true to the laws of Bedouin hospitality, welcomed him. That evening a sheikh of the neutral Hutaim tribe came to Maflak with an ultimatum from Abdallah: they must move out by dawn.

Before the sun came up the tribe, accompanied by Guarmani and his two Hutaim guides, began their trek. There were two hundred horsemen in the advance guard, seven hundred riflemen on camels in the rear and the mass of the tribe and its herds in the centre. They marched for four days and nights, continually harassed by the Wahhabi army, resting only for a few hours at a time. True to his nature Abdallah had reneged on his promise. Every time the Ataiba warriors tried to break through the surrounding Wahhabi forces they were thrown back, like the leopard at bay that Guarmani had hunted while with the Bani Sakhr. By 12 March they had suffered sixty dead and two hundred wounded, and had been robbed of all their flocks.

Eyeing the surrounding country, Maflak spotted a deep gorge surrounded by volcanic outcrops. Here he decided on a final stand. He packed his people in the gorge, placed his cavalry at the entrance and positioned his riflemen in the rocky crags around.

The following morning the Wahhabis attacked. They were beaten off. Next day they tried again, led in person by Abdallah. The two sides fought from dawn to dusk, Guarmani helping to look after the wounded in the gorge. With nightfall Abdallah's army withdrew, 'having neither dislodged us from our eagle's nest nor broken our brave cavalry'.

Above: *R. Calton Woodville's 'A Night March in the Desert' (1884): another example of the nineteenth century Oriental genre. In reality, Bedouin raiders would not be riding on the skyline, where all can see them, but along the lower slopes of the valley in a more discreet manner.*

That night the defenders were awoken by shots, shouts and the sounds of battle. Expecting to be attacked at any moment they listened carefully; but it was not the Wahhabi warcry that they heard but their own Ataiba one. The southern Ataiba, led by their Sultan, ibn Rubayan, with four hundred cavalry and five thousand camels, had come to their rescue. Emerging without warning they fell on the exhausted and disorganized Wahhabis, annihilating them. Abdallah fled from the battlefield while Maflak and ibn Rubayan embraced at the bloody entrance to the gorge.

Guarmani was introduced to ibn Rubayan who was so elated by the victory that when he heard that Guarmani was a horse-dealer, he offered him three beautiful bay stallions for a hundred camels. Two were dark bays and the third was a light bay with black markings. One hundred camels was a lot of money for three horses – twice the normal price – but Guarmani who, like the old Danish cavalrymen Berggren, knew a thing or two about horses, was convinced that they were worth the price. They were not all that Guarmani got. Maflak, who had witnessed the negotiations, was so moved by Guarmani's love of horses that he gave him a fourth bay, a spoil of war. It had white stockings on its hind legs and a star on its forehead.

With the four horses Guarmani's horse-buying expedition was over. He would have liked to return with them to Jerusalem immediately, to ship them back to Europe; but he had another commitment, a political one to Napoleon III, and that forced him to say goodbye to the Ataiba and continue into the Wahhabi domains.

> I nearly wept when Maflak embraced me and I was left alone with my guides on that vast and bloody plain . . . . Jackals, ravens, wolves and vultures were devouring the scattered bodies. My horses trembled with fear. All night I watched over them, caressing them; and at dawn I went in search of grass.[19]

Right: *War in the desert as Guarmani encountered it during his search for Arab horses. Sudden attacks, brief skirmishes, then fleeting retreats to fight another day were the pattern of Arabian warfare from pre-historic times to the reign of ibn Saud.*

Sending one of his Hutaim guides north with the horses, he continued with only one guide, Ali el-Fidawi, towards Abdallah's encampment. About three miles away from it they were surprised by a Wahhabi patrol and led as captives to the Saudi headquarters. Abdallah, suspecting Guarmani of being a Turkish spy, refused to see him. He ordered him to be taken under escort to Unayzah, the town that had rebelled against the Wahhabis during Palgrave's visit. It was just what Guarmani wanted. Not only was it anti-Wahhabi and now loyal to ibn Rashid, it was the equestrian capital of Arabia. 'Its principle commerce was the rearing of horses, brought as colts from the Bedouin and exported to Kuwait, the Gulf, Persia and India.'

At first Guarmani's escort was unfriendly, and treated him as a prisoner; but once out of Abdallah's territory they relaxed, and the head of the escort, a Negro called Anaibar, gave him dates and choice pieces of meat. He told Guarmani that he was safe with them, since the escort was made up of Rashidi rather than Wahhabi soldiers, and that he himself was an official of Talal ibn Rashid.

On his arrival at Unayzah, Guarmani discovered that the town was now under the control of the ibn Rashids. The Emir, Zamil, who had been adopted by the Rashidis as a child, hated the intolerance of the Wahhabis, and gladly provided Guarmani with a letter of introduction to Talal in Hail. From Unayzah they made their way to Buraydah, 'much spoilt and full of ruins', where Palgrave had his first bad experience with the Wahhabis, who had now been driven out; and on 26 March, about a day from Hail, they came to the camp of Bandar, Talal's son and heir. Bandar, having shown off his mares, offered Guarmani (whom he believed to be a Turkish agent) some tobacco. When Guarmani refused Bandar asked him with a smile whether the Wahhabis had overrun Constantinople. Guarmani spent three days there before riding on to Hail.

Right: *David Roberts' 'Arabs of the Beni Said'.*

Left: *The Arab horse. To encourage their care and breeding the Prophet gave an additional share of booty to the soldier with the best cared-for horse. 'Love horses,' said the Prophet's general Omar, 'tend them well, for they are worthy of your tenderness. Treat them like your own children, nourish them like friends of the family, clothe them with care. For the love of Allah, do not neglect this, or you will repent for it in this house and the next.'*

Arabs of the Tribe of the Benssaid. Feb 17th 1832

> While my family mourned me for dead I, in the best of
> health, ate my rice and said my prayers (to God in my heart
> and to Mohammed on my lips) with all due reverence, and
> recalling the sermon on the Mount, not to mention the
> stench of the rotting corpse, resolved not to be amongst the
> poor in spirit and enter Paradise with the fools.[20]

Guarmani and Ali were lodged in one of Talal's guest houses close by the
palace that Palgrave had visited two years earlier. The floor was covered in
mats, carpets and cushions and emerging out of the middle was a structural
pillar, on which Guarmani carved the name of his daughter, 'Zulima'.

Next day, after a breakfast of grapes and camel's milk with honey, he was
presented to Talal by Bandar. The Emir of Jebal Shammar was dispensing
justice, seated by the western wall of the mosque, with his officials and
advisers sitting on his left in rows, according to the order of precedence.
Twenty slaves sat cross-legged in a half-circle in front of him, all covered in
fine black cloaks over red or blue gold-embroidered robes. Each held in his
hand a scimitar in a silver scabbard.

> He put out his hand; I touched it with mine, which I then
> lifted to my mouth, kissing the fingers, and then to my
> forehead, while he did the same with his, and at a sign from
> him, and without uttering a word, I seated myself on the
> ground at his right hand on the mosque's steps. He went
> through eight lawsuits in two hours, then put on his sandals
> and ended the session. He saluted me with a smile, his hand
> on his heart, and I followed suit, doing my best not to laugh.
> I was not used to a dumb reception.[21]

That night, while eating his evening meal of *pilaff* on the palace roof, he
was visited by Bandar and invited into Talal's private apartments. The father
welcomed Guarmani with embraces and talked with him for five hours,
perfuming his beard and forcing on him coffee. By the time Guarmani left it
was early morning.

The three days in Hail were a welcome respite for Guarmani from the
tensions on the road. Like all good Italians Guarmani was not at a loss to pick
out the more interesting features of the town that the Jesuit priest had
possibly missed. The women of Jebal Shammar included some of the most
beautiful in Arabia, possessing 'a purity of line . . . that rivalled the most
graceful beauties of Canova'. They had bronzed skin and almond-eyes, their
faces framed in shiny black hair, oiled by a mixture of palm bark and clarified
fat from sheep's tails.

His first sight at the city gate was the rotting corpse of a Persian Jew. This
unfortunate had come disguised as a Moslem to buy horses for the Shah of
Persia but, when challenged by the townspeople to pronounce the words of
the Faith ('There is no god but God and Mohammed is the Messenger of
God') he had refused and been lynched. This was hardly the neo-Platonic
republic that Palgrave enthused about. 'His fate was sad but what he
deserved. If a man takes risks he must use every subterfuge in his power, or
face the consequences of his enterprise.' Unknown to Guarmani news of a
foreigner's death in Hail had reached his family in Damascus. Everyone
assumed it was him.

From Hail Guarmani rode to Taima, which he had passed through on his
outward journey. There he picked up Mohammed and el-Draibi and collected the money he needed to buy one hundred camels to pay for the horses

he had bought from ibn Rubayan. Then he paid off his Hutaim guide who had been looking after the horses, 'giving him enough to be grateful and happy' and took on two Shammar horsemen as grooms. After a month travelling with complete security through ibn Rashid's domains he was back in Hail.

Right: *The entrance of the Rashidi palace in Hail, built just after Palgrave's visit to the city.*

Left: *Riders in the Nafud as Guarmani must have seen them on his return from Hail.*

Returning to the city he discovered that Talal was preparing for an expedition against the luckless Sherarat who were in arrears with their tribute. It must have been a difficult moment for Guarmani, guest of a prince about to go to war with paupers who only two months earlier had welcomed him as their own guest. He left the city with regrets on 3 May travelling northwards towards Syria with Mohammed, el-Draibi, his four horses and Anaibar, the Ethiopian who had ridded with him since leaving Abdallah's camp. On their first day out they rode with Talal's army.

> At ten o'clock a slave seized the banner, vaulted onto his horse and began the march; the entire army, a thousand men, followed; then came Talal, with Ali his cousin; and lastly there was Anaibar and myself; Anaibar distributing money and gifts to the wives and children of the slaves, who accompanied us for half an hour singing the praises of their great and liberal master.[22]

The next morning he brought a fifth Arab stallion, a grey, from one of the Alaibi accompanying Talal's army. Then he bade farewell to Talal, who gave him his camel as a leavetaking present. With Mohammed, el-Draibi and the two Shammar horsemen Guarmani set off across the Nafud. Strangely enough it proved quite easy. As on his outward journey it poured with rain. At Jawf, which Palgrave had passed through in the other direction, he learnt that Talal was only twenty-five miles away. Rather than fight the impoverished Sherarat he had made peace with them and had now turned his attention on the more dangerous Ruaulla in the north. Guarmani promptly took twenty-four hours off his itinerary and rode over to visit him. When he arrived at Talal's camp Talal rose and embraced him. Guarmani rode back to Jawf that night, paid off his Shammar guides and joined one of the regular caravans to Syria.

Five days out of Jawf, just beyond Rashidi territory, the almost four hundred-strong caravan was attacked by the Ruaulla. The caravan halted and tried to fight, but with only sixty-five rifles their position was helpless. After two hours the caravan surrendered. Realizing he would lose his five stallions, Guarmani signalled to Mohammed and el-Draibi and the three leapt onto three of the stallions, and leading the other two by their halters, galloped through the Ruaulla lines, firing as they rode. Guarmani's stallion was shot under him, but he quickly mounted a second that el-Draibi brought up under fire. The Ruaulla took up the chase. 'Whenever we perceived them separated from each other by the inequality of the ground or the pace of their mounts, we turned to aim, and they hesitated and waited for the others to join them before taking up the chase again.'

They managed to elude their pursuers and laid up in the mountains that night. When they returned to the caravan in the morning they found their fellow travellers had been stripped of everything, the men quite naked and the women in nothing but their underclothes. Guarmani pressed on with his four remaining horses into Syria, where he got some satisfaction in learning that while the Ruaulla had been looting his caravan, a party of Talal's Anaiza irregulars had come up and stolen everything the Ruaulla possessed from their undefended camp. He finally arrived in Damascus with his horses in June 1864, from where he continued to the Lebanese coast and took ship to France. He returned to the Levant after his visit to France, wheeling and dealing for another decade before eventually retiring in Genoa, a prosperous merchant and an expert on horses, where he died in 1884.

Right: *'The Great Caravan of Central Asia', by W. H. Overend. Such caravans as these would have passed through Hail on their way to Mecca.*

Napoleon III's interest in central Arabia awakened her imperial rival, Britain, who could not leave the field open to France without a challenge. The challenge took the form of a somewhat unusual English diplomat, Colonel Lewis Pelly. Although his record was exceptional there seems some mystery and eccentricity in him that denied him the highest honours, which always just eluded him. He was born in 1825 and educated at Rugby. He joined the Indian Army in 1841 and was transferred at the extremely youthful age of twenty-six to what was later called the Indian Political Service, serving as the British Viceroy's representative to the Indian Princely state of Boroda. Next he was fighting in Persia and the Sind with irregular cavalry, before finding himself in the British Legation at Tehran. In 1860 he was sent on a secret mission to India, eight hundred miles through Persia and Afghanistan, alone and virtually unarmed. In India he joined Lord Canning's staff in Calcutta, but a year later he was British Consul in Zanzibar, with special responsibility to gather intelligence on the slave trade. After another swift move, in less than a year he was British Resident in the Gulf, where he was to counter the growing French influence in the Arabian interior. To do this he resolved to go straight to Riyadh. His justification for the journey is so charmingly absurd that it deserves to be savoured in full.

Left: *Sir Lewis Pelly (1825-1892), the first European since Sadlier to visit Riyadh from the Gulf, the first traveller to make the solo ride from Persia via Kandahar to India, and the first British Resident in the Gulf to seek to improve the lot of the inhabitants.*

Right: Not all wells were insignificant pock-marks on a lunar landscape: some, like the Wells of Walra and Abdallah, had been in use for hundreds of years, with reservoirs and interconnecting tunnels, irrigating hundreds of acres.

I confess that when I found . . . it was very difficult for 'Europeans' to enter Arabia on account of the 'extraordinary' jealousy of the population and that to be known as a European traveller . . . in the Wahhabi country . . . would be exceedingly dangerous, possibly even fatal, I was unwilling that this should be supposed to be the case in regard to any Asiatic territory which might be adjacent to my jurisdiction, for it has been my habit to consider that an English officer can go anywhere his duty to the Government requires it.[23]

But his requests to enter Nejd were politely ignored. His persistence finally secured him an unenthusiastic safe-conduct without guide or escort. He went all the same, taking with him a naval officer, a doctor, an Iraqi Christian interpreter, three Indian orderlies, one Persian servant, a Portugese cook and thirty camels; 'much the sort of company that Falstaff would have objected to marching through Coventry with.'

The first ten days took them through a lean and dessicated country. Only one tree broke the monotony of two hundred miles of gravel, sand and sandstone. On the seventh day they reached the hundred Wells of Walra. Five more days took them to Orma. They descended from the plateau into a wide depression, the Dahna Desert, and trekked across the red sand dunes. Beyond the Dahna they passed through the gardens of ruined Diriyyah and arrived in Riyadh on 5 March 1864. It had taken fifteen days.

Faisal's initial reception of Pelly was distant and unfriendly. 'We abominate your religion,' he told Pelly, 'but we hear yours is an orderly government.' After the second audience Faisal seemed to have softened. He told the Englishman 'Riyadh was a curious place for a European to come to; that none had ever been allowed to enter; but that he trusted all would go well.' Pelly became optimistic. 'From something which occurred, I could not but presume that he was a freemason.' Alas for Pelly, it was all a mistake and, in spite of the presents he had brought for Faisal (rifle, pistol, sword and gold watch), he never got the guarantee for an English officer to go anywhere 'which might be adjacent to my jurisdiction'.

On the third day the party left, taken by their guide on a little frequented route north of Hufuf. They arrived at the Gulf on 17 March and boarded the Residency steamer *Berenice* which was lying offshore waiting for them. Pelly himself went on from the *Berenice* to better things, a knighthood, a generalship, a seat in parliament and an invitation (which he turned down) from the King of the Belgiums to administer the Congo.

VI

THE WANDERER

Twelve years went by before another traveller arrived in Hail, years in which the House of Rashid, fed by its own fratricidal blood, grew in power. In 1867 Talal, fearing he was going mad, shot himself. Power was disputed between Talal's brothers, Mtab and Mohammed, and his son, Bandar. Mtab was assassinated by Bandar and Bandar by Mohammed who secured power by slaughtering all his rivals; two cousins had their hands and feet cut off and were left to bleed to death in the palace courtyard. Mohammed ruled for twenty-five years, and was virtually the only Rashidi to die in bed. He was assisted by his cousin, Hamud, the son of Palgrave's old enemy Obied. Hamud was a liberal and popular man who – although never a party to Mohammed's early atrocities – served him loyally. Under the two men's rule Shammar power extended to Jawf in the north, the Hejaz in the west, the semi-independent towns of Buraydah and Unayzah to the south and, by 1887, Riyadh in the east.

To Europe, anxious to prop up a tottering Turkish empire and unaware of the rise of the Rashidis and the temporary demise of the House of Saud, it was all a mystery. No European had visited Hail since Guarmani in 1864. The first to follow him, twelve years later, was the oddest of the Arabian travellers: Charles Montagu Doughty.

Psychologically, the man was a disaster. He came from a family of bishops on his father's side and admirals on his mother's side. His parents died when he was six, he was physically ungainly and had red hair, his schooldays were a misery and he developed a stammer. Rejected by the Navy because of the stammer, he threw himself into the study of geology to escape further humiliations. His fellow undergraduates at Cambridge found him religious to the extreme and socially impossible. In fact the man was deeply lonely. He left Cambridge with a Second class honours degree. 'If you asked him for a collar he upset his whole wardrobe at your feet,' said one examiner.

Left: 'The Letter-writer', by David Roberts. Most of the people could not write, and would come to the letter-writer not only for their letters to be written, but also to ask for letters they had received to be read.

After three years of trying to escape human contact and speech by immersing himself in geology, Doughty suddenly decided to confront them. He took to the study of language and for five years from 1865 to 1870 studied early English at the Bodleian and British Libraries. He attacked his subject with single-minded determination and emerged with an uncompromising conviction of the superiority of 'the divine Muse of Spencer and Venerable Chaucer' over the spoken language. Then in 1874 he quite literally dropped out of the cultural and academic fringes of Victorian society to which he so scarcely belonged, and wandered through Europe as a poor student, ending up the following year in Damascus.

A year in Damascus perfected his Arabic (a language whose harsh gutteral sounds obliterated his stammer) and on 10 November 1876 left Damascus to join the Haj caravan at Mezarib. He intended to travel with the caravan as far as Madain Salih, site of the ancient Nabataean city built out of rock, about half way to Mecca. He called himself Khalil and carried with him a revolver, a cavalry carbine, a box of medicines, a stack of books including a seventeenth-century edition of Chaucer's *Canterbury Tales*, and a profound belief that the Bedouin spoke the Arabic equivalent of Chaucerian English. His total funds were thirteen pounds. Clothed as 'a Syrian of simple fortune' but never slow to proclaim that he was a Nasrani (Christian), he chose to travel at the back of the caravan with the despised Persian Shiites, spat upon by the Sunni Bedouin as they walked along.

Above: *Charles Montagu Doughty (1843-1926). 'I am by nature self-willed, headstrong, and fierce with opponents, but my better reason and suffering in the world have bridled these faults and in part extinguished them.'*

Each morning the pilgrims dismantled their tents, loaded their camels and waited for the cannon shot to signal the departure, in a ritual that had not changed since Varthema's day. 'Without any disorder litters were suddenly heaved and braced upon the bearing beasts, their charges laid upon the kneeling camels, and the thousands of riders, all born in the camel countries, mounted in silence.' With the second shot the Emir el-Haj at the front began to move, Doughty and the Shiites in the rear waiting twenty minutes while the caravan unfolded for their turn to follow. They marched four camels abreast in a column stretching two miles over grey gravel, not stopping till sunset. When the caravan halted the ten thousand beasts and six thousand pilgrims spread out, the former in search of grazing, the latter in search of kindling wood, then ate and slept around their tents, protected by the Ottoman escort. 'A paper lantern after sunset is hung before every one to burn all through the night where a sentinel stands with his musket, and they suffer none to pass their lines unchallenged.' But by midnight the lanterns were out, the unpaid soldiers sparing their candle allowance to sell in the markets on the way to Mecca.

On their way the pilgrims passed stone *kellas*, fortified waterholes on the Haj route. 'The *kellas* stand alone, as it were ships in the immensity of the desert.' They were garrisoned by about half a dozen Algerian soldiers who had come to Syria, with Abd el-Kader, preferring a life in exile to French rule, and making their living as soldiers on the Haj route.

After three weeks the caravan arrived at Madain Salih. 'Khalil, thou shalt see wonders today of houses hewn out of rocks', the pilgrims told him. It was a relief to arrive. Already one Christian had been found in the caravan and killed. Doughty heard a hoarse voice say: 'Now another Nasrani in the caravan, curse Allah his father, he will be dealt with presently.' It was time to leave the caravan. Doughty moved into the *kella*.

There were five in the garrison: Nejm, an old Moor from Fez who had served as a soldier in Algeria, Morocco, Tunisia, Egypt and Turkey; Hasan, who had come to Syria with Nejm; Abd el-Kader, thick in breadth and brain, the complete opposite of his Algerian namesake; Mohammed, the half-Algerian half-Bedouin son of a former *kella* keeper; and Mohammed Ali, the surveyor responsible for several *kellas*. Head of the garrison was Nejm, who sat in the tower with his blunderbuss on his knees entertaining the local Bedouins to coffee.

Doughty spent three months there, studying Madain Salih, his companions, the Bedouin, and himself. The lifelessness of Madain Salih fascinated him. 'It is a marvel that you may view their *suks* (markets) and even the nail holes whereupon they hanged their stuffs over the shop doors, and in many of their shops and shelves, spences and little cellars where they laid up their wares,' Nejm said, offering him some three-thousand-year-old lumps of frankincense.

After Doughty had been there a week the garrison heard the faint cry of a stranger outside the *kella*. Hasan and Mohammed ran out and brought in a nearly naked Turkish dervish. He had walked six hundred miles, trying to catch up with the Haj caravan, 'but though robust his human sufferance was too little for the long way'. The last two hundred miles had been spent following the tracks of the caravan through the desert, where the dervish had been stripped by the Bedouin and almost killed. Mohammed Ali brought him a piece of Aleppo felt cloth, and the garrison gave him the traditional three days' hospitality before sending him on his journey.

Right: *A Nabataean tomb at Madain Salih, drawn by Doughty.*

> The third morrow come, the last of the customary hospitality,
> they were already weary of him; Mohammed Aly, putting a
> bundle of meal in his hand and a little water-skin upon his
> shoulders, brought him forth, and showing the direction bade
> him follow as he could the footprints of the caravan.[1]

A few weeks later the garrison asked some passing Bedouin if they had seen
the dervish. 'Ay, we saw him lying dead, and the felt was under him.'

To inspect the monuments at Madain Salih Doughty secured the services of
Seyd, a Bedouin sheikh with eyes that looked out from 'the lawless lands of
famine'. He was dark in colour, of middle age and middle stature, and no
fool. Seyd managed to contrive with all the Bedouin in the area that none
would act as Doughty's guide, thus ensuring the position for himself.

> Nothing in Zeyd was barbarous and uncivil; his carriage
> was that haughty grace of the wild creatures. In him I have
> not seen any spark of fanatical ill-humour. He could speak
> with me smilingly of his intolerant countrymen; for himself
> he could well imagine that sufficient is Ullah to the
> governance of the world, without fond man's meddling.[2]

Another week went by and, collecting the inscriptions of Madain Salih,
Doughty remained blissfully unaware of the resentment he was causing with
his continual demands on the hospitality of the garrison. If the soldiers had
tolerated the presence of the dervish for only three days, how did they feel
about Doughty after three months? The crisis came with Mohammed Ali,
who was hoping to get the cavalry carbine in return for the food Doughty had
eaten.

> Mohammed Aly, trembling and frantic, leaping up then in
> his place, struck me again in the doorway, with all his tiger's
> force; as he heaped blows I seized his two fists and held
> them fast . . . . He struggled, the red cap fell off his Turk's
> head, and his stomach rising afresh at this new indignity, he
> broke from me. The sickly captain of ruffian troopers for a
> short strife had the brawns of a butcher, and I think three
> peaceable men might not hold him.[3]

Left: *A Bedouin desert camp,*
from a painting by Charles
Tyrwhitt-Drake.

Mohammed Ali then plucked Doughty's beard, a serious Moslem insult, and Doughty, as if wanting to increase his humiliation, gave the man the cavalry carbine he so coveted. No other serious traveller in Arabia – not Niebuhr, Burckhardt, Burton, Palgrave, nor Guarmani – would have made such a disastrous mistake. Doughty's arrogant assertion of his Christianity was a festering provocation to people on whom he was wholly reliant, yet he gave away the very thing that might have saved him from the consequence of that arrogance. It was as if the man was deliberately courting martyrdom.

The Haj caravan returned eight days late from Mecca, and when it finally came it brought smallpox. Doughty's original plan was to return to Damascus with it, but three months in the desert had changed his mind. He was attracted to people who saw him as a mere unbeliever. His social inadequacies were irrelevant beside that one overwhelming fact.

'When the caravan left, Seyd and Doughty rode with it for the first two days. A poor dervish, passing him by and seeing him thirst, offered him water. 'Drink of this, O pilgrim, and refresh thyself.' Doughty took one look at the dirty and discoloured liquid and gave it back. Such behaviour could hardly have endeared him to his fellows. He was on the brink of the unknown. 'The most fanatical and wild Mohammedan region lay before me, where the name of Nasrani is only wont to be said as an injury; how might I have passage amongst a fanatic and sanguinary population?'

They left the caravan on the third day to search for Seyd's tents. They rode all day and found them at nightfall.

'This is Khalil,' Seyd said, introducing Doughty to his unveiled wife Hirfa. 'Take good care of him.'

Next morning Seyd watched Hirfa dismantle the tent and load the camel. Then everyone mounted and rode about ten miles to fresh grazing. They stayed there two days and moved on, keeping up the nomadic pattern for three months. The stay with Seyd gave this European a greater insight into Bedouin life than any before him.

There was little water to drink and Hirfa resented the extra water Doughty used to wash with. 'She thought it unthrift to pour out water thus when all day the thirsty tribesmen have not enough to drink.'

Hirfa was about twenty and already 'the golden youth was faded almost to autumn in her childish face.' She was unsatisfied by her middle-aged husband Seyd. 'Hirfa in her weary spirit desired some fresh young husband, instead of this pallid Seyd, that she mistrusted could not give her children.' She was also attracted to one of Seyd's herdsmen 'whom in her husband's absence she wooed openly.' There were frequent beatings, scratching and screamings as either Seyd or Hirfa threw the other out of the tent. The unlikely Nasrani was regularly called to mediate between the two.

> The woman's lot is here unequal concubinage, and in this necessitous life a weary servitude. The possession in her of parents and tutors has been yielded at some price, (in contempt and constraint of her weaker sex,) to an husband, by whom she may be dismissed in what day he shall have no more pleasure in her. It may be, (though seldom among nomads their will is forced,) that those few flowering years of her youth, with her virginity have been yielded to some man of unlikely age. And his heart is not hers alone; but, if not divided already, she must look to divide her marriage in a time to come with other. And certainly as she withers, which is not long to come, or having no fair adventure to bear male children, she will as thing unprofitable be cast off.[4]

The Nasrani's own single status remained something of an enigma to the Bedouin. Many thought he had rented out his wife while he was away, which was the kind of things Moslems in Arabia thought to be a common practice among Christians. They offered him sisters, daughters, wives. Seyd even offered Hirfa, to rid himself of her. But Doughty managed to offend with his humourless fanaticism. He told them that his religion did not allow him to take 'other men's wives'.

Soon the Bedouin began to dislike his religious arrogance and cold English reserve. Above all they were becoming impatient with his demands on their hospitality, and they wondered when he would go.

One morning, 15 April 1877, one of the herdsmen rushed into the camp shouting that there had been a raid and the camels had been taken in the night. The whole encampment jumped up and armed themselves, preparing for the pursuit. But with their camels gone, there was nothing to pursue on. It was five hours before more camels arrived and the party set off. By then it was too late. Doughty was critical, 'a weak enemy they thus faintly let slip through their fingers for a little wind', yet it is hard to see what else they could have done.

Eventually Seyd and his encampment arrived at Taima, which Carlo Guarmani had visited over a decade earlier. 'Delightful now was the green sight of Taima, the haven of our desert; we approached the tall island of palms, enclosed by long clay orchard-walls, fortified with high towers.' A free township of some two hundred houses, it was taken over by Mohammed ibn Rashid not long before Guarmani's visit. Doughty saw little of it, however: Seyd's tribe owed ibn Rashid five years arrears in taxes, and they did not linger.

From Taima the encampment moved east and south-east in the direction of Hail. Seyd himself could not go to Hail, so Doughty joined a group of passing Bedouins on their way to the city. Typically he brought neither food nor water, expecting others to provide. When they did not, the day became 'a

Above: *The Taima Stone, found by the Frenchman Charles Huber in 1879, two years after Doughty's visit. Huber returned in 1883 with a companion, the German Julius Euting, and transported the stone to Hail. Reflecting the views of their respective governments, the two disliked each other intensely and parted company. Huber was killed by the Bedouin and Euting fled to Jerusalem in fear of his life after getting mixed up in a blood feud. The stone remained in Hail until the Emir wrote to both French and German governments. The French bribed the Ottomans to deport the German agent and got the Stone. It now stands in the Louvre.*

long dying without death'. To add to the torment a small Bedouin girl mocked him from morning to night. The days that followed were no better. 'All about us is an iron wilderness, a bare and black shining beach of heated volcanic stone.'

Unable to keep up, Doughty dropped out. An old man guided him to some Moahib Bedouin. Their route lay across ranges of lava hills; at one point Doughty counted thirty extinct volcanoes. Thrusting himself on the Moahibs as a forsaken traveller, he was taken in with mixed feelings. He outstayed his welcome and, when the tribe moved on to new pastures, they told him that they did not want him. With nowhere to go he followed them pathetically, stumbling along behind, living a thousand humiliations on the way. Reluctantly the Moahibs took him in again, frightened that the Turkish authorities would hold them responsible should any harm come to him. He delayed his journey to Hail and stayed with them throughout the summer, clearly resented as an extra mouth to feed. He met Seyd again, but his former friend showed a distinct disinclination to want to know him. He was even

Right: *A Bedouin woman. 'Few then are the nomad wives whose years can be long happy in marriage.'*

more unpopular when he revisited Taima. The well had caved in three times since his last visit and the blame fell on the Nasrani's evil eye. There he finally left the Moahib, and joined some Bishr Bedouin going to Hail. The Moahib warned him not to go, before he left them. 'Word is come of thee to ibn Rashid that a Nasrani, whom no man knoweth, is wandering with the Arabs and writing, and he is much displeased. The Bedouin eastwards will fear to receive thee lest the Emir should require it of them.' Doughty ignored the warning. As he collected his baggage a Bedouin woman came to him in search of a needle and thread. He told her to go away. She turned on him.

'Ha, Nasrani. But ere long we shall take all these things from thee.'

They left in the rain. It was a humiliating ride. The sheikh of the Bishr coveted Doughty's red Moroccan girdle and threatened to abandon him if he did not give it up. Doughty's exhausted camel could not keep up with the Bishr's fast dromedaries which were averaging fifty miles day and night. The Bishr Bedouins refused to be held up, and only when the Nasrani's camel collapsed in the sand did they rest. When they started again he called to them to stop, but they went on, leaving him in the hands of a single Bishr guide to take him to Hail at his own pace.

As they approached the city Doughty's guide gave him one final warning:

> Khalil, the people where we are going are jealous. Let them not see thee writing, for be sure they will take it amiss; but wouldst thou write, write covertly and put away these leaves of books. Thou wast hitherto with the Bedouin and the Bedouin would know thee what thou art; but hearest thou? They are not like good-hearted in yonder villages.[5]

A few hours later they were in Hail. They saw before them a high castle. 'The Emir's summer palace,' said Doughty's Bishr companion. The city wall was enclosed in a forest of palms. The Bishr guide told Doughty to dismount, there were some low gateways ahead. Doughty realized that this was because he was a Nasrani but, wisely, said nothing. They made their way down the same main street that Palgrave had walked, into the square. The streets were crowded; no one paid any particular attention to them. They stopped and couched their camel outside the castle. Doughty sat down by his luggage and waited; the Bishr guide withdrew as far away as he decently could.

Finally Doughty was greeted by one of ibn Rashid's junior ministers and led into the castle, past the Rashidi's ancient artillery, to the large and pillared reception room that Palgrave and Guarmani had been entertained in a decade earlier. A slave offered him coffee and dates. He drank the coffee but refused the dates, since they were covered in dust. Another bad beginning. His hosts, feeling insulted, curtly summoned him to the Emir.

He made his way down a long corridor, through an iron-plated door guarded by a slave, into a small courtyard. Some of the Emir's soldiers, lounging in the shade, stared at him. He was taken across the courtyard to the Emir's private apartments. Mohammed ibn Rashid was lying, half leaning on his elbow, resting on cushions. He wore his hair in long black braided locks. His face was lean and sallow. Doughty saluted him: 'Salam alaikum.'

There was no reply. Doughty stood there, then the Emir told him to sit.

'From whence comest thou, and what is the purpose of thy voyage?'

'I am arrived from Taima and el-Hejr, and I came down from Syria to visit Madain Salih.'

One of the Rashidi sheikhs sitting with the Emir leaned towards him. 'A man to trust. This is not like him who came hither, thou canst remember Mohammed in what year, but one that tells us all things plainly.'

Right: Detail from 'A Bedouin Encampment' by Eugene Girardet. This painting is probably of a north African landscape, rather than from central Arabia. (Mathaf Gallery, London)

The Emir continued his questions. 'What could move thee to take such a journey?'

Doughty, with his extraordinary knack of saying the wrong thing, announced: 'The liberal sciences.' But said in the plural it became 'tidings' or 'information'. It was like saying: 'I'm a spy.' He explained his meaning, and the Emir let it go. He asked Doughty his profession. The reply was a scholar and a doctor. The Emir asked if he could read and write. He picked up an Arabic history book, opened it at random, pointed, and asked Doughty to read. 'The king slew all his brethren and kindred.' The text was unfortunate. A dark and troubled look came over Mohammed's face. 'Not there!' He told the Nasrani to read somewhere else, then asked him where he wanted to go. 'To Baghdad.'

'Very well, we will send thee to Baghdad.'

On his second day in Hail Doughty met Hamud, Obied's younger son. He was noble, wise and loyal.

Left: *Hamud, Obied's son and Mohammed ibn Rashid's cousin; a man, according to Doughty, of 'clement nature'.*

> The princely Hamud has bound his soul by oath to his cousin the Emir, to live and to die with him; their fathers were brethren and, as none remain of age of the Prince's house, Hamud ibn Rashid is next after Mohammed in authority, is his deputy at home, fights by his side in the field, and bears the style of Emir.[6]

Hamud was friendly to the stranger, inquiring about the telegraph, the Crystal Palace, Paris and oil lamps. Was it true, he asked, that petroleum was made out of human urine? Then he leaned over to the Nasrani and asked him if he had a cure for impotence. The next evening the Emir invited Doughty back to his apartments. Mohammed, who had obviously been talking to his cousin, asked the stranger what exactly a telegraph was. Doughty tried to explain: 'If we may suppose a man laid head and heels between Hail and Istanbul, of such stature that he touched them both; if one burned his feet at Hail, should he not feel it at the instant in his head, which is at Istanbul?'

Mohammed listened carefully. He learnt quickly. The next year he installed a telephone.

The Nasrani was allowed to wander the streets of Hail. At first he was a mere curiosity, then he became the object of hostility. It was frequently suggested that he should say that he was a Moslem, but his replies were provocative and offensive. One man, Anaibar, the same who had guided Guarmani, was particularly irritated. Doughty even tried patronizing Hamud, giving him a lecture on slavery. Hamud, with his good manners, listened. He had to. The Nasrani was providing quinine for Hamud's child who was suffering from malaria.

Doughty must have been a difficult guest. He was quick to demand the benefits of hospitality from others, yet rarely allowed his patients to escape from consultations without full payment. After a fortnight, the Emir became increasingly annoyed at Doughty's unwelcome stay, and departed from Hail on a minor expedition, leaving the affairs of the city in the hands of Hamud. A week later he returned, displeased to see the Nasrani still there. He summoned him to the palace. Doughty greeted him: 'Salam alaikum.' There was no answer. He greeted Hamud. Mohammed abruptly asked him what he was still doing in Hail. Doughty was silent, arrogantly silent. Hamud tactfully suggested that the stranger was tired. Mohammed was impatient.

He was not the only one impatient with the Nasrani's behaviour. One morning the coffee-maker in ibn Rashid's reception room could not take the man's constant presence and hit him with a camel stick. Again it was the good Hamud who saved him.

That same week the Persian Haj caravan arrived in Hail. The streets were packed with pilgrims. One, clad like a Baghdadi merchant, whispered to Doughty as he passed by, asking if he spoke French. Doughty replied: 'I shall understand it. But what countryman art thou?'

'I am an Italian, a Piedmontese of Turin.'

'And what brings you hither upon this hazardous voyage? Good Lord! You might have your throat cut among them. Are you a Moslem?'

'Ay,' he said. 'A man may not always choose, but he must sometimes go with the world.' The mysterious stranger then passed on, into the vastness of Arabia, and Doughty never saw him again.

Finally ibn Rashid had had enough of Doughty and sent one of his officers, Imbarek, to arrange the Nasrani's passage to Khaybar, and let the Turkish authorities deal with this troublesome stranger. Imbarek marched into Doughty's quarters without knocking.

'We have found some Heteym who will convey thee to Khaybar.'

'And when would they depart?'

'Tomorrow or the morning after.'

An hour later Imbarek returned and abruptly told Doughty that he must leave immediately. Doughty demanded to speak to the Emir.

'Have done and delay not, or the Emir will send to take off thy head.'

Doughty now feared that Imbarek had come to slay him. Imbarek's slaves were openly pilfering his belongings and pulling the clothes from his back.

'Imbarek, I no longer trust you,' Doughty said.

At this, Imbarek spat in his face. Doughty demanded protection (*dakilah*) from Imbarek against the slaves. Imbarek ordered the slaves to restore Doughty's possessions to him and allowed him one final interview with Hamud. The good man came to him.

'Was this done at the commandment of the Emir?' asked Doughty.

'Khalil, I can do nothing with the Emir.'

'There is a thing, Hamud.'

'What is it Khalil?'

'Help me in this trouble, for that bread and salt that is between us.'

'What can I do? Mohammed rules us all.'

Right: *Ibn Rashid's stud of Arab thoroughbreds.*

'Speak to Imbarek to do nothing till the hour of the afternoon *majlis* (court of justice), where I may speak to the Emir.'

The court of justice sat each afternoon in the courtyard by the palace. The Emir faced his people. Next to the Emir sat the *kadi* (the judge) who acted as clerk of the court. On either side of them were ranged the sheikhs of Shammar. About one hundred and fifty soldiers sat in a semi-circle in front. The accused and suppliants walked into the semi-circle. Doughty joined them. He waited his turn and approached the Emir.

'I am about to depart,' he said, 'but I would it were with assurance. Today I was mishandled in this place, in a manner which has made me afraid. Thy slaves drew me hither and thither, and have rent my clothing; it was by the setting on of Imbarek, who stands here: he also threatened me, and even spat in my face.'

The Emir spoke to Imbarek then turned to Doughty. 'Fear not, but ours be the care of thy safety, and we will give thee a passport. He spoke to the *kadi* who wrote out a safe conduct. Mohammed signed it and the *kadi* read it out: 'That all unto whose hands this bill may come, who owe obedience to ibn Rashid, know it is the will of the Emir that no one should do any offence to this Nasrani.'

Doughty asked when he should depart.

'At thy pleasure.'

'Tomorrow?'

'Nay, today.'

'Mount,' Imbarek cried. He led him from the court to the Rashidi kitchens for one last meal. Doughty refused it. Ibn Rashid had given him four riyals for his journey and Hamud gave him another four for the quinine. Outside the city walls he met the three Bedouin who would take him to Khaybar. 'My companions were three, the poor owner of my camel, a timid smiling man, and his fanatic neighbour, who called me always the Nasrawi (and not Nasrani), and another and older Heteym, a somewhat stronger-headed holder of his own counsel.' Soon it was nightfall. Doughty and his companions talked as they rode, and he answered their questions 'with the courtesy of the desert'. 'Wherefore did those of Hail persecute him?' they asked. 'The people of Hail are the true Nasranis.'

They rode for three and half hours through the night until they couched their camels and fell asleep in the sand near to the village of Gofar. The men

Left: *The* kahwah *(reception room) in ibn Rashid's palace, which Palgrave, Guarmani and Doughty all passed through.*

Right: *The Jebal Shammar,
approaching it from Doughty's
and Palgrave's 'petrified' lava
beds.*

gave them dates and coffee and the women sewed up Doughty's clothes. They were sedentary Bedouin, tribeless and landless. 'These poor folk, disinherited of the world, spoke to me with human kindness; there was not a word in their talk of Mohammedan fanaticism.'

By the time they left it was one o'clock in the afternoon. They rode over a plain of granite and grit. Next day the landscape rose up into volcanic mountains; they climbed all day through the mountains and did not meet a solitary soul. They went to bed supperless. The night was cold and they could not sleep.

They left before dawn. Soon after daybreak they met a party of Shammar Bedouins. Two rode over to greet them. 'What news from the villages?' they shouted. They looked at the wild-looking stranger with his flaming red hair and beard. Realizing he was a Nasrani one of them raised his spear. Doughty was on foot. He had perversely allowed his three guides so to dominate him that one was riding his camel. One of the guides told the Shammar that the Nasrani had the protection of ibn Rashid. The spear was lowered. The four rode on until they reached another Shammar encampment. 'Give us tobacco and come down and drink coffee with us,' the Shammar said, adding that if Doughty did not come down off his camel they would take the beast.

'Ye believe not in God!' cried Doughty. 'I tell you I have none. By God, it is a shame, man, to molest a stranger, and that only for a pipe of tobacco.' They let him passs when he had sworn again that he had none.

That afternoon, as they rode on through the volcanic chaos, the three Heteym guides met one of their own sheikhs, Eyada. They urged the Nasrani to go with him, but Doughty, remembering the advice he had been given in Hail to find Kasim ibn Borak who would arrange his jouney to Khaybar, refused. They rode on until they reached Kasim's camp. It was sunset. The three Heteym hastily unloaded Doughty's bags and tried to make off with his camel. Doughty siezed the camel by its lower lip and forced it to kneel. Kasim approached, and the three reluctantly realized that they had to stay.

Kasim was an obliging but unenthusiastic host. He was annoyed with both ibn Rashid and the three guides for forcing the Nasrani on him, but made the best of it. Next morning he told his guest he would pass him on to a nearby Hanna sheikh who could provide a guide for him to Khaybar. His three Heteym guides would take him there. The guides 'swore mighty oaths to convey me straightway to Hannas' and the next day the four of them rode out of Kasim's camp. At the first Bedouin tent they came to they dumped Doughty's baggage and made off on his camel.

'Where is thy oath, man?'

'His oath was not binding, which was made to a Nasrawy.'

Doughty sat down in the desert and wept. An old woman took pity on him.

'Be not sorrowful, for I am thy mother's sister.' She told him of a nearby sheikh. His name was Eyada, the same Eyada Doughty had passed the day before. She led him to her tent and he sat there until her husband came home. He arrived with three grown sons and a large herd of camels, sheep and goats. He was called Thaifullah and was a good man. He gave his guest some hot milk and said he could stay the night. 'We have nothing here to eat, no dates, no rice, no bread, but drink this which the Lord provideth.' The Nasrani blessed him.

In the morning the old woman gave Doughty a bowl of buttermilk while Thaifullah loaded the Nasrani's baggage on one of his own camels. The two mounted the camel and rode off in search of Eyada's encampment.

They found his tents pitched in a shelving hollow. Doughty looked out over the surrounding landscape. 'I saw a vast blackness beyond . . . and rosy mountains of granite. Sandstones lying as a tongue between the crystalline mountains and overlaid by lavas, reach southward to Khaybar.'

They alighted outside Eyada's tent. Doughty told his story but Eyada refused to take him in. The Nasrani pleaded. The sheikh turned to some nearby Bedouins.

'Which of you will convey this man to Khaybar and receive from him what –? Three riyals?'

'I will carry him, if he gives me this money,' said an on-looker whom Eyada addressed as Ghroceyb.

The Nasrani agreed. Ghroceyb made ready then returned to Eyada's tent. 'Give me four riyals. I have a debt and this would help me.'

Eyada, who knew more about Ghroceyb's debt than Doughty, advised him to give four and to go with him. Doughty agreed. Ghroceyb, relieved, looked up at the sky.

Above: *Arriving at an oasis. After the barren emptiness of the desert the oasis, with its extravagant exuberance, was like paradise in a dessicated Hell.*

'See how the sun is already mounted. Let us pass the day here and tomorrow we set forward.'

'Today,' said Eyada, firmly.

They rode off into a volcanic waste. Doughty asked Ghroceyb how far they were from Khaybar. 'Three days,' he replied. Two passed by. The closer they got to Khaybar the more reluctant Ghroceyb became. Khaybar was Turkish and Ghroceyb had killed a man in Turkish territory. The debt that he told Doughty of when he demanded four riyals was a blood debt, and it had not yet been paid.

As they approached the town the hard volcanic shell melted into a forest of palms. They rode down into the valley where the shabby town lay half-hidden by palms. The water in the valley was stagnant and the earth covered in salt crusts. It was humid, and there were a lot of flies. 'A heavy presentation of evil lay upon my heart, as we rode into this deadly drowned atmosphere.'

Khaybar had hardly changed since Guarmani's visit. The old Jewish town was still inhabited by a colony of Negroes. The houses were two-storeyed, with animals on the ground floor and people above. Ghroceyb led him through a rickety gate made out of rough palm tree boards to the house of a friend, Abd el-Hadi. They couched their camels outside the house and climbed up a ladder of palm tree trunks to the first floor. There they quenched their thirst from el-Hadi's sweating goatskin. 'The water, drawn, they said, from the spring head under the basalt, tasted of the ditch.' People came from all over the town to stare at Doughty. Abd el-Hadi served coffee to them all. It was nearly midnight before the last of them left.

'Will they serve supper, or is it not time to sleep?' Doughty asked Ghroceyb.

'I think they have killed for thee; I saw them bring a sheep to the terrace.'

When morning came Ghroceyb, fearful of his blood debt, slipped out of the town. 'Farewell,' he said, 'and if there was any difference between us, forgive it, Khalil.' He kissed Doughty's hand and left.

Right: 'Look yonder!' The overwhelming feeling of releif on arriving at an oasis in the desert.

Abd el-Hadi took his guest into the palm forest around the town. He showed him the spring where Khaybar's water came from, and asked about the representative of Turkish power in the town, the Dowla. 'Are you afraid of the Dowla? Is the Dowla better, or ibn Rashid's government? The Dowla delivered us from the Bedouin, but is more burdensome.'

They passed through the burial ground. 'That funeral earth is chapped and ghastly, bulging over her enwombed corses, like a garden soil in spring-time, which is pushed by the new-aspiring plants.'

From the cemetery el-Hadi took him to the Dowla. They went to the barracks where they drank coffee with a sorry bunch of Turks, Albanians, Egyptians, Kurds and Africans, none of whom had been paid for two years. As they left, climbing down the ladder, Doughty heard a voice say: 'He is an enemy.' 'Let him alone awhile,' another said. Doughty asked Abd el-Hadi where the Dowla was. 'You did not see him! He sat in the midst of the hearth.'

Again, Doughty made no attempt to disguise his Christianity, oblivious to the difficulties he might be giving his host. 'This man has little understanding of the world,' said one villager.

Some soldiers came and summoned Doughty to the barracks. He told them he was a Nasrani and an Englishman and they thrust him to the stairs. He shook the dust off and found himself surrounded by a mob of frightened and angry townspeople. They dragged him to the Dowla. 'I had secretly taken my pistol under my tunic at the first alarm.' The Dowla interrogated him, and said: 'If any books should be found with thee, or . . . charts of countries, thou shalt never see them more: they must all be sent to the Pasha at Medina.' He asked the Nasrani where he had come from. 'From Hail; I have here also a passport from ibn Rashid.' The Dowla looked at it mystified; he could not read. 'Call me here the Sheikh Salih, to read and write for us.'

Salih, old and lame, arrived carrying a long inkstand and a large sheet of paper. The Dowla searched Doughty's baggage; Salih listed the contents.

'What is this?'

'A medicine box.'

'Open it.'

A soldier took out Doughty's compass, wrapped in cloth. Another soldier thought it was soap. The search went on. Comb, books, tape measure, tea. He tried to show Sheikh Salih his circular passport from the Governor of Syria, but it was written in such elegant Turkish that Salih could not understand it. Then the soldiers reached his revolver holster. 'Where is the pistol?' Doughty said nothing. 'It is plain that ibn Rashid has taken it from him,' someone exclaimed. 'A pistol among them is always preciously preserved in a gay holster; and they could not imagine that I should wear a naked pistol under my bare shirt. After this I thought, will they search my person? But that is regarded amongst them as an extreme outrage; and there would be too many witnesses.'

The Dowla asked him where his money was. 'Reach me that tin, where you saw the tea: in the midst is my purse, – and in it, you see, are six riyals! Salih wrote down six riyals. 'I have taken them for their better keeping,' said the Dowla. Doughty looked around in despair. Abd el-Hadi, his host of the previous evening, came up to him. 'Take comfort, there shall be no evil happen to thee.' The Dowla began to soften. 'Abd el-Hadi, let him return to lodge with thee,' he said. 'He can cure the sick.' Abd el-Hadi replied that he would be happy to receive the Nasrani, if only he became a Moslem. 'Then he must lodge with the soldiery.'

The Nasrani stood in the street alone, penniless, a prisoner. He searched the hostile crowd for a friendly face.

Below: *Detail from Adolf von Meckel's 'A Land Without Shade'. 'Great was the day's heat upon the kerchiefed heads of them who herded the camels; for the sun which may be borne in journeying, that is whilst we are passing through the air, is intolerable even to Nomads who stand still.' (Mathaf Gallery, London)*

I saw the large manly presence standing erect in the backward of the throng – for he had lately arrived – of a very swarthy Arabian; he was sheykhly clad, and carried the sword, and I guessed he might be some chief man of the irregular soldiery. Now he came to me, and dropping (in their sudden manner) upon the hams of the legs, he sat before me with the confident smiling humour of a strong man; and spoke to me pleasantly. I wondered to see his swarthiness, – yet such are commonly the Arabians in the Hejaz – and he not less to see a man so 'white and red.' This was Mohammed en-Nejumy . . . who from the morrow became to me as a father at Kheybar.[7]

To Doughty, Mohammed en-Nejumy was his only friend. He never recognized the debt that he owed the Dowla. Several times over the following weeks the Dowla saved his life. When the townspeople threatened to kill him, it was the Dowla who stopped them. 'What are these Nasranis? Listen all of you. It is a strong nation. Were not two or three Nasranis murdered some

years ago at Jeddah? Well, what followed? There came great warships of their nation and bombarded the place.' Then he had paused and thought. 'But you the Khaybara know not what is a ship.'

Each morning and evening Doughty had to present himself to the Dowla, but was free during the daytime to wander where he wanted. The longer he stayed in Khaybar the more he hated the Dowla. He had no sense when dealing with people of middle ground. So drawn to extremes himself, he saw all others in terms of these extremes. Men were either good or bad, and the Dowla was bad. It never occurred to Doughty to see the situation from the Dowla's point of view: a score of unpaid soldiers, a provocative stranger whose presence threatened the peace, a potential spy scandal. He was blind to shades of grey.

Doughty spent most of his time with Mohammed en-Nejumy, utilizing his knowledge of geology to help Mohammed dig a well. Geology and simple practical tasks brought out the best and least neurotic in the man, and the long hours of physical labour gave the two a chance to know each other.

Mohammed was the son of a Turkish soldier from Medina. He himself had been a Turkish soldier and he had the blood of two men on his conscience. His father died and he had gambled away his inheritance, ending up as a dustman working for eightpence a day. A friend of his father's generously gave him sufficient capital to buy a sick horse in Khaybar, heal it, and sell it in Medina for double the price. He was now a leading merchant.

It was not the first time he had helped a stranger. Once a Medina tradesman, stripped and wounded, was cared for by Mohammed and sent on his way to Medina. 'And now when I come there and he hears that I am in the city, he brings me home and makes feast and rejoicing.'

Another time the Bedouin dragged a naked man into Khaybar on a noose. They said they would kill him for withholding ten riyals from them. 'The Nejumy will redeem me,' he pleaded, and the Nejumy did. 'I clothed him and gave him a waterskin, and dates and flour for the journey, and let him go. A week later the poor man returned with ten riyals, and driving a fat sheep for me.' Honesty indeed.

Strangely enough, this saintly man was a tyrant in his own house, beating his wife and son. When Doughty started preaching to him he would have none of it. 'I snub my wife because a woman must be kept in subjection, for else they do begin to despise their husbands.'

Doughty spent as much time as he could with Mohammed, for only with him could he escape the hostility of the rest of Khaybar. 'Ah, Khalil,' Mohammed said. 'Thou canst imagine all their malice.' The Dowla was getting increasingly restless; he feared there would be a riot and that he would be blamed for any harm that would come to the Nasrani. The final straw came for the Dowla when he received reports that the Nasrani was making magical spells, and that a couple of Bedouin nomads had tried to take a shot at him.

Left: *Doughty's drawing of Khaybar, an African village in the middle of Arabia, and originally a Jewish town.*

Right: A suk *in an Arab town. Already Palgrave had recognized the gradual demise of the Bedouin and the rise of the new cosmopolitan bourgeoisie. It was more pronounced in Doughty's time. Soon they would dominate the economy of Arabia, paving the way for the petroleum society and dragging the protesting Bedouin into the twentieth century.*

What hadst thou done, Khalil? What is it that I hear of thee? The chief persons come to me accusing thee. And I do tell thee the truth, this people is no more well-minded towards thee. Observe that which I say to you, and go no more beyond the gates of the village. I say go not. I may protect thee in the village, in the daytime: by night go not out of thy chamber, lest some evil befall thee, and the blame be laid upon me.[8]

Doughty was getting equally impatient with the Dowla. It was three weeks before the letter was sent to the Pasha at Medina, carried in the hands of a reliable Bedouin, Dakhil. Days passed waiting for his return. Doughty confided to Mohammed his fear that the Pasha would order his death – in fact fairly unlikely considering the relationship between the British and Turkish empires and the Dowla's awareness of warships.

'Look Khalil, if there cometh an evil tiding from the Pasha, I will redeem thee,' said Mohammed. 'If I see the danger instant I will steal thee away.'

That night Dakhil returned with a letter from the Pasha ordering the Dowla to 'send all the stranger's books and papers which he brought with him from ibn Rashid.' The Dowla informed Doughty of the contents. 'I will also write to the Pasha,' insisted Doughty. 'And here is my English passport, which I will send with the rest.'

'No', the Dowla yelled. 'This Nasrani, who lives today only by my benefit, will chop words with me. Oh, wherefore with my pistol. Wherefore, I say, did I not blow out his brains at first?'

Doughty's reckless assertion of his Englishness and the superiority of the English coming from a vagabond, was too much even for Mohammed. He

'heard me with impatience, when I said to him that we were not the subjects of the Sultan.' When Doughty told Mohammed that without English goods and technology the Ottoman army would be naked, Mohammed put him in his place. 'It is very well that the Engleys . . . should labour for the Sultan.'

Weeks passed. Doughty had already endured this 'black captivity' for two months. Mohammed's well was finished. One day the Dowla came up to him. 'Good news, Khalil. Thy books are come again, and the Pasha writes, "send him to ibn Rashid." '

The Turkish authorities were refusing to take him back into the Hejaz. They were sending him back where he had come from. Doughty asked the Dowla for his six riyals back. The Dowla no longer had them. He played for time. Next day Doughty asked him again.

Left: *Detail from 'Approach to Mount Sinai', by David Roberts. Doughty would have travelled through similarly barren landscape towards Hail.*

'I will restore them at thy departure.'

'Have you any right to detain them?'

'Say no more – a Nasrani to speak to me thus! – or I will give thee a buffet.'

'If thou strike me, it will be at thy peril.' The Dowla, furious, struck him in the face. Doughty turned to Mohammed. He got little sympathy.

'You have no wit to be a traveller,' he said. He paused a moment. 'If thou say among the Moslems, that thou art a Moslem, will your people kill thee when you return home? Art thou afraid of this, Khalil?' Doughty was silent. When they next met over coffee Mohammed said to Abdallah: 'I have found a man that will not befriend himself. I can in no wise persuade Sheykh Khalil. But if all the Moslems were like faithful in their religion, I say, the world would not be able to resist us.'

Finally the Dowla gave Doughty back his six riyals (by selling a cow that he had commandeered in lieu of tax). Doughty was now ready to leave, but leaving was not as easy as he thought. Khaybar was not on any of the main caravan routes and there was little traffic north-east towards Hail. Dakhil, the reliable messenger, offered to take him but asked too much. Instead, Doughty found a Bishr Bedouin, Eyad, who agreed to take him for five riyals. 'Eyad, a Bedouin, and by military adoption a townsman of Medina, was one who had drunk very nigh the dregs of the mischiefs and vility of one and the other life.' His camel looked as if it had been through the same. Eyad insisted on being paid all five riyals in advance. Doughty agreed, after considerable persuasion from the Dowla.

He went to say goodbye to Mohammed, dividing his medicines with him and buying him a new gun stock and a tunic. When the Nasrani offensively offered Mohammed some small change in his pocket, Mohammed refused it. 'Nay, Khalil, but leave me happy with the remembrance, and take it not away from me by requiting me. Only this I desire of thee that thou sometimes say, "The Lord remember him for good." '

> So I ever used the Arabian hospitality to my possibility: yet now I sinned in so doing, against that charitable integrity, the human affection, which was in Mohammed; and which, like the waxen powder upon summer fruits, is deflowered under any rude handling.[9]

Mohammed accompanied him on foot a little way out of the town then took his hand. 'The world, and death, and the inhumanity of religions parted us for ever.'

Doughty and Eyad, accompanied by a young Bedouin boy, Merjan, walked out into the volcanic wastes. Relations soon soured, and Doughty insisted that Eyad should leave his matchlock behind whenever he went out of Doughty's sight.

On the third day Doughty encountered Eyada for the third time. 'Eyada saluted me, but looked askance upon my rafiks, and they were strange with him and silent. This is the custom of the desert, when nomads meeting with nomads are in doubt of each other whether friends or foemen.'

'Fear nothing,' said Eyada.

Doughty asked after Ghroceyb. Ghroceyb, Eyada told him, had said that the Nasrani had tried to steal his camel.

They went on. Next day they encountered none other than Doughty's old guide Salih, who had walked out on him three months earlier. It must have been an embarrassing moment for Salih, but he handled it well and killed a kid. By now a distinct distance had developed between Eyad and Merjan on one side and Doughty on the other. Merjan in particular was tired and exhausted by the long hours of travelling. He had a habit of walking in front of Doughty's camel.

'Step on, lad, or let me pass,' Doughty said impatiently.

Merjan turned and raised his gun. Eyad tried to intervene.

'Forgive him, Khalil.'

Doughty, who had dismounted, spoke provocatively to Eyad.

'Was there ever a Bedouin who threatened death to his *rafik*?'

'No, by Allah.'

'But this is a Nasrani,' shouted Merjan. 'With a Nasrani who need to keep the law? Is not this an enemy of Allah?'

Doughty, a big man, wrestled the gun from Merjan and started beating him with his riding stick. Eyad tried to stop him, grabbing his arms from behind. Merjan took advantage of Eyad's intervention to kick the Nasrani in the groin. He went to pick up a large stone but Eyad released Doughty and calmed the two down.

'We have all done foolishly. What will be said when this is told another day?'

The days that followed were silent, heavy with recriminations. Their tiny world moved across the volcanic emptiness at war with itself. Relief came only at night, when they happened upon Bedouin encampments. 'I speak many times of Arab hospitality, since of this I have been often questioned in Europe; and for a memorial of worthy persons. The hospitality of the worsted booths, the gentle entertainment of passengers and strangers in a land full of misery and fear, we have seen to be religious.'

As they got closer to Hail they learnt that ibn Rashid was not in the city, but on an expedition in the north. The acting Emir was Anaibar, who had befriended Guarmani and been so irritated by Doughty on his earlier visit. The nearer they got to the city, the more Doughty felt himself going towards martyrdom.

> I walked in the mornings two hours, as much as at afternoon, that my companions might ride; and to spare their sickly *thelul* (camel) I climbed to the saddle, as she stood, like a bedouin; but the humanity which I showed them, to my possibility, hardened their ungenerous hearts. Seeing them weary, and Eyad complaining that his soles were worn to the quick, I went on walking barefoot to Gofar, and bade them ride still.[10]

Left: *Travellers – townsmen from their clothes and merchants by their baggage – resting in the desert.*

Right: *The court of ibn Rashid's palace at Hail.*

Right: *The court of ibn Rashid's palace at Hail.*

They entered Hail. The city was almost deserted, most of the citizens having departed with ibn Rashid. The few in the streets were unfriendly. 'It is he indeed. Now it may please Allah he will be put to death.' Anaibar greeted him coldly. He was taken to the guest house. Outside the children threw stones at him. Anaibar spoke to him: 'Khalil,' he said, 'we cannot send thee forward, and thou must depart tomorrow.'

'Send me to the Emir in the north with the Medina letter, if I may not abide his coming in Hail.'

'Here rest tonight and in the morning depart'. He shot the palm of one of his hands across the other. 'I durst not suffer thee to remain in Hail, where so many are ready to kill thee, and I must answer to the Emir. Sleep here this night, and please Allah without mishap, and mount when you see the morning light.' Doughty wanted to go to Buraydah and Unayzah, the two semi-independent towns in the south. Anaibar insisted that he go back to Khaybar. Doughty envisaged a lifetime spent shuttling between Hail and Khaybar. Anaibar turned to Eyad and Merjan. They were to take him back

Eyad was terrified of what would happen to him if he returned to Khaybar with the Nasrani. 'I durst not do it, Anaibar.'

It is not permitted thee to say nay,' cried Anaibar. 'I command you upon your heads to convey Khalil to Khaybar.'

Next morning Eyad led him out of town. 'Let us hasten from them; and as for Merjan, I know not what is become of him. I will carry thee to Gofar, and leave thee there. No, Khalil, I am not treacherous, but I durst not, I cannot, return with thee to Khaybar: at Gofar I will leave thee.'

They stopped after a couple of miles and waited for Merjan. He arrived with a bundle of dates and barleymeal balanced on his head. It was a tense journey. 'Eyad had caught some fanatical suspicion in Hail, . . . that the Nasrani encroached continually upon the dominion of the Sultan, and that Khalil's nation, although not enemies, were not well-wishers, in their hearts, to the religion of Islam.' Two days later, amid a volcanic landscape, they stopped at a Heteym encampment.

'Khalil, we leave thee here,' said Eyad as he rode away, 'these are good folk.' The head of the encampment, Maatuk, urged the stranger to follow. 'Hasten after them with your bags or they will be quite gone.' Doughty did not move. Instead he asked Maatuk if he could stay. Maatuk shouted at him to follow the others. Doughty stood and demanded protection (*dakilah*). Again Maatuk told him to go, but he would not. Maatuk started beating him with a tent stake. Doughty sought refuge in the harem. 'What wrong ye do to chase away the stranger,' said Maatuk's wife. Maatuk calmed down and accepted his duties as a host. He would take the stranger to ibn Nahal, his sheikh, who would find him a guide to Buraydah.

Doughty was pleased: Eyad's departure had freed him from Khaybar. Ibn Nahal, however, showed no wish to help the Nasrani, so Maatuk, anxious to be rid of him, passed him on to two brothers, Motlog and Tollog. Motlog found a man who would take the Nasrani to Buraydah. His name was Hamed, and he had just arrived after a one-hundred-and-thirty-mile journey from the west. He collected up his belongings, turned to his wife, said: 'Woman, I go with the stranger to Buraydah,' and left with him.

The journey took over a week. Thanks to Hamed, it was unnaturally uneventful. Buraydah, when they arrived, was 'a great clay town built in this waste sand with enclosing walls and towers and streets and houses.' As they entered Hamed gave Doughty some advice.

> If at any time I have displeased thee, forgive it me; and say hast thou found me a good *rafik?* Khalil, thou seest Boreyda, and today I am to leave thee in this place. And when thou art in any of their villages, say not I am a Nasrani, for then they will utterly hate thee; but pray as they do, so long as thou shalt sojourn in the country, and in nothing let it be seen that thou art not of the Moslems.[11]

They walked into the town. The streets were empty. Hamed drew up the camel outside the Emir's guesthouse. A surly porter let them in, and served them with 'a churlish wheaten mess boiled in water.' Hamed rose and left. Doughty was alone. The porter, joined by coffee server and a black swordsman, approached him. He asked the porter where he could sleep. The porter asked why he did not pray and angrily pushed him into a darkened room. 'All was silent within and sounding as a chapel. I groped and felt clay pillars, and trod on ashes of an hearth: and lay down there upon the hard earthen floor. My pistol was in the bottom of my bags, which the porter had locked up in another place: I found my pen-knife, and thought in my heart, they should not go away with whole skins, if any would do me a mischief.' He was woken an hour later by the porter. 'Up and follow me, thou art called before the sheikhs to the coffee hall.' He was taken to another room. His interrogators sat around drinking coffee.

'Art thou the Nasrani that was lately in Hail?'

'I am he.'

'Why then didst thou not go to Khaybar?' Doughty excused himself, saying that his camel was sick. 'What are the papers with thee? Go and fetch them, for will we have those instantly, and carry them to the Emir.'

The porter unlocked the storeroom where Doughty's bags were. A crowd of soldiers and household slaves followed. A slave hit Doughty; another grabbed his papers.

'If thou hast any silver commit it to me, for they will rob you,' whispered the porter. Doughty looked at him. He had no reason to trust the porter any more than the rest of them. The crowd were taking his belongings.

'Thieves' Doughty shouted.

'Shout not or by Allah . .' one threatened.

His barometer was torn from his neck. He was jostled, pushed and

Right: *A romantic western view of the secrets of an Arab harem. The harem in which Doughty took refuge would have been much less exotic than this. Detail from 'Femmes au Harem' by Eugene Giraud. (Mathaf Gallery, London)*

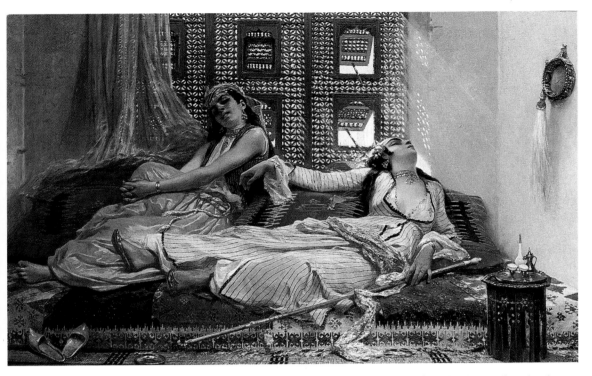

manhandled. Suddenly it stopped. An officer of the Emir stood at the door.

'What has happened?'

'They have stripped the Nasrani,' the porter said.

'Who has done this?' Doughty's assailants had retreated into the shadows. 'Bring the stranger his clothes,' the officer cried out, and turned to Doughty. 'All that they have robbed shall be restored, upon pain of cutting off the hand.'

'He refused to say *"La ilah ill'Allah"*,' they said.

'This is their falsehood,' cried Doughty, not above a white lie when it proved necessary. 'I said it four or five times. And hearken, I will say it again. *"La ilah ill'Allah"*.'

The Emir's officer, whose name was Jeyber, drove the crowd out of the room and left Doughty to sleep. He returned in the morning. 'Now shall we visit the Emir?' Jeyber took him to a street in front of the palace. 'A sordid fellow was sitting there like Job in the dust of the street.' Doughty asked Jeyber where the Emir was. 'He is the Emir.' Doughty, once over the shock, complained of his treatment. The Emir, who had heard reports of the Nasrani's behaviour in Hail, was unimpressed. He told the stranger he must depart the next morning for Unayzah.

Doughty spent the day in Buraydah, accompanied by Jeyber, 'a great civil township' compared with Hail, 'a half-Bedouin town-village with a foreign *suk* (market)'. As in Hail, he saw little. Everywhere he went there were hostile crowds. He returned to the guest house at midday to sleep, but was awakened by the creaking of his door. He tried to focus his eyes. It was a prostitute.

'Suffer me to sleep in thy bosom,' she said.

Doughty refused. 'Who could have sent thus lurid quean?' he wondered. 'The Arabs are the basest of enemies, – hoped they to find an occasion to accuse the Nasrani?'

The poor girl was in utter misery. 'Aha! The cursed Nasrani! And I was about to be slain, by faithful men; that were in the way, sent by the Emir, to

do it! and I might not now escape them.' Doughty threw her out. She went away. A crowd gathered outside the house. They banged on the door and broke it down. Doughty sought refuge in the harem.

'My sisters, you must defend me with your tongues.'

The women went out to face the angry mob. 'Ye seek Khalil the Nasrani? But here is not Khalil: ye fools, he is not here, away with you.' The crowd was unconvinced. 'Khalil is not here. He went forth. Go and seek the Nasrani, go.' Eventually Jeyber came and drove them off. He went into the yard. Doughty emerged from this hiding place and looked at him. Jeyber shrugged his shoulders. 'They are clamouring to the Emir for thy death. No Nasrani, they say, ever entered Buraydah.' Doughty returned indoors.

Early next morning Jeyber came to him and prepared coffee. Doughty, packing his baggage, heard the steps of the Emir. He came in accompanied by a Bedouin.

'This is he that will carry thee on his camel to Unayzah. Rise and bring out thy things.'

The Bedouin saddled his camel couched by his house and led Doughty out of Buraydah. They rode into the desert. Doughty asked him when they would arrive at Unayzah. 'By sunset,' the man replied. They arrived in the suburbs as night was falling, where the Bedouin calmly unloaded Doughty's baggage and rode off. 'This was the cruellest fortune that had befallen me in Arabia; to be abandoned here without a chief town, in the midst of the fanatical Nejd.' A man came out of his house and looked at Doughty, then bid his daughter fetch some water. The stranger drank greedily. Several elders came to inspect him. As they watched they heard the call to prayer.

'Come and pray, come,' they said.

'I have prayed already.'

'Thou dost not pray,' they said with troubled looks.

Doughty said nothing. They let it pass, loaded the unbeliever's baggage onto a mule, and took him to the house of Ali, the local policeman, on the edge of the city. He stayed there that night and was taken to the Emir Zamil in the morning. Zamil was a small man with a mild face and understanding eyes. He took Doughty's hand and made him sit by him. The stranger announced that he was a Nasrani and an Englishman and asked to be sent to the coast. He showed Zamil his papers. Zamil read them. There was an uneasy look on his face.

'It is well,' he said after a pause. 'In the meantime go not about publishing thyself to the people, "I am a Nasrani". Say to them "I am a runaway Ottoman soldier",' and added, 'Walk not in the public places.'

Later that morning Doughty met Ali, Zamil's uncle and deputy.

'This stranger is a *hakim*, a traveller from Damascus,' Zamil said, introducing Doughty.

Ali refused to acknowledge his existence.

'He is a passenger. He may stay a few days.'

Doughty returned with the policeman and was given a small shop where he could practise medicine. He sat in his shop booth and watched the passers-by. A lean and consumptive man approached him.

'Hast thou a knowledge of medicines?' he asked, taking his hand. 'Wilt thou visit my sick mother?' The man led Doughty to a large house not far away. His name was Abdallah el-Kenneyny. He was a kind man and one of the richest merchants in the town. He asked Doughty what on earth he was doing proclaiming himself to be a Nasrani so loudly.

'Should I not speak truth as well here as in my own country?'

'We have a tongue to further us and our friends and to elude our enemies.'

'Truth may walk through the world unarmed.'

El-Kenneyny introduced Doughty to his mother, then took him to the coffee room. Doughty looked around and saw a pile of books. He picked one up. It was an encyclopedia, and its owner's spectacles fell out from a page dealing with artesian wells: a common interest. They talked until evening. 'I passed this one good day in Arabia,' Doughty later wrote; 'and all the rest were evil because of the people's fanaticism.'

Next day the stranger was driven out of his lodgings by the angry populace. Ali the policeman found him another house owned by one of his patients, who charged an exorbitant rent. It was a busy time for a *hakim*: there was an outbreak of smallpox. In the evenings he escaped from both patients and the

Below: *It was under palm trees such as these, outside Unayzah, that Doughty stayed six weeks, pronounced* haram *(unclean), and forbidden entrance to the town.*

157

hostile townspeople to el-Kenneyny's house, where he met the other merchants of the town, including Abdallah el-Bessam, who – like el-Kenneyny – became a good friend. Their travels had given them a cosmopolitan outlook and they were the most sophisticated people Doughty met in Arabia. El-Kenneyny and el-Bessam became more than friends, they became benefactors, el-Bessam undertaking to arrange his journey to Jeddah and el-Kenneyny offering to advance him money.

The warmth of Unayzah's new bourgeoisie did not extend to the majority of the fifteen thousand inhabitants, and Doughty's benefactors were attacked in the mosques at the regular Friday sermon. 'It is an evil example, that certain principal persons favoured a misbelieving stranger; might they not in so doing provoke the Lord to anger? And all might see that the seasonable rain was withheld.' Doughty felt outcast and estranged from his friends. 'Cold is the outlaw's life, and marked with a natural constraint of heart, an alienation of the street faces, a daily standing-off of the faint-hearted, and of certain my seeming friends.' He noticed it more in el-Bessam than in el-Kenneyny. 'There was a strife in his single mind, betwixt his hospitable human fellowship, and the duty he owed unto God.'

Doughty's landlady's daughter got smallpox. He moved out of the house, sleeping in the streets, driven from corner to corner and dodging the stones that the children threw at him. 'The simple sort of liberal were bye and bye afraid to convene with me, and many of my former acquaintances seemed now to shun.' Only el-Kenneyny, and to a lesser extent el-Bessam, remained loyal. One day he returned to his house to find excreta on the doorstep.

A few weeks later, Doughty was awoken by Ali, the Emir's uncle, who told him he must leave that night. He was allowed to lodge in a palm grove outside the walls of the town, where el-Kenneyny visited him. He told the Nasrani he would bring food and clothing and advised him to do nothing but wait until a caravan had been found that was going to Jeddah. He then asked Doughty if there was anything else he wanted. Yes, money, Doughty replied. El-Kenneyny cashed him a cheque. 'The bill, for which he sent me on the morrow the just exchange in silver, came to my hands after a year in Europe: it had been paid in Beirut.'

Doughty stayed in the palm grove for six weeks. It was owned by one ibn Rasheyd, a local merchant who had just returned from Basra by caravan. 'The poor field labourers of Rasheyd's garden were my friends: ere the third day, they had forgiven me my alien religion, saying that they would they thought it might be as good as their own; and they would I might live always with them.'

What none of them could fathom were the motives for the Nasrani's journey. Only ibn Rasheyd, man of the world, had an explanation. 'I know the manners of them. This is a Frank, and very likely a poor man who has hired out his wife, to win money against his coming home; for, trust me, they do so all of them.'

The weeks went by. Doughty heard nothing more from el-Kenneyny, whose daughter had died of smallpox. Buraydah and Unayzah were in a state of semi-war with each other and the Holy Men attacked anyone seen aiding the Nasrani. Doughty despaired. He wrote a letter to el-Kenneyny; 'I am slain with weariness and hunger.' His message was delivered 'and at sunrise on the morrow came Abdallah's serving lad, who brought girdle-bread and butter, with a skin of buttermilk; and his master's word bidding me be of good comfort; and they (the friends) would ere long be able to provide for my departure.'

Finally, his friend found a caravan bound for Mecca carrying butter. There were kinsmen of both el-Kenneyny and el-Bessam on it. El-Kenneyny sent

Above: 'An Arab Sheykh in his Travelling Dress,' from the painting of Burton in Arab dress by Thomas Seddon, 1854.

Doughty a camel and an invitation to his own palm grove some two miles away. It was the night before Doughty's departure. Both el-Kenneyny and el-Bessam were there. Next morning el-Kenneyny walked a little way with Doughty, then turned to say farewell. Doughty looked at him. Consumption and his daughter's death had broken him. 'He stood sad and silent.' They said goodbye. Three years later el-Kenneyny was dead.

The caravan set off, and Doughty discovered that no one in the caravan was going to Jeddah. They were all going to Mecca, hardly the place for a self-proclaimed Nasrani. Frequently during the journey Doughty became the object of hostility, but he was always saved by either the el-Kenneyny or el-Bessam kinsmen. Hostility bubbled up over the question of water. To many on the caravan Doughty was unclean and they disliked sharing their water with him. Doughty, with the religious fanatic's inability to see the other fanatic's point of view, put this down to malice.

Right: *Charles Montagu Doughty, T. E. Lawrence's 'Master Arabian', painted by Eric Kennington. 'The sun made me an Arab, but never warped me to Orientalism.'*

As we rode forth I turned and saw my companions drinking covertly. Besides, they had drunk their fills in my absence, after protesting to me that there was not any; and I had thirsted all day. I thought, might I drink this once, I could suffer till the morning. I called the fellow to pour me out a little . . . but they denied me with horrible cursing.[12]

Three weeks later, the caravan entered Holy Ground, two days from Mecca. All except Doughty washed, shaved and donned the pilgrim's robe. The Nasrani could no longer remain with the caravan.

'Khalil,' el-Bessam's son said, 'I am in doubt if we may find anyone . . . to accompany thee to the coast.'

They stopped at a caravanserai. There el-Bessam's son came upon a cousin taking carpets to Taif. He introduced him to the Nasrani. As they spoke they heard a fanatical voice in the shadows shouting: 'He shall be a Moslem!' There were sounds of scuffling. El-Bessam's cousin, realizing the seriousness of the situation, urged Doughty to mount immediately. He hesitated. The rest of the caravan had ridden away. The man urged him again. Doughty mounted his camel but the exhausted beast would not move.

'Dismount, dismount,' cried the same fanatical voice. 'Let me alone I say, and I will kill the *kafir* (unbeliever).'

Doughty looked round. The man had a knife. Doughty whispered to el-Bessam's cousin to ride back to the butter caravan for help. He refused.

'Only say, Khalil, thou art a Moslem, it is but a word, to appease them, and tomorrow thou shalt be in Jeddah.'

Doughty refused. A crowd gathered. 'Those Mecca faces were black as the hues of the damned in the day of doom: the men stood silent, and holding in their swarthy hands their weapons.' An old Negro slave, Maabub, slave to the Sherif of Mecca and a man with some authority, intervened.

'Remember Jeddah bombarded! And that was for the blood of some of this stranger's people. Take heed what thou doest. They are the Engleys, who for one that is slain of them will send great battleships and beat down a city.'

The crowd waited for Maabub to withdraw, then started rifling Doughty's posssessions. Maabub came limping back and persuaded them to return Doughty's belongings to him. The crowd were getting increasingly out of control. Maabub turned to Doughty's original tormentor, Salem.

Left: *Haj pilgrims gathered in Mecca. 'Prayer at Sunset, Outside the Kaaba' by Etienne Dinet. (Mathaf Gallery, London)*

Right: *An Arab caravan in
the desert, following a well-
used route, past the remains of
less fortunate travellers.*

'If thou have any cause against this stranger, it must be laid before our lord
the Sherif,' he said. 'I commit him to thee.'

The fanatical Salem happily agreed. 'I hope it may please the Sherif to hang
this Nasrani, or cut off his head.'

'Thus Maabub who had appeased the storm, commited me to the wolf.'

Doughty rode in the custody of Salem with a small local caravan to Taif.

'Dreadest thou to die?' jeered Salem.

'I have not so lived, Moslem, that I must fear to die.'

After a while the two men's fanaticism cooled. Salem even began to call the
Nasrani 'Khalil'. Though malignant, and yet more greedy, there remained a
human kindness in him; for understanding that I was thirsty, he dismounted
and went to his camels to fetch me water.' But the rest of the caravan still saw
him with hositility, and Salem's moods took sudden turns.

One night as they rode with the caravan, Doughty, thinking he was about
to be attacked by a robber, drew the revolver he had managed to keep hidden
up to that moment. The 'robber' turned out to be one of the cameleers on the
caravan. Salem heard about it next morning and roughly woke him.

'The thing that thou hast in thy breast, what is it? Show it to me.'

'I have shown you all in my saddlebags; it is infamous to search a man's
person.'

The cameleer at whom Doughty had aimed his revolver joined in. 'He has
a pistol, and he would have shot me last night.'

'Show it, without more, all that thou hast with thee in thy bosom,' Salem
shouted, taking out his knife.

Doughty resorted to moral blackmail. 'Remember the bread and salt which
we have eaten together, Salem.'

'Show it all to me, or now, by Allah, I will slay thee with this knife.'

Doughty took out the revolver. 'What should I do now? The world was
before me; I thought, shall I fire?' The head of the caravan they were
travelling with, Fheyd, aggressively grabbed the revolver, and fired off five of
its bullets into the air.

'Leave one of them,' Salem shouted. Fheyd left the last one in the chamber.

Suddenly Doughty was knocked from behind. He went out cold. Fheyd
had hit him on the back of the head with his driving-stick.

'Why have you done this?' he asked when he came to.

'Because thou didst withhold the pistol.'

'Is the pistol mine or thine? I might have shot thee dead, but I remembered the mercy of Allah.'

Maabub, who was also going to Taif and heard the shots, intervened again. 'Are you men who have so dealt with this stranger?' he harangued. He turned to Salem. 'Thou art to bring this stranger to our lord Hasseyn at Taif, and do him no wrong by the way.'

'Is not this a Nasrani?' replied Salem. 'He might kill us all by the way; we did but take his pistol because we were afraid.'

'Have you taken his silver from him . . . because ye were afraid?' retorted Maabub.

The caravan continued towards Taif, Doughty a prisoner of Salem. They rode through the night and arrived at Taif, where to Salem's anger and embarrassment, Doughty was welcomed with hospitality and respect by the Turkish commander.

> Colonel Mohammed awaited me on the landing; and brought me into his chamber. The tunic was rent on my back, my mantle was old and torn; the hair was grown down under my kerchief to the shoulders, and the beard fallen and unkempt. I had bloodshot eyes, half-blinded, and the scorched skin was cracked to the quick upon my face.[13]

Above: *Richard Burton's tomb in Mortlake Roman Catholic Cemetery. Rejected by both Westminster Abbey and St Paul's Cathedral, and rejecting in turn cremation, he told his wife: 'I don't want to burn before my time – but I would like to lie in an Arab tent.'*

It was August 1878. He had been in Arabia two years. After four days in Taif Doughty rode to Jeddah and took ship to Aden, India and eventually England.

The same time that Charles Montagu Doughty was on his first visit to Hail another traveller arrived in Arabia. He had been there before.

He was twenty-four years older but otherwise had not changed, except to become more cantankerous. It was none other than Richard Burton. He was leading an expedition for the Khedive of Egypt in search of gold, accompanied by a French mining engineer and an escort of Egyptian soldiers. They arrived from the Red Sea in the extreme north and made their way to the desert around Ma'an. The expedition originated from a memory Burton had of an old Egyptian who had made the Haj and who, on his way back, had found a rock of gold. In their three-week search Burton found new plants, old inscriptions, some fascinating geological specimens that turned out to be three-thousand-year-old camel droppings, but no gold.

He returned a few months later with a larger party of four Europeans, six Egyptian officers, thirty-two soldiers, thirty quarrymen and a Greek cook. In four months they covered two thousand five hundred miles, bringing back twenty-five tons of samples, but still no gold. Burton returned to England, his exploring life over.

A year later Doughty arrived back in England. Immediately he set foot in his native country his stammer returned. He had difficulty eating and communicating, and escaped by taking a house in Naples where he wrote his massive and uncompromising *Travels in Arabia Deserta*. It was rejected by four publishers, one of which suggested that it should be 'practically rewritten by a literary man.'

It finally appeared in 1888, ten years later. One of its first reviewers was Richard Burton, who found Doughty's martyr complex infuriating and his passiveness revolting. Yet he could despise neither the man nor the book. The very extremities that Doughty had gone to left Burton reeling. As for the book, it was 'a twice-told tale writ large . . . which, despite its affectations and eccentricities, its prejudices and misjudgements, is right well told.'

Right: *Richard Burton, as arrogant and aggressive as on his first visit to Arabia twenty-four years earlier.*
'I wore thine image, Fame, Within a heart well fit to be thy shrine.'

VII

THE LAST ROMANTICS

A year after Doughty's departure from Jeddah two very different travellers arrived in Hail. They came as neither 'Orientalists' nor secret agents, nor even 'loners'. They came as 'persons of distinction from England', paying a social call on their opposite numbers in the Nejd. To Wilfrid and Lady Anne Blunt there was nothing abnormal in this. To them the inhabitant of Arabia was a Bedouin, and the Bedouin was the 'gentleman of the desert'. So it was perfectly natural for one gentleman and his wife to visit another. That the majority of the population of Arabia were townspeople was immaterial. Townspeople – except the rich ones who were expected to be of good Bedouin blood – were quite plainly *not* gentlemen.

The Blunts came from as fine a pedigree as the greyhounds they brought with them. She was the granddaughter of Lord Byron. Her mother died when Anne was fifteen and she went to live with her grandmother, the dowager Lady Byron. Her music master was Joachim, her drawing master Ruskin, and she had an annual income of three thousand pounds a year. He had a no less perfect pedigree. In his own words, he was 'born under circumstances peculiarly fortunate as I think for happiness. Those of an English country gentleman of the XIXth Century; my father a Sussex squire of fair estate, owning some four thousand acres'.

Yet neither had a happy childhood. Anne was terrified of her grandmother and, after seeing first her mother and then her brother die, she took to a life of solitude, wandering from one place in Europe to another. Wilfrid's childhood was even lonelier. His father died, school was 'hell on earth' and his mother became a Catholic convert. When he heard the news the young Wilfrid, 'filled with unspeakable shame, burst into tears'. For five years Wilfrid's soul was fought over by a Calvinist nanny and a Catholic mother. In the end the nanny was sacked and Wilfrid became a Catholic. His catholicism held steady for twelve years until his brother died and his sister announced that she wanted to become a nun. First he began 'looking on God as my enemy', then he 'began to disbelieve in His existence altogether'. Yet until the end of his life he maintained 'a belief in holy places and holy people quite apart from any religious creed'.

Left: *Wilfrid and Lady Anne Blunt, with hawk, horse and greyhound, who visited ibn Rashid in Hail. 'Our quality of English people was a sufficient passport for us in his eyes.'*

Left: *One of the Bedouin encampments in the Syrian Desert that the Blunts passed through on their way to Hail.*

They met in Rome. She was recovering from the news of her father's remarriage and he was recovering from one of his many tortured love affairs. 'She thought herself plainer than she was, and had none of the ways of a pretty woman, though in truth she had that sort of prettiness that a bird has . . . . Her colouring, indeed, I used to think was like a robin's with its bright black eyes, its russet plumage and its tinge of crimson red.' Years later, after they had separated, he was to recognize her deeper qualities. 'There was never anyone as courageous as she was. The only thing she was afraid of was the sea.'

This was their second visit to the desert; their first had been to Mesopotamia where they had visited the Bedouin tribes of the Euphrates. They had already been to the tourist spots of the Arab world: Algeria, Egypt, Syria and Turkey. It was not until their first contact with the Bedouin of Arabia that Lady Anne felt that she had met her equals.

> We . . . saw below us a scattered camp of about twenty-five tents, a great number of camels and a few mares, perhaps half a dozen. I got on my mare so as to arrive with becoming dignity . . . we both, I think, felt rather shy at this our first visit, arriving as strangers and unannounced. No one came to meet us or seemed to pay the least attention to our party, and we rode on without looking to the right or to the left towards the largest tent we could see . . . . Nobody moved until we had come inside the tent, and Wilfrid had said in a loud voice 'Salaam Aleykoum', to which everybody – for there were perhaps a dozen people sitting there – answered also in a loud voice, 'Aleykoum salaam' . . . . Hatmoud's tent was a very poor one . . . . The men, however, were better behaved than most of those in whose tents we had been, and have asked no impertinent questions.[1]

Their travelling companion was called Mohammed ibn Aruk, son of a Tadmur sheikh, again of the highest pedigree. In 1760, when Wahhabism had first emerged in central Arabia, his ancestors, three brothers, had fled the Nejd. One of the Aruks had gone to Tadmur, another to Jawf, the third 'tradition knew not whither'. When Mohammed announced that he intended to go to central Arabia, to find his long lost cousins and arrange a marriage with one of them, the Blunts eagerly offered to accompany him.

Right: *The caravanserai, encapsulating all the splendid havoc and confusion of a railway station. 'The Arrival of the Caravan, Khan Asad Pasha, Damascus', by Charles Robertson. (Mathaf Gallery, London)*

To us too, imbued as we were with the fancies of the Desert, Nejd had long assumed a romantic colouring of a holy land; and when it was decided that we were to visit Jebal Shammar, the metropolis of Bedouin life, our expedition presented itself as an almost pious undertaking; so it is hardly an exaggeration, even now that it is over, and we are once more in Europe, to speak of it as a pilgrimage. Our pilgrimage then it is, though the religion in whose name we travelled was only one of romance.[2]

When they left him to return to England with promises to meet again the following year, the Blunts offered Mohammed a choice between becoming a blood brother of Wilfrid or a large tip. Mohammed – not one to let an opportunity be missed – opted for blood brotherhood. The Blunts hardly expected less.

The three rendezvoused in Damascus on 6 December 1878, and were joined by Hanna, another of the previous year's travelling companions, 'the most courageous of cowards and cooks.' Both Mohammed and Hanna had brought their own retainers, 'to share the advantages of being in our service and to stand by their patron in case of need,' mused Anne. 'Servants like to travel in pairs.' This proved to be quite fortunate to Lady Anne. 'It is a great advantage in travelling that the servants should be as much as possible strangers to each other, and of different race or creed, as this prevents any combination among them for mutiny or disobedience.'

It was a busy week. There were camels to be bought ('In choosing camels,' said Lady Anne, 'the principle points to look at are breadth of chest, depth of barrel, shortness of leg, and for condition roundness of flank.'), and calls to be made on 'persons of distinction', one of whom was Mrs Digby. Mrs Digby had married a Bedouin – 'In appearance he shows all the characteristics of good Bedouin blood' – and had replaced Lady Hester Stanhope as Britain's most interesting monument in the Levant. She lived in a house just outside Damascus surrounded by trees and gardens. The gardens were beautiful, with a narrow stream running through, and the paths bordered by English flowers. There was a pelican by the fountain and turtle doves in the trees. The main house was hardly furnished, almost empty in its bare and abstract Arab style, but in the garden was an annex, packed with arm-chairs, sofas, pictures, books and other portable Victoriana.

They also went to see old exiled Abd el-Kader, still running the guardhouses on the Hejaz road, but passing more and more of his time as a man of letters, with all the dignity of an elder statesman; something of a monument himself. Anne described him as 'a charming old man, whose character would do honour to any nation or any creed.' During the Levant's periodic Christian, Moslem and Jewish massacres he had opened his doors to everyone, irrespective of their religion. He proudly gave the two travellers a copy of a book his son had written on the Arab horse and talked to them about his youth when he had travelled across north Africa on foot to make the pilgrimage to Mecca, tactfully avoiding the subject of colonialism. 'His smile was that of an old man, but his eyes were still bright and piercing like a falcon's. It is easy to see, however, that they will never flash again with anything like anger. Abd el-Kader has long possessed that highest philosophy of noble minds according to Arab doctrine, patience.'

They left Damascus unobtrusively, claiming that they were travelling to Baghdad, to avoid attracting too much attention. Wilfrid was dressed as a Bedouin while Anne wore a Bedouin cloak over her ordinary travelling ulster; 'not exactly as a disguise, for we did not wish, even if we could have done so, not to pass as Europeans, but in order to avoid attracting more notice than was necessary.' It was Friday, 13 December.

> Our caravan, waiting at the gate, presented a very picturesque appearance. Each of the *deluls* carries a gay pair of saddlebags in carpet-work, with long worsted tassels hanging down on each side half way to the ground, and there are ornamented *reshmehs* or headstalls to match. The camels, too, though less decorated, have a gay look; and Wilfrid on the chestnut mare ridden in a halter wants nothing but a long lance to make him a complete Bedouin.[3]

Left: *Mezarib, four days south of Damascus, is the first stop of the Haj caravan. Set on a lake, it is where Varthema, Guarmani, Doughty and the Blunts all camped on their travels in Arabia.*

Above: *Bosra. 'The entrance of the town is rather striking, as the old Roman road, which has run in a straight line for miles, terminates in a gateway of the regular classic style, beyond which lies a mass of ruins and pillars.'*

They took a last look back to the minarets of Damascus protruding over palm trees, turned their backs on the city and were off. The first part of the journey was along the Haj road, on a black and shiny volcanic surface. The villages they passed through were black and shiny too, dreary little places even in the sunlight. There were neither crops nor trees: it was a drought year. The Arabs called it *Abu Hadlan*, father of leanness. To the east they could see the blue line of the Hauren mountains. After four days amid a landscape 'as uninteresting as the plains of Germany or northern France', they arrived at Mezarib, where Doughty had joined his Haj caravan. It was nightfall. The next morning they awoke and looked out of the tent.

> The view from our tents was extremely pretty, a fine range of distant hills, the Adjlun to the south-west, and about a mile off a little lake looking very blue and bright, with a rather handsome ruined khan or castle in the foreground. To the left the tents of the Suk, mostly white and of a Turkish pattern. There are about a hundred and fifty of them in four rows, making a kind of street. The village of Mezarib stands on an island in the lake, connected by a stone causeway with the shore, but the Suk is on the mainland. There is a great concourse of people with horses, and donkeys, and camels, and more are constantly coming from each quarter of the compass. They have not as yet paid much attention to us, so that we have been able to make ourselves comfortable.[4]

Left: *An engraving of the sandstorm, based on a sketch by Lady Anne. 'The beasts looked gigantic yet helpless, like antediluvian creatures overwhelmed in a flood.'*

They stayed two days, spending most of their time paying social calls, and left on 18 December, abandoning the Haj road and going due east, across the Hauran mountains to Jawf. Their route took them past the ancient ruins of Bosra where their sleep was disturbed by the baying of dogs. Anne had never heard anything so melancholy and unearthly.

A string of sheikhs entertained them on the way. True gentlemen, they never asked any personal questions until after everyone had eaten heartily. But invariably the host would eventually enquire who on earth these extraordinary people were. 'Mohammed's answer that we were English persons of distinction, on our way to Jawf, and that he was Mohammed, the son of Abdallah of Tadmur, made quite a *coup de théâtre*, and it is easy to see that we have at last come to the right place.'

On their second day out from Mezarib Mohammed entertained them to a story. There was an old man about to die. He was very poor. He called over to him his son and said: 'I have nothing to leave behind me for your good but advice, and my advice is this: build for yourself houses all over the world.' The boy, who had no money, did not know how to put the advice into practice, so he set out on a journey to find a wise man who would enlighten him. His search took him to every part of the world, and everywhere he passed through he made friends. Finally he found the wise man to whom he told his story. The wise man looked at him and said he had already accomplished what his father had said. 'For you have friends everywhere, and is not your friend's house your house?'

They were in high spirits. Their route took them under immense clouds of sand-grouse; Wilfrid bagged eight with one shot. That night they slept in a high volcanic crater, sheltered from the wind and concealed from raiders. In the morning they climbed up to its edge and looked out on the desert before them: 'It was a wonderful sight with its broken tells and strange chaotic wadis, all black with volcanic boulders, looking blacker still against the yellow morning sky.'

Christmas Eve took them across that same bleak windswept surface. The only living thing they encountered was a solitary hare, which the Blunts' greyhounds chased unsuccessfully for a couple of hundred yards. 'We were all too cold for much talking, and sat huddled up on our *deluls* with our backs to the wind, and our heads wrapped in our cloaks.' Evening was an improvement. 'Hanna has made us a capital curry, which with soup and burghul and a plum-pudding from a tin, makes not a bad dinner.'

When Lady Anne awoke on Christmas Day the 'black wilderness had become like a nightmare with its horrible boulders and little tortuous paths'. After a couple of miles the nightmare faded away, the neurotic landscape giving way to open plains feeding herds of gazelle. Wilfrid was so anxious to get one for their Christmas dinner that he was away from the caravan for three quarters of an hour. The gazelles eluded him and when he came back empty-handed Mohammed was furious; not for coming back meatless but for leaving the caravan without telling anyone. 'He was perfectly right and we were to blame,' Lady Anne felt, 'for we are on a serious journey, not a sporting tour.' Then, suddenly, their Christmas dinner trotted towards them, a young camel lost from a herd. Stray camels are prized in the desert and it was not long before it had been killed, cut and its best bits grilled on a fire. It was a splendid feast. 'People talk sometimes of camel meat, as if it were something not only unpalatable, but offensive. But it is in reality very good; when young it resembles mutton, even when old it is only tough, and never has any unpleasant taste as far as my experience goes; indeed if served up without bones it could hardly be distinguished from mutton.'

That night there was a sandstorm and the Blunts' tent was blown down on top of them. The sandstorm continued through to the next day and the servants (for all intents and purposes Mohammed ibn Aruk was regarded by the Blunts as a servant) proposed that they should all stay where they were. The Blunts would have none of it.

> The sun shone feebly at intervals through the driving sand, but it was all we could do to keep the caravan together, and not lose sight of each other. At one moment we all had to stop and turn tail to the wind, covering our eyes and heads with our cloaks, waiting till the burst was over. Nothing could have faced it. Still we were far from having any idea of danger, for there really is none in these storms, and had plenty of time to notice how very picturesque the situation was, the camels driven along at speed, all huddled together for protection, with their long necks stretched out, and heads low, tags and ropes flying, and men's cloaks streaming in the wind, all seen through the yellow haze of sand which made them look as though walking in the air. The beasts looked gigantic yet helpless, like antediluvian creatures overwhelmed in a flood.[5]

Right: Sheikh Abdallah el-Kamis' fortified house in Kaf, ibn Rashid's northernmost outpost, where the Blunts arrived on Boxing Day.

Next day the sands were still. There had been rain in the night and they rode off over a firm surface at eight o'clock. They crossed a wide plain packed with damp, coarse sand until noon, by which time the sands had dried, and they came upon the tracks of the salt caravans from Bosra to Kaf. They followed the salt road through a deep wadi, its sides exposing alternate layers of yellow sandstone and black rocks. As they rode through their greyhounds surprised a jerboa, which, with its prodigious hops, almost escaped – until it hopped into the mouth of one of the greyhounds.

The jerboa was not the only casualty that day. Lady Anne sprained her knee after a fall from her horse. 'The pain is indescribable, and I fear I will be lame for some time to come.' But they saw no reason to curtail the journey. That night she limped into Kaf, which Carlo Guarmani had passed through fifteen years earlier.

Abdallah el-Kamis, the local sheikh, gave them a room in his house. It looked out onto a small courtyard where the sheikh kept his two-year-old colt. The walls were of mud and there were neither windows nor chimney. The principal room of the house was the *kahwah*, the coffee room. It was there that the Blunts learnt that Kaf had only recently been taken over by ibn Rashid ('They are very enthusiastic about the "Emir" '), and Mohammed discovered the first of his long lost cousins, 'an untidy half-witted young man', who told Mohammed he could find more of his relations in Jawf.

On 29 December, in a bitter east wind, they set out for Jawf, marching across rocky promontories and sandy inlets. The ground was rough and broken, and the sand sprinkled with grit. The wind blew all day and the pain in Lady Anne's leg distracted her from thinking. The next day they found themselves on a lifeless volcanic terrain which continued through to the following day. They passed the end of the year in 'one of the most desolate places in the world'. It was so cold that even the locusts died in the night. New Year revealed gazelle and hyena tracks leading to a tiny spring. Its name was *Maasreh* (little by little). Lady Anne took a realistic attitude to the insects swarming in the pool. 'There is nothing more suspicious in the desert than perfectly clear water free from animal life.'

Night was cold since they could not light a fire for fear of Bedouin raiders. They sat huddled together while their Sherari guide briefed them on the recent politics of the Nejd, and how Mohammed ibn Rashid had killed Bandar, the legitimate Emir, and cut off the hands and feet of his cousins, leaving them to die in the palace courtyard. 'This is very tiresome,' thought Lady Anne, 'as it may be a reason for our not going on to Nejd after all.

By now the caravan had taken on a routine. They rose at dawn, ate a biscuit and drank coffee, then struck camp and set off immediately, rarely stopping, but chewing a few dates and rusks on the way, until about four o'clock when they stopped, unloaded and set up camp again. Coffee came at five and dinner – with meat when Wilfrid could shoot it – at sunset.

Right: The ghazu, *with Lady Anne on the ground and Wilfrid being hit on the head with the butt of Lady Anne's rifle.*

Left: A halt on the journey. Two of Wilfrid's greyhounds lie exhausted in the sand.

Below: *The castle at Jawf. In the middle distance in front of the castle are the Blunts' very European-looking tent (where they were able to write and sketch in privacy) and Mohammed's and the servant's Bedouin tents.*

All went well until 3 January when Anne and Wilfrid, separated from the rest of the caravan and dismounted, were attacked by a Ruaulla raiding party. Wilfrid jumped to his feet. 'Get on your mare,' he shouted to Anne, 'This is a *ghazu*.' Lady Anne struggled to mount with her strained knee but was knocked down by a spear. Wilfrid, unable to get at his own gun, was hit over the head with the stock of Lady Anne's rifle. Lady Anne, with great presence of mind, shouted '*Anna dakilah!*' ('I am under your protection.') Only then did the raiders realize that she was a woman.

'Who are you?' they asked in surprise.

'English.'

The Ruaulla were so nonplussed that they gave all the Blunts' belongings back to them. 'Arabs are always good-humoured, whatever else their faults, and presently we were all on very good terms, sitting in a circle in the sand, eating dates and passing round the pipe of peace. They are our guests now. . . . We liked the look of these young Ruaulla. In spite of their rough behaviour we could see that they were gentlemen.'

Two days later, after passing over a gravel plain and a range of red, yellow and purple stoned hills, the Blunts' party, reduced to their last pint of water, reached Jawf, 'a large oasis of palms, surrounded by a wall with towers at intervals, and a little town clustering round the black castle.'

Set on a plain of white sand surrounded by a few outlying oases, it was far smaller than the Bedouin had led them to expect, but the Bedouin were accustomed to judging places by the size of encampments, and anything larger would appear vast. The Blunts rode through dark and narrow lanes crowded with armed men who 'answered our "Salaam Aleykoum" simply without moving, and let us pass on without any particular demonstration of hospitality'. There was very little response until Mohammed inquired about his cousins, whereupon everyone warmed to him and pointed the way. The relatives lived about a quarter of a mile away, a little outside the town, in one of the outlying oases that they had seen on their way in.

Left:*The sword dance of the soldiers in Jawf, 'one performer beating on a drum made of palm wood and horse hide, while the rest held their swords over their shoulders . and chanted in solemn measure, dancing as solemnly.'*

Hussain, the senior of the cousins, welcomed them with coffee and produced a litter of other cousins to meet them.

> Mohammed was kissed and hugged, and it was all he could do to pacify these injured relatives by promising to stay a week with each, as soon as our visit to Hussain should be over. Blood here is thicker than water. The sudden appearance of a twentieth cousin is enough to set everybody by the ears.[6]

The Blunts settled down in their tent in the little palm garden behind the house while Hussain killed a sheep in celebration. Just after they had eaten it two soldiers appeared at the door. 'They were very gaily dressed in silk *jibbehs,* and embroidered shirts under their drab woollen *abbas.* They wore red cotton *kefiyehs* on their heads, bound with white rope, and their swords were silver-hilted.' They came from the castle with a message from Dowass, the acting governor, inviting the Blunts to stay at the castle. Lady Anne and Wilfrid were sad to leave the hospitality of Hussain, but it was an invitation they could hardly refuse. The castle had been built about eleven years earlier, after Palgrave's and Guarmani's time, but its architecture – towers, loopholes and courtyards – was positively medieval. With the governor 'on tour', the deputy governor and his six soldiers acted as hosts. The oasis town, they told their guests, had originally belonged to the Ruaulla, but it had been taken over by ibn Rashid about twenty years earlier, just before Palgrave's and Guarmani's visit. There had been a couple of pro-Ruaulla revolts in the early days but they had been subdued by Mtab ibn Rashid, the brother of Talal, and he had felled the palm trees, the town's livelihood, as punishment.

Four years earlier the Ottomans in Syria had sent a military expedition to take over the town, but ibn Rashid threatened to discontinue the tribute he paid to the pro-Turkish Sherif of Mecca if the troops were not withdrawn. The troops were withdrawn.

> The greatness of ibn Saud and the Wahhabis is now a thing of the past, and Mohammed ibn Rashid is now the most powerful ruler in Arabia. . . . You may travel anywhere, they say, from Jawf to Kasim without escort. The roads are safe everywhere. A robbery has not been known on the Emir's highway for many years, and people found loafing about near the roads have their heads cut off.[7]

The deputy governor and his soldiers were cheerful and civil, assuring the Blunts that ibn Rashid would be delighted to receive them. In the evenings they ate a first hors-d'oeuvre resembling wall-paper paste, a second hors-d'oeuvre of chopped onions mixed with rancid butter, and a third hors-d'oeuvre of bread soaked in water. This was followed by boiled lamb and fillet of antelope. Lady Anne considered these hors-d'oeuvres to be disgusting, the lamb bearable and the antelope 'one of the best meats I have ever tasted'. After dinner came sword-dances. Only after that could the Blunts retire to their tent, 'at liberty to write or make sketches by the moonlight, things we dare not do in the daytime.'

From Jawf they went on to Meskakeh, about twenty miles away, where more of Mohammed's cousins were to be found. It was a slightly larger town, with about seven hundred houses. Mohammed's cousin Nassr received Wilfrid, who was Mohammed's blood brother, as his own blood cousin.

They stayed three days with Nassr. To Anne he resembled an old Scottish laird, 'poor and penurious, but aware of having better blood in his veins than his neighbours'. Mohammed's main interest lay in his first cousins, two daughters of Jazi ibn Aruk who lived next door. The elder, Asr, was good-looking and short-tempered; the younger, Muttra, good-looking and placid. Mohammed, inevitably, wanted Muttra, but Jazi was anxious to get rid of Asr. A family counsel was convened in Wilfrid's tent with Wilfrid presiding to find a way out of the deadlock. Mohammed ibn Aruk sat on one side of him and Jazi ibn Aruk on the other. Every ibn Aruk for miles around was packed into the tent. Wilfrid hammered out an agreement whereby Mohammed would have Muttra in a year's time; then Asr almost upset the entire counsel by getting into a violent temper at her younger sister getting married before her, and tormented old Jazi into withdrawing his consent. Lady Anne would have none of this. She spoke to the mother.

Right: 'A Halt in the Desert' by John Frederick Lewis (1805-1876), with either the Dead Sea or Lake Tiberias in the background.

I said it was no use arguing about that all over again; that if she and her husband were not really able to manage their daughters, we must look elsewhere for Mohammed; that I hoped and trusted Asr would not be so foolish as to stand in the way of her sister's happiness, for it would not profit her. This bad temper of hers made it more than ever certain that she could not marry Mohammed, and, in fine, that the family must make up their minds, yes or no, about Muttra, and at once, for we were leaving Meskakeh presently, and must have the matter settled. I then saw the two girls, and spoke to them in the same strain, and with such effect that a few hours later, Mohammed, who had fallen into low spirits about the affair, now came with a joyful countenance to say that the marriage contract would be signed that evening.[8]

While Lady Anne was arranging Mohammed's marriage, she still found time to make travel arrangements. She had found the governor of Jawf, Johar, who was a Negro, and was trying to extract from him a letter of introduction to ibn Rashid. Johar was fat and vain, and had put on his finest clothes (silk robes and a shirt so stiff with starch that it cracked every time he moved) 'as barbaric a despot as one need wish to see'. He kept them waiting for ten minutes and then affected the languid air of a royal personage. The man was quite plainly *not* a gentleman and an obligatory 'present' brought the necessary letter of introduction and the names of two reliable guides. 'Carpets were then spread, and we all sat down on the roof and had breakfast, boiled meat over the rice, and then after the usual washings and *el hamdu lillahs* we retired, extremely pleased to get away from the flies and the hot sun of Johar's roof; and not a little thankful for the good turn things had taken with us.' They were also extremely relieved; as Wilfrid remarked on the way back, he was just the sort of capricous despot who would as soon have ordered their heads off as order breakfast.

Next day it rained until noon. The sky was shattered by thunder and lightning. They made their final preparations for departure and the following morning the ibn Aruk cousins came out to say goodbye to them.

In spite of their noble birth and their Nejdean traditions, they have the failing of town Arabs in regard to money, and it was a shock to our feelings that Nassr, our host, expected a small present of money. . . . Such small disappointments, however, must be borne, and borne cheerfully, for people are not perfect anywhere, and a traveller has no right to expect more abroad than he would find at home.[9]

Below: *Johar, the Governor of Jawf, with his narghile.*

Their course lay due south over pure white sand dunes which gave way to a steep and broken surface that levelled off into a plain of gravel. Beyond the gravel were the red sands of the Nafud Desert. Its colour was what surprised them most: rhubarb and magnesia. In a few minutes their mares had cantered onto it and were standing with their hooves in the first waves of the desert. In the soft dawn of the following morning the sands looked almost crimson.

They continued through the dunes, sometimes riding round them, sometimes dismounting and leading their camels and mares over them, keeping to the hard windward side as much as they could, until they came upon a single Bedouin tent. But by the time the two English visitors had ridden up to it, the tent had been dismantled and loaded on the camels for a quick departure. Soon afterwards they reached an encampment of Ruaulla

Right:*Meskakeh, about twenty miles east of Jawf, with its ancient citadel perched a hundred feet up on a cliff.*

slaves by a well, over two hundred feet deep. Just as they were tying all their pieces of rope together, in the hope of reaching the water at the bottom of the well, a passing Bedouin, who recognized the Blunts from their earlier visit to the Euphrates, offered them his own rope and happily drew all their water. They stayed there all day.

> A camel foal was born today by the well. I went to look at the little creature which was left behind with its mother, when the rest were driven home. I noticed that it had none of those bare places (callosities) which the older camels get on their knees and chest from kneeling down, and that its knees were bruised by its struggles to rise. We helped it up, and in three hours' time it was able to trot away with its mother.[10]

Radi, their Negro guide (the name means 'Willing') provided by the governor of Jawf, proved quite an acquisition; old, dry and withered, he sat on his horse ('an ancient bag of bones that looks as if it will never last through the journey') mostly silent, occasionally pointing out to the party bones of less fortunate travellers who had tried to cross the Nafud before them.

> I find that Radi makes out his course almost entirely by landmarks. On every high sand-hill he gets down from his *delul*, and pulls some ghada branches, which are very brittle, and adds them to piles of wood he has formerly made. These can be seen a good way off. We have learned, too, to make out a sort of road after all, of an intermittent kind, marked by the dung of camels, and occasionally on the side of a steep slope there is a distinct footway. Along this line our guide feels his way, here and there making a cast, as hounds do when they are off the scent.[11]

On the fourth day they encountered the two conical peaks of Aalem, that had guided Wallin, Palgrave and Guarmani to Hail. Lady Anne and Wilfrid left the caravan and galloped towards the peaks. After so long among sand dunes they felt as if they had been lost at sea and found a desert island. Lady Anne filled a bottle with sand to make an hour-glass when she got home.

Left: The Blunts' journey from Damascus, via Mezarib, Bosra, Kaf, Jawf, Meskakeh and Hail, to Meshed Ali.

By the next day the labour of trudging through the red sands was beginning to tell. Water was short and two of the camels were weakening. 'Fresh grass there is none, and last year's crop stands white and withered still without signs of life. . . . Today all our Mahometans [*sic*] have begun to say their prayers for the first time since the journey began.' Two days later at sunset the exhausted caravan arrived at the oasis of Jubbah, two-thirds of the way across. As they rode on Radi regaled them with more tales of Mohammed ibn Rashid's early atrocities.

> We felt as if we were going towards a wild beast's den. In the meantime, however, there were four days before us, four days of respite, and of that tranquillity which the desert only gives, and we agreed to enjoy it to the utmost. There is something in the air of Nejd, which would exhilarate even a condemned man, and we were far from being condemned. It is impossible to feel really distressed or really anxious, with such a bright sun and such pure delicious air. We might feel that there was danger, but we could not feel nervous.[12]

The last four days were easy, and on their second night, almost at their journey's end, they killed a sheep. The following noon they saw ahead of them the outlines of Jebal Shammar, a line of spires, domes and pinnacles with loopholes between the peaks through which you could see the sky. The next day they rode to the top of a low ridge and saw Hail in front of them.

The town was not particularly imposing, most of the houses being hidden in palm groves, and the wall surrounding it little more than ten feet high. The only building visible was a large castle close to the entrance, and this Radi told us was the ksar, ibn Rashid's palace. In spite of my preoccupations, I shall never forget the vivid impression made on me, as we entered the town, by the extraordinary spick and span neatness of the walls and streets, giving almost an air of unreality.[13]

Their reception – totally different from Doughty's – was everything they could have desired. Twenty magnificently dressed men ('The sons of sheikhs', said Mohammed) and a tall elderly man, splendid in his scarlet with snow-white beard and a long wand ('The Emir', said Mohammed), came out to greet them. The old man motioned to them to enter the castle. He turned out to be the court chamberlain and the twenty 'sheikhs' were only servants. They were led into the same imposing reception room in which Palgrave had been entertained. Speeches were made, coffee was served and finally Mohammed ibn Rashid entered. To Anne he was like Richard III: dark, lean, sallow, thin-lipped with piercing restless eyes, 'a conscious-stricked face . . . that fears an assassin'. He was robed in purple and carried on his belt a gold-hilted sword ornamented with turquoises and rubies.

After a quarter of an hour of formalities they were served dates and bread with rancid butter, then taken outside to watch ibn Rashid preside over the court of justice, the same one at which Doughty had appeared as a suppliant two years earlier.

In front of the Emir stood half a dozen suppliants. No case lasted more than three minutes and the whole thing was over in half an hour. The Emir rose, bowed and returned to the palace, the two 'persons of distinction from England' wearily stretched their legs after being cramped in a squatting position for so long and were shown the guest house.

It was divided into two sections, one for the men and one for the women, with a courtyard between. 'All was exceedingly simple, but in decent repair and clean, the only ornaments being certain patterns, scratched out in white from the brown wash which covered the walls.' Here they made themselves comfortable, glad to rest. Hardly had they lain down when there was a knock at the door. The Emir had invited them to another audience, this time in private. For the Blunts and Mohammed ibn Aruk it seemed an opportune moment to present their gifts.

Below: *The camel foal born by the well in the Nafud Desert, from a sketch by Lady Anne.*

We had brought presents with us, the duty of displaying which we left to Mohammed, who expatiated on their value and nature with all the art of a bazaar merchant. As for us, we were a little ashamed of their insignificance, for we had no conception of ibn Rashid's true position when we left Damascus, and the scarlet cloth *jibbeh* we had considered the *ne plus ultra* of splendour for him, looked shabby among the gorgeous dresses worn in Hail. We had added to the cloak and other clothes, which are the usual gifts of ceremony, a revolver in a handsome embroidered case, a good telescope, and a Winchester rifle; . . . but ibn Rashid, though far too well-bred not to admire and approve, cared evidently little for these things, having seen them all before. Even the rifle was no novelty, for he had an exactly similar one in his armoury.[14]

They were saved from further embarrassment by the call to prayer. Mohammed ibn Rashid politely excused himself, begging his guests to remain seated. When he returned from his prayers he offered to show them his gardens. In the first was a menagerie with tame gazelles, ibexes and oryxes (Varthema's unicorns); in the second lemon trees, orange trees and pomegranates; and in the third ibn Rashid's prize mares. This display of wealth ended in the royal kitchens, where the Emir showed off seven monstrous cauldrons, each capable of boiling three whole camels. His table, he boasted, fed two hundred people, on forty sheep and seven cames a day.

The following morning Lady Anne visited ibn Rashid's harem to pay her respects to his favourite wife, Amusheh. The harem was almost a town in itself, and Anne's guide led her through so many courtyards and alleys that she thought she would never be able to get back by herself.

Above: *Ibn Rashid showing off his pet gazelles, which he bred in captivity and fed with dates from his hands.*

> At last, however, after crossing a very large courtyard, we stopped at a small door. This was open, and through it I could see a number of people sitting round a fire within. . . . All the persons present rose to their feet as I arrived. Amusheh could easily be singled out from among the crowd, even before she advanced to do the honours. She possessed a certain distinction of appearance and manner which would be recognised anywhere, and completely eclipsed the rest of the company. . . . Her face . . . is sufficiently good looking, with a well cut nose and mouth, and something singularly sparkling and brilliant. Hedusheh and Lulya, the two next wives, who were present, had gold brocade as rich as hers, and lips and cheeks smeared as red as hers with carmine, and eyes with borders kohled as black as hers, but lacked her charm. . . . We sat together on one carpet spread over a mattress, cushions being ranged along the wall behind us for us to lean against, and the fire in front scorching our faces while we talked.[15]

They were dressed in what can only be described as very expensive sacks of 'gold interwoven with silk', presenting an appearance of 'splendid shapeless-

Left: *The Blunts' house, just off the main street in Hail and less than two hundred yards from the palace: there was a kahwah (reception room), a harem, (private bedroom), and a couple of cubbyholes for Mohammed and the servants.*

ness'. Around her neck Amusheh wore gold, turquoises and pearls, her hair hung in four long hennaed plaits and on her left nostril was a two-inch nose ring, 'a most inconvenient ornament', that she fiddled with while she talked. After prayers Amusheh led Lady Anne to her own private apartment upstairs. It was well-carpeted and furnished with a large bed covered by a velvet and gold counterpane. The bedroom was clearly something of an embarrassment to Lady Anne, especially since the Emir made two visits to the private parts of his palace while she was there, but she managed to cope with the situation, showing the same fortitude she had displayed over the insect-ridden water. It was a relief to be in the fresh air again.

That evening the couple from England were invited to pass the after-dinner hours with the Emir. It was then that they received their one and only test. 'A fat vulgar-looking fellow' was introduced and after addressing Wilfrid in what appeared to be gibberish, turned to ibn Rashid and said: 'There, I told you he was no Englishman.' After some confused cross-questioning, Wilfrid discovered that his interrogator had been a stoker on board one of the British East India Company steam ships in the Gulf. The language he had been speaking, the Blunts were surprised to discover, had been English. Distinguishing two phrases from the chaos ('werry good' and 'chief engineer') Wilfrid gave their Arabic equivalent and his nationality was established.

Another of the Emir's guests that evening was Nassr ibn Rashid, a Wahhabi sheikh from the Dahna Desert. He was small, old and good-humoured, 'not one of those disagreeable ones described by Mr Palgrave', and sat amongst the illustrious company conspicuous in 'the plainest possible dress'. He was evidently not too extreme a Wahhabi, for when the call to prayer was sounded and ibn Rashid's entourage went off to pray, he discreetly stayed behind to smoke some tobacco with Wilfrid, quietly returning the pipe to its owner before the others returned.

But the greatest hit that evening was with Hamud, Obied's son who had befriended Doughty.

> He was a man who at once inspired confidence, and we have no cause to regret having acted on our first impression of his character. He has always, they say, refused to take presents from the Emir; and has never approved of his conduct, though he has sided with him politically, and serves him faithfully as a brother. His manners are certainly as distinguished as can be found anywhere in the world, and he is besides intelligent and well-informed.[16]

Below: *An evening in the palace with ibn Rashid.*

It all seemed like a romance come true, a meeting place of two milleniums. Yet curiously enough the Rashidi millenium seems to have been far more in tune with the modern world than the Blunts, and the Emir took particular pride in showing his guests a telephone, a new-fangled device which neither of the English visitors had experienced before.

All went well for the first few days, then suddenly the Emir's hospitality cooled. On the fourth day the presents of game and lamb ceased, on the fifth the Blunts were surprised not to be invited to the usual evening soirée, and on the sixth Wilfrid called at the palace and was curtly informed that the Emir was not 'at home'. It turned out that Mohammed ibn Aruk had so aggrandized his position to the Court that ibn Rashid had got bored with them. What was particularly galling to the Blunts was that Mohammed had presented himself as someone who had taken the foreigners in under his protection, which was not at all how the Blunts saw it. He even claimed that the Blunts' camels, mares and servants were his own.

Left: *Rashidi horsemen outside Hail. 'Hamud then suddenly put his mare into a gallop, and one after another the rest of the party joined him in a sham fight; galloping, doubling and shouting as though they would bring the sky about their ears'.*

> This under ordinary circumstances might have been a matter of small consequence, and we should not have grudged him a little self-glorification at our expense, conscious as we were of having owed the success of our journey hitherto, mainly to his fidelity. But unfortunately the secondary *rôle* which he would have assigned to us, made our relations with the Emir not only embarrassing, but positively dangerous.[17]

Fortunately Wilfrid met the Emir's chief slave and bodyguard, Mubarek, in the street, learned from him of Mohammed's behaviour and put everything right again.

> That very evening we were sent for once more to the palace, and received with the old cordiality. It is, too, I think very creditable to the arrangements of the Hail court, that no explanations of any sort were entered into. . . . Still the incident was a lesson and a warning, a lesson that we were Europeans still among Asiatics, a warning that Hail was a lion's den, though fortunately we were friends with the lion.[18]

The Blunts began to concentrate their minds on moving on. The Persian Haj caravan was camped outside the city returning from Mecca to Meshed Ali. They decided to leave with it.

On almost their last day in Hail the Emir invited them to go riding with him. The Blunts joined him and his court in the open ground outside the city walls, the same place where Obied had given the letter to Palgrave and Bandar had ridden with Guarmani. Mohammed ibn Rashid was splendidly dressed in flowing silks, with bare feet. He rode a white mare.

> It was one of those mornings one only finds in Nejd. The air brilliant and sparkling to a degree one cannot imagine in Europe, and filling one with a sense of life such as one remembers to have had in childhood, and which gives one a wish to shout. The sky was of an intense blue, and the hills in front of us carved out of sapphire, and the plain, crisp and even as a billiard table, sloping gently upward towards them.[19]

The Blunts galloped up to ibn Rashid who gave the signal to advance. Hamud, riding close to the Emir, put his horse into a gallop. One by one the riders joined him in a 'barbaric display', galloping, doubling up, charging and shouting, until only the Emir, the Blunts, and a sad Persian adolescent nobleman who was to die on the pilgrim caravan returning home were left riding with dignity. At last the Emir could resist no longer and, seizing a palm stick from a slave, galloped off with the others. In a few seconds he was transformed back into the Bedouin that he once had been, his silks thrown back and his long plaits streaming in the wind, 'charging into the throng, and pursuing and being pursued, and shouting as if he had never felt a care, and never committed a crime in his life.'

It was time to bid farewell.

> Our last interview with ibn Rashid was charactistic. He was not at the *ksar*, but in a house he had close to the Mecca gate, where from a little window he can watch unperceived the goings-on of the Haj encamped below him. We found him all alone, for he had lost all fear of our being assassins now, at his window like a bird of prey, calculating no doubt how many more silver pieces he should be able to make out of the Persians before they were well out of his clutches.[20]

Wilfrid made a small speech of thanks, begging the Emir to consider him his ambassador in Europe should he ever need one. The Emir thanked him and proposed that they should delay their departure to join him in a minor campaign against rebel tribes. The Blunts politely declined. 'Our heads, in fact, had been in the jaws of the lion long enough, and now our only object was to get quietly and decorously out of the den.' An hour later they had mounted and were riding out of the town, by the same gate that they had come in by. 'Then looking back, we each drew a long breath, for Hail with all the charm of its strangeness, and its interesting inhabitants, had come to be like a prison to us, and at one time when we had had that quarrel with Mohammed, had seemed very like a tomb.'

They looked ahead. In the foreground stretched a plain of coarse reddish sand; across the sand lay a long belt of green barley. Beyond the barley the desert faded from red to orange and from orange to a shimmering sheet of

Right: *David Roberts' 'Mount Seir, Wadi el Gohr', near Petra. Dated 1839, this picture was completed thirty years after Burckhardt first rediscovered Petra.*

water reflecting the blue sky. It was only a mirage. Crossing the mirage was the line of pilgrims, five miles long, with the green and red banner of the Haj in front.

They put their horses into a gallop and rode up to the banner, and on for a couple of hours. But only ten miles out of Hail the standard was planted and the Haj unrolled its camp. The Blunts put up their tent a few hundred yards from the bulk of the caravan passengers. They sat in their tent and listened to the Shiite elder chanting the call to prayer. Outside the mares were munching barley. It was a cold night.

Next morning they discovered that only half the caravan had left Hail. The other half was still detained awaiting their camels. The Emir el-Haj was Ambar, the brother of Anaibar, who had ridden with Guarmani and Doughty. He ordered the caravan to move another two miles to fresh grazing then halted again. The caravan stopped by a small pool at which the Blunts, together with the Persian dervishes who walked ahead of the caravan, arrived before the bulk. For the first and last time Lady Anne was not quite sure of the drinking water. The dervishes had 'an unpleasant habit of washing in the water first, and drinking it afterwards, which we are told is part of their religious ritual.'

The caravan stayed two days. The long hours of boredom gave the Blunts the opportunity of thoroughly inspecting the pilgrims before delivering judgement. Since the Persians lacked 'blood' and, compared to the Bedouin were like Dutch cart-horses to ibn Rashid's mares, the judgement was pretty damning. Lady Anne decided not to waste her time on Persians and spent the day 'profitably at home restuffing my saddle, which was sadly in want of it'.

When the caravan eventually moved on 5 February it shuffled a mere ten miles to another patch of grazing. As it reached the wadi where it was to spread out again, Wilfrid and Lady Anne climbed up on a rock to watch it go by. It was a curious sight. In front of the caravan were the dervishes, walking so fast they were almost running, 'wild dirty people, but quite amenable, and quite ready to converse if they know Arabic'; next came the respectable bourgeoisie, walking out of piety; behind them, some way behind, came the Emir el-Haj with his banner and escorting dromedaries; and finally there was

Left: *The Persian Haj caravan, with Ambar beneath the green banner which proclaimed 'There is no god but God', on its way to Meshed Ali.*

Right: *Chasing hyena. 'It would have escaped had we not got in front and barred the way.'*

Right: *Chasing hyena. 'It would have escaped had we not got in front and barred the way.'*

the mass of the pilgrims, some in litters, some perched awkwardly two on a camel, some walking. One pilgrim in a litter was smoking a long-tubed narghile, the other end carried by a servant walking ten feet in front.

Frustrated by the delays the Blunts decided to go ahead, making their own way to Meshed Ali. A Bedouin boy called Izzar, on his way to Mesopotamia with three camels, agreed to act as their guide. They enjoyed the pace. Two days after leaving the caravan they spotted a hyena. The greyhounds gave chase and the beast made off as fast as it could over the broken ground. The dogs continually attacked it but it went on running regardlessly until Wilfrid and Lady Anne galloped ahead and cut off its retreat.

> I never saw so cowardly a creature, for though much bigger than any dog, it never offered to turn round and defend itself as a boar or even the jackal would have done, and the dogs were so persistent in their attacks, that Wilfrid had great difficulty in getting a clear shot at it, which he did at last, rolling it over as it cantered along almost under the feet of our camels.[21]

Surprisingly the Moslems in the party did not regard the corpse as unclean. They even called it *kosh lahm* (capital meat). It was flayed and quartered on the spot. Though Anne could only bring herself to taste a morsel, Wilfrid, who made a meal of it, pronounced it perfectly edible.

Short of food after the delays with the Haj caravan, the Blunts now took to locusts. After trying them several different ways they came to the conclusion that they were best plain boiled and dipped in salt. Wilfrid thought they would hold their own as an hors-d'oeuvre in the best Paris restaurants; the more practical Anne had her doubts.

They continued across the desert for five days, then something totally unexpected happened. They had just made camp for the night when six men on dromedaries galloped straight towards them. At first everyone thought it was a raid. The riders galloped up to the tents and stopped. They dismounted from their camels; Mohammed welcomed them and offered them coffee; they accepted. Only after coffee did Mohammed feel able to ask them where they were going to and who they were.

They said they were going to Hail to find a distant cousin of their sheikh, who was reported to be there, a guest of ibn Rashid. Their sheikh was called Muttlak ibn Aruk and the man they were looking for was Mohammed ibn Aruk. Mohammed gasped in astonishment; he had found his long lost cousins, the descendants of the third brother who had parted company from the other two, 'tradition knew not whither'.

Muttlak's tents were only a day away and they rode there the following

Left: 'An Encampment of Pilgrims near Jericho', by David Roberts. 'When I remember how, years ago, I read that romantic account of Mr Palgrave, which nobody believed, of an ideal state in the heart of Arabia, and of a happy land which nobody but he had seen, and how impossibly remote and unreal it all appeared . . . I feel that we have achieved something which is not given to every one to do.'

morning. 'There was of course a great deal of kissing and embracing between Mohammed and his new-found relations, and Wilfrid came in for his share of it.' Anne heartily approved of the new cousins, particularly Muttlak himself.

> He has an expression of extreme kindness and gentleness which is very attractive, and we already like him better than any of Mohammed's Jawf relations. Unlike the ibn Aruks of Jawf and Tadmur, this branch of the family has remained Bedouin, and unmixed by any fellahin alliances. Mohammed's rather vulgar pretentions to birth and dignity have fallen ashamed before the simplicity of this good old man.[22]

They stayed in Muttlak's encampment for three days, at the end of which Muttlak announced that he would travel with them as far as Meshed Ali. When it was time to go the Blunts left with genuine sorrow.

'You shall be our sheikh whenever you return to us,' Muttlak's people told Wilfrid. 'Muttlak will not be jealous. We will make war for you on all your enemies, and be friends with your friends.'

'It is strange,' thought Anne, 'what friendship we have made with these simple-hearted people in a few hours. We are the first Europeans they have seen, and they look upon us as beings of a superior world.'

Muttlak's equipment for the journey to Meshed Ali was the simplest; the clothes he stood up in and a black camel which he shared with a single attendant, Muttlak in the saddle and the attendant kneeling behind him.

'There,' Wilfrid said to Mohammed, 'that is how your ancestors left Nejd.'

When they rejoined the pilgrim road they found the two halves of the Haj caravan together. During the three days in Muttlak's encampment the pilgrims had caught up. They rejoined the caravan but only two days later the line of pilgrims stopped again. This time the delay was ordered by the Emir el-Haj to elicit a contribution from the pilgrims for his own private pocket.

The Blunts were annoyed. 'He has made it known that two mejidies a head is what he expects, and that he will not move until the sum is forthcoming. This will be a nice little purse for him, something like eight hundred pounds.' The next few days, determined to make up for lost time, the Emir el-Haj hurried the caravan on at thirty miles a day. It was difficult country. The camels were getting leaner, the pilgrims thirstier. Camels collapsed, lying down and dying on the road. Two pilgrims died of thirst when they were separated from the rest of the caravan (one was the rather sad Persian prince the Blunts had met in Hail). Finally the caravan staggered into the first of the settlements beyond the Arabian deserts. 'A cry of "stop thief" already announces that we have returned to the Turkish Empire! It has not been heard since we left Mezarib.' Ahead of them stood the gilt dome of Meshed Ali, shining across the desert.

Wilfrid and Lady Anne's pilgrimage was not at an end. From his experiences with ibn Rashid and the Bedouins, Wilfrid saw their political system of 'shepherd rule' as the perfect form of government. Combining anarchy and aristocracy, rule by the few with consent by the many, who were free to withdraw their consent whenever they wanted, it was 'a community living as our idealists have dreamed . . . without compulsion of any kind, whose only law was public opinion, and whose only order a principle of honour.' It was another mirage, but a very old one.

For the next forty years the Blunts devoted themselves to the cause of Arab independence, to which they later added Indian independence, Egyptian independence and lastly Irish independence; the two dividing their time between their estate in Egypt where they bred horses and their estate in Sussex where they bred dreams. As the dreams manifestly failed to turn into reality, so Wilfrid became more bitter, his anti-imperialist ideals degenerating into crude self-aggrandizement and anti-semitism.

By 1906 it had all become too much for Lady Anne. The couple separated, he living in Sussex and she in Egypt where she died in 1917, the year of the Arab Revolt. According to his daughter, Lady Wentworth, he had 'played havoc with her heart, wrecked her life and, jealous of her intellectual gifts, appropriated the credit of her brains to himself with shameless arrogance'.

Wilfrid, lonely and cantankerous to the end, continued until 1922. The free Arab state he had dreamed of was a reality; the Irish Free State that he had suffered imprisonment for was about to come into existence; the first steps in the Indianization of the Indian Civil Service (a step which would lead inevitably to independence) had been taken; and Egyptian nationalism, led by Zargoul Pasha, was awakening from a troubled sleep. It would mean the end of the British Empire, but Wilfrid Blunt was confident enough of his own position in English society not to feel threatened and to accept the consequences. 'For a hundred years we did good in the world; for a hundred we shall have done evil, and then the world will hear of us no more.'

They were words of prophecy, but only one man recognized the eighty-two-year-old semi-recluse as a prophet, T. E. Lawrence. To him Blunt and Doughty were the 'master Arabians', while to Blunt Lawrence was the man who had made his dream of a free Arab state a reality. The two met in Blunt's drawing room on his estate in Sussex. The old man was sitting in a monumental arm-chair, dressed in Bedouin robes, 'a fire yet flickering over the ashes of an old fury.' They talked for a while but not too long. The terrifying patriarch in the arm-chair was very tired. Lawrence rose to go. The old man presented his visitor with a copy of his poems, inscribing it, with a withered shaky hand:'To T. E. Lawrence in admiration of his courage and honesty in public and much else, from Wilfred Scawen Blunt.'

A few days weeks later Wilfrid Blunt was dead, buried in a copse on his Sussex estate, without religious rites.

VIII

THE TWENTIETH-CENTURY TRAVELLERS

In 1908 the first motor car arrived in Arabia. Its owner was an Englishman, Captain William Shakespear (a distant relative of William Shakespeare but without the 'e'), assistant to the British Political Resident in Kuwait. His background could not have been more conventional: British-in-India family, strong-minded mother, draughty boarding schools, Indian Army and Viceroy's Political Department. He believed in Curzon's claim ('the message is carved in granite, it is hewn out of the rock of doom – that our work is righteous and that it shall endure') as firmly as he believed in God. Less conventionally British had been his last leave. He had spent it motoring from Persia, through Mesopotamia (which Arab nationalists were already beginning to call Iraq) and the Balkans, to England. The Bedouin of Arabia found his camel travelling equally unconventional. He took with him a crate of wine, a collapsible bath and a copy of W. G. Palgrave's account of his journey through Arabia. Considering that two of the most fundamental characteristics of desert travel are lack of water and lack of privacy, it is difficult to imagine when he had much chance to indulge in any of these things. As for his views on the Bedouin, he liked them 'because they were men.'

He had already made several excursions into the desert by camel and motor-car, when he met the Wahhabi ruler, Abdul Aziz ibn Saud, in Kuwait. Ibn Saud was thirty-one years old, over six foot tall, and had a 'frank open face, and after initial reserve, has a genial and courteous manner'. Hating Arab food, Shakespear dined the young king on roast lamb with mint sauce, roast potatoes and tinned asparagus. They liked the food and each other.

'You are my friend,' ibn Saud told Shakespear after the meal, and invited him to visit Riyadh.

Shakespear jumped at the opportunity. No European had been to Riyadh

Left: The Empty Quarter, photographed by Bertram Thomas, the quiet and self-effacing Englishman who first crossed it.

since Pelly half a century earlier. The others – Doughty, the Blunts, the Frenchman Charles Huber who was killed by his guides, Julius Enting and the tragic and teutonic Baron Nolde, who rode through Arabia in full Prussian uniform complete with spiked helmet and then committed suicide – had reached only the edges of Wahhabi domains. Shakespear was going to the heart. He spent the next four years battling with British officialdom to get permission to go.

In the half century since Palgrave's and Pelly's visit, a veil had been drawn across the centre of the Peninsula, and the whole balance of power had altered. The turn of the century saw the House of Rashid at the height of its prestige, and the House of Saud was at its lowest ebb. Buraydah and Unayzah were occupied by the Rashidis, and the Nejd was divided between the Rashidis and the Turks, the Turks occupying Hasa and the Rashidis Riyadh. The Saud family itself was in exile in Kuwait.

In 1902 Saudi power reasserted itself and recaptured Riyadh. The taking of the Nejd capital has become part of the legend of Saudi Arabian history, as the Long March has for China. It is as simple as it is heroic. Forty men left Kuwait, collecting Bedouin on the way, and making eventually for Riyadh by a long and indirect approach. They rode south, and further south, and further south still heading into the depths of the Empty Quarter. So many dropped out that by the time they stopped they were only a handful more than the original forty. Deep in the the Empty Quarter, hidden by sand dunes, they lost themselves for fifty days, only visiting the water-holes at night, and brushing away their tracks as they came and went. It took seven nights, averaging thirty miles a night, to get back to Riyadh. They crept into the city during the small hours, making their approach from the south where the tomato ketchup factory now stands. Once inside, they commandeered a house directly opposite the palace, held the harem hostage, and rushed the Rashidi governor when he came out of the palace half an hour after daybreak. He tried to escape through the palace postern gate but Abdul Aziz grabbed his legs. A Rashidi guard tried to kill the Saudi leader; someone threw a spear at him and missed. In the postern gate the governor was stretched; the Rashidi guards inside the postern pulled his head and the Saudis outside pulled his legs. He freed one leg and kicked Abdul Aziz ibn Saud in the

Above: 'Bedouin Caravan' painted by R. Talbot Kelly in 1893, just fifteen years before the first motor car arrived in Arabia. (Mathaf Gallery, London)

190

groin. Ibn Saud let go with a cry and the governor scrambled through the postern. The Rashidis tried to close the door on the intruders, but too late; one of ibn Saud's cousins, Abdallah ibn Jalawi, got in after the governor and the rest followed. The governor sprinted towards the mosque. He never made it.

Abdul Aziz ibn Saud built up his army and rapidly it became one of the most powerful forces in the Peninsula. Its shock troops were the *Ikhwan*, the Warriors of God, who had spread the Wahhabi empire so ruthlessly one hundred years earlier. In 1904 he seized Buraydah and Unayzah, in 1906 he defeated the Rashidi army at Raudbat el-Muhanna, killing the Rashidi Emir, Abdul Aziz ibn Rashid, and in 1913 he cleared the Turks out of Hasa.

With the death of its monarch, the House of Rashid went through another bout of fratricide which killed not only three Emirs and a regent, but any genuine Shammar nationalism that might have been growing up. From then on the Rashidis were irreversibly divided between two factions, one pro-Turkish and pan-Islamic, and the other pro-Wahhabi and nationalist. Power alternated between the two groups and by the beginning of the second decade of the century the pro-Wahhabi nationalist faction, led by the regent, Zamil ibn Subhan, dominated the Shammar.

Meanwhile in the west a railway had been built from Damascus to Medina, giving the Sherif of Mecca a strategic and political importance that he had never had before, and giving hundreds of thousands of pilgrims the chance to complete the Haj, which they had never had before.

The present Sherif, Hussain, had spent less than half a lifetime in Arabia, although he could trace his descent directly back to Mohammed. Hussain was fifty-four years old and had been born in Istanbul. He came to power in 1908, the year absolute despotism was abolished in Turkey and the Young Turks came to power. In the convulsions that followed he utilized both his deviousness and his ambition to gain a measure of independence unknown since Mohammed Ali's occupation a hundred years earlier. 'He smiled rarely,' wrote one English diplomat. 'His eyes were grey, lustrous and cold.'

As the three Bedouin powers of Riyadh, Mecca and Hail adopted anti-Turkish attitudes in unison, a relative newcomer to Arabian society was flexing its muscles in the towns: the new bourgeoisie, outward-looking, reformist, cosmopolitan and secular, epitomized by el-Kenneyny and el-Bessam, who had cared for Doughty. In 1901 the first secular schools were opened in Jeddah, paid for by Jeddah merchants. They were disapproved of by the Turks for being nationalist, the Sherif for being irreligious and the British for fostering those 'half-educated natives' that they so deplored.

Where all four groups were united was in their opposition to the Turks. By 1911 the nationalist mood was so favourable that the rulers of Riyadh, Hail,

Right: *'Love your camel,' the Prophet said. The photograph was taken by Captain Shakespear.*

Mecca, the Yemen and Asir were exchanging letters with the aim of creating a federation of Arabian States strong enough to eject the Turks and keep out the British. But the alliance was too weak to withstand the opposing ambitions of ibn Saud and Sherif Hussain, the suspicions of the reformist middle classes, the assassination of the pro-nationalist Rashidi Regent, Zamil, and the strenuous opposition of the British government who, under the guise of non-interference in Turkish affairs, worked to maintain what Lord Crewe called: 'a weak and disunited Arabia, split into little principalities as far as possible under our suzerainty – but incapable of co-ordinated action against us.'

It was to maintain this policy of profitable non-interference that His Majesty's Government delayed four years before granting Captain Shakespear permission to visit his friend in Riyadh. Even then permission was only granted because the Viceroy wrote a personal letter to London pointing out that 'it would be most unfortunate if, for political reasons, Englishmen are always to be excluded from exploration in central Arabia while the field is left open to foreigners.'

By 1914, when Shakespear's permission came, two rivals – one of them a foreigner – had beaten him to it. The first of these, a Dane called Barclay Raunkaier, had actually been helped by Shakespear, against the express wishes of His Majesty's Government. Raunkaier left Kuwait in February 1912 with fifty men and a hundred camels. He was twenty-three years old and could not speak a word of Arabic. The nightmare that followed rivalled Doughty's. In Buraydah the Emir commandeered his binoculars and revolver. He described the Emir as having 'curly black hair, hanging unplaited. One eye is sightless and filled with matter, the other seems to be scowling, his lips are thick, the face is bloated and the fingers swollen.' When he got to Riyadh he found Abdul Aziz was away and was entertained by Abdul Aziz's father, Abdul Rahman. Raunkaier almost died of tuberculosis, his guides stole all his possessions, he did not eat for four days and the water he drank smelt so foul he had to hold his nose.

The second was an Englishman, Gerald Leachman of the Royal Sussex Regiment, who arrived in Hail on his first trip to Arabia in 1909. Leachman was capable; he had fought in the Boer War in South Africa, explored central Asia and travelled with the Anaiza Bedouin in the Syrian Desert. He was with

Left: *Shakespear's photograph of the Saudi army on the march, with the green standard at the front.*

Above: *The first photograph of Abdul Aziz ibn Saud, when he was Emir of Nejd, taken by Shakespear. A decade later he became King of Arabia.*

their army when it was attacked and overwhelmed by the Rashidi forces, taken prisoner and found himself treated like a guest of honour, staying with the Rashidis for several months before continuing to Basra. His second trip to Arabia in 1912 took him from Damascus, via Jawf, Hail, Buraydah (he arrived on Christmas Day) and Riyadh (where he was almost killed) to the Gulf. It was an epic journey; no one had done it since Palgrave. Shakespear did his best to hide his envy.

Captain Shakespear rode out of Kuwait in January 1914. He had decided to combine a visit to Riyadh with a diagonal crossing of Arabia through Riyadh, Unayzah, Buraydah and Jawf, finishing his journey at Suez, where he would take more conventional transport to London. Shakespear took with him his private cameleer, Abdul Aziz ibn Hassan, seven assistant cameleers, two servants, an arsenal of rifles, a camera, his favourite camel, Dhabia, several crates of good *château* wine, a well-thumbed copy of Palgrave and his collapsible bath. For the first half of the journey it rained almost every day. It was so cold the water in the goatskin froze during the night. After a week one of the *rafiks* bolted with Shakespear's spare suit which he had been keeping for when he arrived in London, and at the first well they came to they were confronted by hostile Bedouin and denied water. It was three days before they could replenish their water at Hafar, where Shakespear had his first bath. After Hafar came the red sands of the Dahna Desert. They trudged for days. Beyond the dunes, which change their colour from pink in the morning through orange at high noon to purple at dusk, lay Zilfi. Shakespear celebrated his arrival there with a bottle of Moselle. After a bath he was invited to coffee by Abdallah ibn Suleimen, whose family had befriended Palgrave half a century earlier. He arrived at Riyadh in early March, where he was warmly greeted by Abdul Aziz ibn Saud.

He was not the first Englishman to visit Riyadh. Sadlier, Palgrave, Pelly and Leachman had been there before. But he was the first to describe the city in such detail, and the first to record it on film. His friendship with ibn Saud, his status as a diplomat and his easy-going and open personality protected him from Wahhabi intolerance and he was free to go where he liked. He left the desert city on 12 March. Ibn Saud was taking his army out on an expedition and Shakespear rode with him for two days. They chatted together at the rear of the column about military technology. Ibn Saud was riding a superb white horse. A few miles out Shakespear put his camel into a canter and rode off to the column's right flank where he dismounted and took out his camera. At the head of the column was the green standard, proclaiming that there was no god but God. Behind came the escort on their camels, each leading a mare by the halter. Following the escort were the infantry, riding camels without the attendant mares. Every man had a bandoleer across his shoulder, and a rifle hanging from the saddle. It was an unforgettable sight.

He left the Saudi army on the second day, travelling well to the west on the main Buraydah road through unknown territory. The Bedouin children he passed did not wear clothes until they married, he noted, and covered their pudènda with a 'horse's eye' fringe. It rained, he was attacked by raiders, he lost his way and eventually arrived in Unayzah on 26 March. Like Doughty, he was struck by its cosmopolitanism, and spent hours with the Emir, Saleh ibn Zamil, and the merchant community, smoking his pipe and discoursing on world affairs. On 28 March he made the eighteen-mile journey to Buraydah and, like Doughty, he found it the least friendly place he visited, but the culture shock that he suffered was worse. Shakespear met a man called Abdallah el-Khalifa who spoke English with an American accent. He had stowed away on a ship to New York and had driven a taxi cab there for six years before returning to Arabia.

From Buraydah Shakespear took a semi-circular route around the eastern edge of Jebal Shammar for Jawf, avoiding Hail where he was uncertain of his reception. Endless wind replaced endless rain, Shakespear was constantly sick, and the water, which looked 'like urine', was so filthy that he was unable to develop his photographic plates. He wore an Army greatcoat and woollen gloves to protect himself from the cold and when he developed toothache the pain was so intolerable that he borrowed a pair of rusty forceps from one of his *rafiks* and pulled out the tooth, a lower molar, himself. A few days later they encountered an old man who thought they were railway surveyors looking for a route between Kuwait and Suez. He too spoke with an American accent. His name was Mohammed el-Rawaf, and he had been chief groom for the camels at the Chicago Exhibition fifteen years earlier.

On 26 April, plagued by locusts, they came into Jawf. With the demise of the power of Hail, effective control lay with the Ruaulla, under their chief, Nuri ibn Shaalan. Shakespear handled Nuri perfectly. Nuri's favourite subjects were medicines and guns. Shakespear showed the chief first his medicine chest and then his arsenal. They challenged each other to a test of marksmanship. Shakespear won, but only just. When he left after two days, the twelve-year-old boy-Sultan, Nawaf bin Nuri bin Shaalan, burst into tears.

Five days north-west of Jawf they were attacked by raiders. They made a defensive camp and kept the Bedouin at bay until mid-afternoon when they made a break for it. It was as hot as a frying pan. They rode all night to the refuge of the grasping and bloodthirsty Sheikh Audah of the Abu Taiya. They were into the fire. Audah was one of the most infamous characters in Arabia. Once he had torn the heart out of a vanquished foe and eaten it. Shakespear had given away so many presents en route in return for hospitality that all he had left was twenty-seven pounds. He offered ten pounds on credit, but Audah would not accept this, and took twenty pounds in cash instead. Three years later Audah was riding with T. E. Lawrence. 'When he dies,' wrote Lawrence, 'the Middle Ages of the desert will have ended.'

Above: *Gertrude Bell, the most eminent woman Orientalist of her day, born in Durham in 1868, died in Baghdad in 1926. 'Scholar, historian, archaeologist, explorer, poet, mountaineer, gardener, distinguished servant of the state,' according to the plaque at her family home in Hull.*

Above: *Sheikh Audah of the Abu Taiya, painted by Eric Kennington. Audah blackmailed Shakespear, was chivalrous to Gertrude Bell and fought with Lawrence. He ceremoniously smashed his Turkish-made false teeth when he joined the Revolt.*

The trek that followed was the hardest in the entire journey. Days were agonizingly hot and nights freezing cold. Fears of raiders forced Shakespear to do without the discomforts of European clothes and pith helmet and everyone to go without the comforts of warm food. It was too risky to light a fire. Shakespear got sunstroke, his body was 'one huge ache' and the desert was utterly devoid of grazing for the stumbling camels. On 12 May they crossed the Hejaz Railway beneath moonlight, a single track running from one dark horizon to the other. On the other side of the railway was the old Haj road, which Varthema, Pitts and Doughty had travelled down. It was totally deserted. There was little food. The party had sustained themselves on dates and camel milk. Now the camels were lame. 'I would like to sleep for ever,' he wrote. 'It was the worst day of my life.'

On 17 May they arrived in Sinai, stopping at the Egyptian police post at Kontilla. Shakespear had a bath and followed it with a dinner of Bovril consommé, salmon in Worcester sauce, mutton pilau with carrots and celery, tapioca and vanilla blancmange. For drinks there was Vermouth, the last bottle of Moselle and a good port. Shakespear had reason to celebrate. He had covered one thousand eight hundred miles, two-thirds of it through unexplored territory, crossing the tracks of virtually every other major Arabian explorer, both Arab and European, on the way.

At about the same time that Captain William Shakespear was preparing to leave Kuwait, another English traveller, Gertrude Bell, was leaving Damascus for Hail. Like that other extraordinary Englishwoman who went to Hail, Lady Anne Blunt, she was a 'person of distinction', and moved in the very highest circles of her day. She was forty-four, had a strong round face, and was inclined towards dumpiness. She was also recovering from an impossible love affair. 'I want to cut all links with the world,' she wrote.

She sailed for Beirut, visiting an English intelligence officer, T. E. Lawrence, who was spying on the Germans in Lebanon, on the way. In Damascus she was introduced to Mohammed el-Bessam, son of the man who had helped Doughty in Unayzah, who found her guides and servants, and advised her to take plenty of money. She left Damascus on 16 December 1913. It was a bitterly cold winter.

Gertrude Bell rode for over three weeks south and west through the Syrian Desert to Ziza on the Hejaz Railway. There both the Turkish and British authorities tried to stop her, so she slipped out of Ziza at night without her passport and with only half her guides. She did not need the additional men: she was protected by her sex. She was even treated well by the heart-eating Sheikh Audah. On 25 February she arrived in Hail. 'I hope the Hail people will be polite,' she wrote. 'The Emir is away raiding and his uncle is left in charge.'

The uncle, Ibrahim, brother of the anti-Turkish regent Zamil, took to the strange spectacle of another Englishwoman as well as he could. She was taken to the magnificent colonnaded reception room, with which she was familiar through the writings of Palgrave, Doughty and Blunt, then led to a guest house outside the walls where she was confined – in the very best of surroundings – for ten days. 'It was like a story from *The Arabian Nights*, but I did not find it particularly enjoyable to be one of the dramatis personae.' She passed the time talking to Turkiyyeh, a thick-set woman with magnificent black hair, the court chatterbox. She found Hail expensive, even for a state guest, and asked Ibrahim if she could draw a cheque on the State Treasury for two hundred pounds. Ibrahim explained that the Chancellor of the Exchequer was away with the Emir and Regent and there was no one who could authorize a payment so large. She brusquely told him that she would leave the next day and he, equally brusquely, returned her gifts.

Left: *'Damascus', painted by Max Schmidt in 1844.*

She went to Ibrahim and spoke her mind, 'without any Oriental paraphrases', then got up and marched out, 'a thing that is only done by sheikhs, you understand'. That evening the chief eunuch arrived with the money and told her she could leave the next morning. She replied that she had no intention of leaving next morning; she wanted to see the town first. The following morning she was ceremoniously shown the sights, with as much discretion from her hosts as she allowed.

> Though it is a town like any other, of streets and houses,
> Hail retains something of the wilderness. There is no clatter
> of civil life. Silent ways are paved with desert dust . . . the
> creak of wheels is not heard. The noiseless slow footfall of
> the camel is all the traffic here.[1]

She left Hail the next day on the same route as the Blunts. Three weeks later she was in Baghdad.

Both Captain Shakespear and Gertrude Bell were in Europe when war broke out with Turkey, Shakespear training a unit in Aldershot and Gertrude doing war-work in Boulogne. The War completely overturned Britain's traditional policy of support for the Ottomans ('Turkey is as good an occupier of the road to India as any active Arab sovereign,' Lord Palmerston once said). Hail, where the pro-Turkish faction was now in the ascendancy, supported the Ottomans, but the other two rulers, ibn Saud and Sherif Hussain, were no longer petty potentates to be kept weak and at arm's length; they were potential allies. Shakespear was whipped out of Aldershot and Gertrude Bell called back from Boulogne. She went to Cairo and then to Baghdad, he to the Gulf and then ibn Saud.

He sailed first to India and then to Kuwait, which he left with a dozen camels on 12 December. He found ibn Saud's camp at Khufaisa, about two hundred miles north of Riyadh, on the last day of the year. All he could see was a sea of billowing tents. The Saudi army was assembled, wild and wiry, bare-footed and bearded. There was a continual sound of drumming, soon joined in counterpoint by the clatter of Shakespear's typewriter, banging out reports to his employers.

Left: *Ibn Saud, Sir Percy Cox (British Resident in the Gulf), and Gertrude Bell in March 1917.*

Right: *Shakespear, with pipe, pith helmet and pet hawk, Shalwah, at Thammila el-Gaa in December 1909.*

Abdul Aziz, who is animated by an intense patriotism for his country, and a profound veneration for his religion and a single-minded desire to do his best for his people by obtaining for them lasting peace and security, now finds himself in a difficult position. He trusted the British government as no other . . . now he is asked to commit himself to open war with his most powerful and bitter enemies by a power which six months before told him it could not intervene on his behalf.[2]

Ibn Saud was justifiably suspicious of the British government's volte-face, but since the Rashidi army, his traditional enemy, was only two days away, he decided to challenge them to battle. As the Saudi army prepared to march, Abdul Aziz recieved a letter from the Sherif of Mecca, Hussain. The Turks were pressurizing him to declare a Holy War against Britain. Ibn Saud advised him to play for time. It was their last civilized communication.

Shakespear, in khaki and pith helmet, left with the army on 22 January 1915. The army he rode with was six thousand strong, and he was at the height of his optimism. 'Ibn Saud,' he wrote to Gertrude Bell, whom he had met in London, 'is making preparations for a big raid on ibn Rashid with a view of wiping him out practically and I shouldn't be surprised if I reached Hail in the course of the next month or two as Din Saud's political adviser!' To his brother he was more thoughtful. 'There is never any knowing what these bedawin will do; they are quite capable of being firm friends up to the battle and then suddenly changing their minds and going over to the other side in the middle of it.'

They camped that night less than a day from ibn Rashid's army, between Zilfi and Buraydah. It was icy cold. Abdul Aziz told Shakespear that he did not want the Englishman present at the battle.

'If I go now, I desert not only you but my own country,' he replied.

Abdul Aziz accepted his words but asked him at least to change into Bedouin clothing. Again Shakespear refused.

Next morning he ate a good breakfast and mounted a ridge with his camera to get a good view of the forthcoming battle, standing out on the skyline in his ostentatious pith helmet. On the plain below the Saudi infantry were ranged in the sand dunes before him. Behind were some Saudi gunners manning a field gun captured from the Turks when the Saudis overran Hasa.

The Shammar cavalry charged the Saudi infantry and the Saudi cavalry were unable to stop them. He took up his camera (which, with its tripod looked like a machine gun) and started focusing it. The Saudi infantry broke. The tall Nasrani in his pith helmet abandoned his camera and started shouting instructions to the Saudi gunners behind him. One of the gunners, Hussain, urged him to remove his pith helmet. He did so. The Shammar cavalry were coming onto them. The Saudi gunners hastily buried their guns and fled. The bare-headed Englishman was alone on the ridge. The first Shammar bullet hit him in the leg, the second in the arm, the third in the head. He went on firing until he fell. After the battle the Turks found his pith helmet and took it to Medina, displaying it in triumph outside the city, proof of Nasrani interference in Arabia.

The death of Shakespear ended all Saudi involvement in the First World War. Unable to defeat the Turkish-backed forces of Hail, suspicious of his rival, Sherif Hussain, and mistrusting the British, ibn Saud withdrew into neutrality. The British, unable to gain a quick success in the centre, turned to the Hejaz, where the ambitious Hussain ibn Ali, seeing the chance of obtaining an Arab kingdom for his Hashemite family with him at its head, willingly welcomed them.

Hussain ibn Ali's revolt in the Hejaz broke out on 5 June 1916 in Mecca. 'Just before daybreak on Saturday, the 9th Shaaban,' wrote the Mecca newspaper *Al-Qibla*, 'a sustained rifle fire was opened on the barracks at Mecca and on the Hamidiya building in which are housed the offices of the Government.' By 9 July all the garrisons of southern Hejaz had surrendered and Medina was under seige. That November, to ibn Saud's fury, Hussain ibn Ali declared himself King of the Arabs.

To the gathering crowd of British orientalists, viewing the world from the veranda of Shepheard's Hotel in Cairo, it was like a dream come true: a Bedouin revolution on the side of the British; and since the Bedouin were the gentlemen of the desert, it would be a revolution conducted by gentlemen. The Orientalists, all employed by the 'Arab Bureau', were an impressive bunch, and all excellently qualified – in their own estimation. Diplomats, academics, archaeologists and 'Old Sudan Hands', their pedigrees were pure. They were very good at talking to Emirs and princes, but other Arabs were merely figures on a landscape, a landscape which they had painted with their own confident imperial brush-strokes. Virtually everything they knew about Arabia came from books, first Doughty's and the Blunts', and later from Guarmani's book, which they resurrected from the Franciscan monks in Jerusalem and translated into English. The most eminent of them all, T. E. Lawrence, actually said that a student of Doughty knew more about the Bedouin than the Bedouin themselves. Their information on Arabia was forty years out of date, and their support for the conservative Sherif and his even more conservative Bedouins, and rejection of the parvenu ibn Saud, seem perfectly understandable in the circumstances. Like Burton and Blunt they were obsessed with 'blood' and the Sherif, with his family tree stretching right back to the Prophet, had 'blood'. That the Bedouin were only one factor in Arabian society, that reasonably sophisticated societies were growing up in the towns of the Hejaz, and that ibn Saud's Nejd state, and alliance of townspeople, cultivators and Bedouin was a much closer reflection of Arabian society than the Sherif's 'blood', were all ignored.

The townspeople had become radicalized and the revolt of the Young Turks had given heart to their hopes for reform and constitutional democracy. They viewed with horror the Sherif's abolition of the Turkish civil code and its replacement by Koranic law. T. E. Lawrence recognized this:

Particularly in Mecca and Jeddah public opinion was against the Arab state. The mass of the citizens were foreigners – Egyptians, Indians, Javanese, African and others – quite unable to sympathise with Arab inspirations especially as voiced by Beduin; for the Beduin lived on what he could extract from the stranger on his roads or in his valleys, and he and the townsman bore each other a perpetual grudge.[3]

But he did nothing about it. Nor did any of the other Orientalists, even if any had recognized it, which they should have done, had they been objective readers of Doughty. The attitude of the Orientalist to the townsman is best expressed by Sir Mark Sykes in his travel 'entertainment' *Dar-al-Islam*. He asked a Bedouin boy what was better, houses or tents? 'Tents,' the boy replied.

From that one sentence I knew there was hope for the East and that hope is not found on the adoption of spring-sided boots and bad manners by native Christians, but in the wild, brave, manly race who having learnt, have weight and character enough to retain their own nationality.[4]

The fact that the Bedouin army could not have stayed in the field without the logistical back-up of the men in 'spring-sided boots' was not really noticed.

Right: *T. E. Lawrence, painted by James McBey, Damascus, 1918.*

Of all the Orientalists in Arabia in the First World War, one towers above all others, Lawrence of Arabia. It is not easy to write about him. As the psychologist Kathryn Tidrick puts it, 'there is a constant struggle between dislike of a man who so assiduously propagated his own legend and a desire to be fair to someone who presents too easy a target for ridicule.' Lawrence was the first to write openly about Doughty's masochism.

While still a child, T. E. Lawrence discovered he was the illegitimate son of an Anglo-Irish baronet, and he yearned for recognition from his father's family. He developed a passion for medieval romances as an adolescent, writing his Oxford history thesis on the Crusades. His hope, he proclaimed in *Seven Pillars of Wisdom*, was to be a general and knighted by the age of thirty. Instead he became an archaeologist and joined the British Secret Service, reporting on German influence in the Levant. When the Hejaz Revolt started he was in Cairo, editing the Arab Bureau's *Arab Bulletin*, gathering intelligence from all over the Peninsula.

When Lawrence arrived in the Hejaz in 1916 the Revolt was foundering. The Turks had brought sufficient forces into Medina by rail to forestall an Arab assault, while their modern German artillery kept the Bedouin (who were unused to shells) far from the city's walls. It was Lawrence's genius to recognize that success for the Arabs lay not in capturing Medina and cutting the Hejaz Railway, but in bleeding Turkey dry of soldiers trying to defend the city and the railways; a policy that admirably fitted into the British scheme of diverting Turkish troops from the Suez and Mesopotamian fronts

Below: *Ajman Bedouin on the march in the Nejd, photographed by Shakespear in 1911.*

Above: *Harry St John Philby* *(1885-1960), 'The greatest explorer of them all.'*

to waste themselves in the strategically insignificant sands of Arabia. In June 1917 he captured Aquaba and, leaving half the Hashemite forces to invest Medina and harass the railway line, he took the other half north and entered Damascus in triumph a little over a year later.

Neither his desert journeys (he never ventured into unknown territory), nor his genius as a guerrilla leader (which he undoubtably had), nor his vulgar egotism, concern us. What concerns us is his view of the Bedouin, which so epitomized the Orientalists of his day. Like other travellers in Arabia, he looked at the Bedouin and he saw himself; conservative, accepting hierarchy as the will of God, and fundamentally out of sympathy with democracy and men in spring-sided boots.

The British in Cairo, however, had no intention of letting ibn Saud sit on one side for the duration of the War. His domains divided the Turks in Hejaz and Sinai from those in Mesopotamia. There had been almost no contact with him since Shakespear's death. Someone had to be sent to ibn Saud. The man they sent has been dubbed by his son 'The greatest explorer of them all'. He was the extraordinary, exuberant, extrovert, egocentric and self-exaggerated Harry St John Philby.

He was a complete contrast to Doughty and Lawrence. Born in 1885, he went to Westminster and Oxford before joining the Indian Civil Service – the first socialist in the Service, he later claimed. In November 1915, with Britain occupying large areas of southern Mesopotamia, he was transferred to the Gulf. Three years earlier his son had been born, whom he named Kim after his Kipling hero.

Morality was simple for Harry St John Philby. There were but two forces in the world; the forces of good, which were invariably allied behind Harry St John Philby, and the forces of evil, usually aligned behind His Majesty's Government; between those two neither compromise nor compassion was possible. When his boss in Mesopotamia said that he had 'an innate and ineradicable tendency to find flaws in everything from governments to fountain pens', he replied that the had never yet found a perfect government or a perfect fountain pen.

British attention in Arabia was still centred on the Sherif of Mecca. Ibn Saud's hoped-for attack on the Rashidis would be no more than a side-show. Two missions were to be sent to him, one under Ronald Storrs setting out from the Hejaz, the other, with Philby as one of its three members, striking west from the Gulf. The Storrs Mission was refused permission to approach Riyadh by Hussain on the grounds that the country beyond Hejaz was lawless; an attempt to undermine ibn Saud's authority. He could not stop the Gulf Mission.

The mission arrived on the Arabian coast at Uqayr in the Gulf of Bahrain in a dhow towed by the inaptly named HMS *Lawrence*. It was 14 November 1917, one week after the Russian Revolution. With Philby was Lt.-Col. Cunliffe-Owen, a senior Orientalist, and his Scottish batman, Private Schofield. The third senior member of the mission, Col. R. E. A. Hamilton, had already reached Riyadh overland from Kuwait. Like Shakespear they all wore khaki, riding boots and pith helmets.

They disembarked to find that nothing was ready. They had been expected two days earlier and all their camels had been sent back out to graze. When the baggage camels arrived, the Englishmen were so impatient that they set off before their *deluls* had been rounded up. It was a very uncomfortable ride. The caravan, carrying rifles, food, water, mapping equipment, cameras, cypher boxes and ten thousand pounds in gold, climbed one monotonous ridge after another, following the beaten track to Hufuf.

There, on his first day in Arabia, Harry St John Philby got his first taste of the desert and its people. A natural extrovert, he excelled in a community where privacy and social distance were unthinkable and unmentionable, and loved talking at the Bedouin around the camp fire, identifying different tribes, detecting truth from falsehood, exchanging pipes and prejudices. Above all he loved eating with them in the democracy of the jostling circle around the steaming dish, scooping up rice, mutton and butter in his right fingers and neatly flicking the ball into his mouth without letting his fingers touch his lips, pontificating between mouthfuls.

Above: The vast expanse of the Empty Quarter. This photograph of a lava plain at Harrat el-Buqum, south of Jaruba, was taken by Philby on his first crossing.

The quieter, less conspicuous Cunliffe-Owen, seeing Schofield's embarrassment at eating with his fingers, stuck to bully beef with knives and forks, to keep him company. The unstoppable Philby hardly noticed the eminent Orientalist. He had an attractive habit of treating eminent Orientalists very much as they treated townspeople – as if they did not exist. ('I didn't hear what you said but I disagree with you,' he said to one a few months later.) Indeed, there were times in the empty wastes of Arabia when nobody appeared to exist at all – except Harry St John Philby.

Next day, after crossing high 'sand billows' and following the dried-up course of the Wadi Shatar, they reached the palm waves of Hasa. A day later they came into Hufuf. Philby was hardly the first to get there, (Sadlier, Palgrave and Leachman had been there before), but he was undoubtedly the loudest. The city had been taken by ibn Saud from the Turks in 1913, and its population of thirty thousand made it the largest city in his domains. Its wealth lay in its water and springs, and Philby visited the same hot springs that Palgrave had stopped at half a century earlier.

> It is one of the beauty spots of the Province, and much resorted to by both sexes for bathing, the ladies being relegated by custom to the southern extremity of the lake where high reeds and the shade of a palm-grove provided some approach to privacy.[5]

He was equally pleased with Hufuf's mosque 'whose great dome and graceful minaret, blending the salient features of Byzantine and Saracen architecture, contribute to make it without exception the most beautiful building in all central and eastern Arabia.' Cunliffe-Owen, who made no claims to local architectural expertise after a mere three days in the country, was less pleased with the town's arsenal. Of the four machine-guns the British had given to ibn Saud, he found three of them still in their packing cases. As for the four Saudis who had been trained by the British to use the guns, three were dead and the fourth had forgotten everything he had been taught.

They left two days later, accompanied (to Philby's utter delight) by a demented dervish on his way to Mecca. The governor of Hufuf had insisted they wear Arab clothes. Convinced that they would suffer sunstroke if they abandoned their pith helmets, they compromised, cutting off the Prussian balconies of the helmets and wearing them under their Arab headdresses. Philby loved the long following robes that gave him the appearance of a minor prophet; Cunliffe-Owen was quite plainly embarrassed; while poor Schofield, 'for all his willing efforts, never came within measurable distance of looking like an Arab'.

Their first challenge was the Dahna Desert. For Philby it was no challenge. 'The terrors of this barrier of sand have been grossly exaggerated.' Beyond the Dahna lay ridge upon ridge of sand and stone, and beyond the ridges was a great chasm. They descended the escarpment on foot and remounted their camels at the bottom. They were on the Turabi Plain. 'Here was grass, green grass, in plenty and scattered bushes of stunted acacia.' Their first sign of life was a solitary gazelle.

Five days out of Hufuf they arrived in Riyadh. Their camels strained up towards a line of pointed hillocks and from the summit they looked out over the folds of the grey valley to the emerald green gardens of the Wahhabi city beyond, the clay towers of its walls showing dimly through the screen of palms. Three horsemen galloped through the gates to welcome them. One was Ibrahim ibn Jurraia, Master of Ceremonies and Captain of the Guard. Philby took an intense dislike to him, which was unfortunate since Ibrahim was to be his constant companion throughout his stay in Arabia. They were too alike to tolerate each other: both insisted on monopolizing attention and conversation, both regarded themselves as expert on everything from military strategy to pressure lamps, and both were convinced that they were invariably in the right. It was a stormy relationship and the dislike was mutual.

Ibrahim led them to the edge of the belt of palm trees surrounding the city and waited; it was Friday and the gates had been closed for prayers. After a few minutes the gates opened and they rode into Riyadh. They continued into the city centre where the crowds were pouring out of the mosque. Ibrahim took them to the palace where they dismounted, stretched, wiped the flies and sweat off their faces, and were led down a corridor to the royal apartments. They were received by an old man, ibn Saud's father, who, as senior member of the family, greeted them. He was no stranger at playing host to Europeans; he remembered Pelly's visit in 1865.

As Philby talked he became aware of another presence, a tall and upright figure in white robes, with a kind and manly face, standing apart. It was ibn Saud. At that first meeting, Philby was completely taken by the man, and already knew that he would hitch his own to this man's star, come what may.

Right: *Detail from 'Descent to the Valley of Jordan', by David Roberts.*

In between audiences with ibn Saud Philby wandered around the town, correcting Palgrave's description of the city, 'in all modesty and without any personal claim to infallibility', on the way. The buildings were made of mud brick, with the palace, which took up about a quarter of the area of the city, in the centre. In front of the palace, in the wide square that ibn Saud had rushed across to kill the Rashidi governor, was the *suk*, selling leatherwork, saddles, tea and coffee, sugar, spices, rifles, ammunition and field binoculars, and several flocks of sheep. On the other side of the *suk* was the mosque, typical of 'Wahhabi architecture and of considerable merit', judged Philby.

Altogether Philby estimated that he spent a quarter of his time in Riyadh in audiences with ibn Saud. The stumbling block was Britain's support for the Hashemite cause. Ibn Saud constantly pointed out the vast sums of gold and crates of arms being sent to the Hejaz in contrast to the pittance and out-dated Winchesters being sent to him, and voiced his fear that the Sherif would use those weapons against him after the War. In vain did Cunliffe-Owen argue that the Sherif was taking an active part in the fighting and that Britain was getting her money's worth; in vain did he remind ibn Saud of the unopened crates of machine guns in Hufuf. Philby, having hitched his star, was already taking ibn Saud's side, ridiculing Cunliffe-Owen's explanations.

On one occasion ibn Saud visited them in their apartments. He arrived so unexpectedly that Philby and Cunliffe-Owen hardly had time to put out their pipes and hide their tobacco tins. Ibn Saud had far too much respect for the laws of hospitality to object while he was there, but after he left he sent a slave round to fumigate the room with incense.

What particularly irritated ibn Saud was the Sherif's refusal to allow the Storrs Mission through the Hejaz. He saw it as a deliberate attempt to minimize Saudi claims to control central Arabia. Philby had a suggestion: 'There is only one way of ensuring that Mr. Storrs shall come; let me go with an escort from you to Taif to bring him back with me.' It would mean an east to west crossing of the Peninsula. No one had done it since Sadlier, and it would be irrefutable proof of ibn Saud's claim to control central Arabia. 'I should confess, perhaps, that my motives in making that proposal were of a mixed character, and not wholly based on the actual requirements of the situation, but that is a trifle and I have never regretted my action.'

Left: *Shakespear's* rafiks *take a coffee break in the desert.*

Right: *Shakespear's photograph of the* suk *at Riyadh looking west, with the sea of palm trees skirting the city in the background.*

Hamilton had already left for Kuwait, driven mad by Philby's manic tactlessness and exuberance. Cunliffe-Owen and Schofield soon followed him. Philby sent a message to his masters in Kuwait and left Riyadh before they had a chance to reply. 'Henceforth in all my wanderings in Arabia I was alone.'

He left on 9 December, alone but for a mere thirty-man escort headed by Ibrahim. He had not only adopted Arab dress, he had abandoned everything European except for his surveying equipment, rifle, brandy bottle, lime juice bottle, quinine tablets and tobacco. When he reached the coast, the surveying equipment and rifle were still in perfect condition, the brandy bottle was one dose short, the lime bottle unopened, and the quinine almost untouched. 'Only the tobacco was seriously depleted, and that not wholly by myself.'

They were travelling west, on the old Haj route to Mecca, the same that Sadlier had taken for the earlier part of his journey. Ten miles out of Riyadh they passed Diriyyah, still a ruin after its destruction by Ibrahim Pasha. From there, the way led through alternate stretches of sand, gravel and loam in a defile defined by hundred-foot high cliffs. At the end of the defile was a ruined village, an echo of Diriyyah, half covered in sand. They continued through the chaotic jumble of rocks and ridges that surrounds Riyadh, west-south-west into the Nafud and across wave after wave of undulating sand dunes. The ground was firm. it was pouring with rain. Beyond the sand dunes they saw herds of gazelle. They were on an open plain. In the middle of it, astride the Pilgrim Road, lay the buildings and plantations of Quwayiyah and Mizul, 'a charming vision of green fertility in the midst of desolation.'

Their next stop was Qusariyah, the last watering place before Khurmah, two hundred miles and seven days away. They made an early start. It was 17 December. They dropped into a broad bushy depression teeming with game, then climbed up onto the Sira plain, a strip of black gravel, and into the craggy upheavals of the central Arabian highlands. These covered ten thousand square miles and took five days to cross. Philby never forgot it; the landscape left him with 'memories which words cannot describe nor time efface'.

Above: *Looking east from Wadi Nu'man near Shaddah village in the Hejaz. The photograph was taken by Philby on his journey across Arabia in 1930.*

Beyond the highlands lay Subai country, where they saw their first evidence of life since Qusariyah: sheep's droppings. They sat around their camp fire listening to the howl of wolves in the night. Next morning, heading westwards, they saw three riders in the distance. Philby scanned the horizon with his binoculars. The three rode on. Thinking they might be the scouts of a larger raiding party, he was all for pressing on. Ibrahim, to Philby's intense irritation, was for more thoughtful action.

'Let us leave our mark behind us and halt for breakfast.'

One of the escort dismounted and drew in the sand with a stick the brands of ibn Saud, the Sherif and the tribes from which the escort came.

'But if that is sufficient,' Philby asked Ibrahim, 'what is there to prevent any party of travellers, whether accompanied by *rafiqs*, or not, from proclaiming a false identity to elude pursuit, or a gang of raiders doing the same to lure the unwary into ambush?'

'Such a thing is never done.'

They continued through sand dunes, Philby riding with four of the escort ahead, the main party behind. Suddenly they were staring into the barrels of a dozen rifles. They had walked straight into an ambush, their rifles still hanging from their saddle-frames. There was nothing to do but raise their arms and feel very foolish. The rest of the party rode up, and there was much shouting and arguing. Sa'd, one of the escort, discreetly drew Philby away so none of the ambushers realized that they had captured a Nasrani.

The men turned out to be merchants from Shaqr in the Nejd, on their way back from Khurmah, who thought Philby's escort were raiders and decided to pre-empt their attack. The two caravans camped side by side that night and went their opposite way the next morning. Philby's thirty trekked on eastward. They were getting tired. It was six days since they had had fresh water, and all they had eaten was rice and dates. Philby's own camel had gone lame. They came into Khurmah next day, a seedy oasis of mud-bricked houses with outbursts of palm trees around.

Khurmah was disputed territory. Its governor, appointed by the Sherif of Mecca, had become a Wahhabi convert and Khurmah was in the process of changing its political allegiance. Any other diplomat on a mission like his would have winced at the idea of passing through Khurmah, but Philby, though many things, was never a diplomat. He drove his camel through Wahhabi and Hashemite sensitivities like Burton driving his coach and four through the flowerbeds of his Oxford college.

They left Khurmah and its troubles behind them. The worst stretch was over, but there were now new fears. They were in no-man's-land between

Hashemite and Wahhabi Arabia, where no Emir ruled. They strained their eyes searching for raiders. One night they thought they had ridden right in to the middle of some. 'Hundreds of them!' the scouts exclaimed. They took their rifles from their saddles, drew back the bolts and waited. Nothing happened. They cautiously advanced. It was a herd of camels moving to new grazing. 'The tracks of baby camels and of a few horses mingled with the heavier marks of the ponderous milch cattle,' wrote Philby. 'Their story was written on the plain for all to read who passed that way.'

On Christmas Day Philby entered Taif in triumph. No one was there to greet him. It did not matter; no one knew who he was. They soon would. He had proved them all wrong. He had proved that ibn Saud controlled most of central Arabia, and that a man could travel from one side of Arabia to the other with ibn Saud's passport. Sherif Hussain, when he learnt of Philby's arrival, was furious, but Philby did not care. 'It's not often one gets the chance that I have had of making a fool of a king.' When he got to Cairo and proved all the Orientalist establishment supporting the Sherif wrong, his triumph knew no bounds. 'The only difference between me and Lawrence,' he later roared, 'was that I was right.'

'Get your facts right,' Philby once advised his son Kim, 'then always go through to the end with whatever you think right.' Father – like son – did just exactly that.

He returned to Arabia in 1918 to coordinate ibn Saud's hoped-for campaign against ibn Rashid. The Saudi, remembering Shakespear, refused to have another Nasrani die fighting for him, and insisted that Philby leave the Wahhabi army for the duration of the campaign. He went off happily to explore the Wadi Awasir, near the oasis of Sulayyil, on the edge of the Rub el-Khali, the Empty Quarter, the vast stretch of unknown sands taking up most of the southern part of the Peninsula. He returned to Kuwait, after being the first European to visit the Wahhabi stronghold of Sulayyil, only to discover that neither his nor ibn Saud's services were required any longer. The War was almost over and the British now wanted to retain the northern state of Hail as a buffer between ibn Saud and the Sherif. Philby recognized the aim immediately. It was the same old policy of 'a weak and disunited Arabia, split into little principalities', a subtle betrayal of the British promise to the Arabs of genuine independence.

Right: *'The Wilderness of Engedi'*, by David Roberts.

Philby moved to Mesopotamia, now occupied by the British, where he worked under Gertrude Bell. He resigned after three years in protest at Britain foisting the Sherif's son Faisal on the throne, as a consolation prize for being thrown out of Syria by the French. The British justification for their action was that Britain had promised kingdoms and not republics when they made their promises to the Arabs, and they had kept their promises. It was another cynical betrayal by Britain, and squashed Philby's hopes for the radical Arab republic (with himself as Chief Political Adviser) that he dreamed of. Instead he found himself Chief Political Adviser to another of the Sherif's despised sons, Abdallah, for whom the British had created the kingdom of Trans-Jordan. With him was a young assistant, Bertram Thomas, a quiet and serious man, the very antithesis of Philby. Since Philby regarded the very existence of this Ruritanian kingdom as another betrayal of Britain's promise, the job could hardly last. In 1925 he was unemployed.

Philby marked time, but ibn Saud did not. He took Hail in 1921 after another bout of Rashidi fratricide and moved his army towards the Hejaz. Every respectable ruler indulging in conquests needs a fig leaf. Ibn Saud's was the disputed oasis of Khurmah which Philby had ridden through so tactlessly in 1917.

The Hejaz was hardly in a position to resist. Its ruler, Hussain, was quietly going mad. The state had degenerated into despotism, the urban middle-classes and embryo proletariat in Jeddah were restless, while the Bedouin army that had helped to defeat the Turks, without pay, arms or discipline, was withering away. 'Imagine,' reported the British consul in Jeddah, 'a cunning, lying, credulous, suspicious, obstinate, vain, conceited, ignorant, greedy, cruel, Arab sheikh suddenly thrust into a position where he has to deal with all sorts of questions he doesn't understand and where there is no power to restrain him, and you have a picture of King Hussain.'

In 1924 the Saudi forces swept into Taif, where the fanatical *Ikhwan* slaughtered the inhabitants. Mecca panicked, but when the Wahhabis captured it ibn Saud ensured that there was no repetition of the Taif massacre; in consolation the *Ikhwan* were permitted to make a bonfire of a thousand hookahs. The Sherif fled to Jeddah, only to find he had walked straight into the middle of a revolution and was forced to abdicate. A Constitutional Democratic Government of the Hejaz was proclaimed, but the infant state was too weak to survive the relentless Wahhabi pressure. The army commander-in-chief, a former physical training instructor in the

Left: *Jeddah, the pilgrim port on the Red Sea, where the streets 'kept their air from year's end to year's end.' (T. E. Lawrence)*

Above: *The road from Taif to Mecca, taken by Philby.*

Turkish Navy, ordered barbed wire to be strung, arms to be distributed and trenches to be dug. There was no barbed wire, the rifles were useless and the trenches were never dug because manual labour is something that only slaves do, and since all slaves were liberated there was no one left to do it. Searching the Treasury, the Chancellor of the Exchequer discovered that Hussain had gone off into exile with eight hundred thousand pounds in gold sovereigns; the state's coffers were empty. To keep the Air Force in the sky the Ministry of War was obliged to pay its White Russian pilots a bottle of whisky and a five pound bonus every time they brought their planes down without damage.

Philby, watching the scene from Trans-Jordan, was in a dilemma. The Hejaz state, though not a republic (Hussain's son, Ali, was the constitutional head), appealed to his democratic sensibilities. The fact that it was treated with disapproval by His Majesty's Government could only be to its credit. Ibn Saud, on the other hand, was an absolute monarch. Philby had no difficulty squaring this, by putting himself in the middle of the square. He would mediate between the two sides and out of his mediation would emerge a radical Arab state, thoroughly anti-imperialist and pro-Philby, with ibn Saud as its constitutional monarch. The Hejazians, clutching at straws, welcomed him; the British told him to mind his own business or risk his pension; and ibn Saud listened, then attacked and took Jeddah without any further ado.

Philby was not disillusioned. His hero now controlled almost all Arabia; the Hejaz misunderstanding was another mere trifle in the great Philby scheme of things. He would 'go through to the end'. He moved to Arabia. 'You have always done what you want, in spite of all the governments in the world *and* me,' his long-suffering wife, Dora, wrote to him.

From his gigantic and baroque half-timber palace in Jeddah, the *Bait Baghdadi*, he set up an import agency, *Sharqieh*. Almost everything modern that came into Arabia in the late twenties and early thirties – radios, Ford motor cars, washing machines, even fire engines – mostly things that he later objected to, passed through his hands. From here Philby advised ibn Saud, warned about the designs of perfidious Albion, listened hunched over the radio to cricket Test Match commentaries, dashed off every *Times* crossword he could lay his hands on, and met – and frequently quarrelled with – every foreigner in Jeddah. In between politics, *Sharqieh* and bed he found time to become a Moslem convert and complete the Haj, though he continued to see mosques as he had previously seen churches, as places of essentially architectural interest.

The British despaired. 'Philby was in his most heroic Prometheus mood,' read one report; 'to his desire to bring the light of science to mankind, is now added a quite ferocious intention to expose the alleged duplicity of HMG towards the Arabs of the Peninsula.'

Crusades, commerce and conversions were not enough for Philby. He wanted to secure immortality by the accomplishment of some great work. The great work was to be the Empty Quarter, the last large totally unexplored region left in the world, which he had glimpsed in 1918. He had wanted to go in 1931, but there was fighting on the borders with the Yemen, where ibn Saud was extending Saudi Arabia's frontiers to their furthest limit and it was a year before ibn Saud gave his permission to go. The delay robbed him of a First. That year Bertram Thomas, Philby's quiet and serious assistant in Jordan, made the first crossing of the Empty Quarter from south to north, leaving Salalah on the southern coast and arriving at Doha on the Arabian Gulf.

Above: Bertram Thomas on the first crossing of the Empty Quarter, 1931.

Thomas had gone from Trans-Jordan to Muscat, from where he had made numerous excursions to the edge of the Empty Quarter, winning the confidence of the Bait Kathir and Rashidi (no relation to the Rashidis of Hail) Bedouins by accepting their standards and their way of life.

He arrived at Salalah in Dhofar in an Arab dhow only to find that his way was barred by tribal war. He spent a month in the mountains, and was about to return to Muscat and abandon the attempt when his Rashidi guides arrived. He told their leader, Salih bin Kanut, of his plans to cross the Quarter. Salih, a swarthy man with frank and open countenance and a reputation as a fearless warrior, demurred. The centre of the 'Sands', as the Bedouin called the Empty Quarter, was uninhabitable and almost impenetrable. There were only the Rashidi in the south and the Murra in the north.

'You don't understand. What you are asking is not in my power to do. Within Rashid teritory I can, and will, take you where you wish, God sparing us from the enemy, but where you want to go is Murra territory. I am no *rabia* for the Murra, and dare not enter their marches myself without their consent and protection.' In the end he agreed to take Thomas with his men as far as the Murra, where he could negotiate a new passage for the second part of the crossing.

Right: Sand dunes in the Empty Quarter, as seen by Thomas.

Thomas left on 10 December 1930 with an escort of forty. His Rashidi companions asked him why he wanted to travel in such a god-forsaken place. He replied that he liked travelling, and that in his tribe, the Inglezis, the pursuit of 'ilm (science) was regarded as highly as war among the Rashidi. His first day out took him past frankincense trees. They had no central trunks and gave the appearance of branches springing straight from the ground. The incense collectors made incisions in the branches like rubber collectors, which exuded resinous tears. These were collected after ten days and dried before being exported to India.

He could be marvellously English at times. 'Fighting is all very well when the time comes,' he lectured one Rashidi, 'but how do you think we English became strong if it was not by work? How do you think we get our ships and our rifles?'

'Money', the Bedouin laconically replied.

Yet he was never laughable. What distinguished him from the stereotype Englishman was his ability to adapt not only to the Bedouin's ways, but to his sense of time (measuring the days by a camel's grazing) and his sense of fatalism. 'The desert holds a philosophy of the inevitability of events . . . . In the acceptance of destiny is comfort.'

He came across oryx, gazelle, fox, wild cat, badger, hedgehog, snake, scorpion and lizard; watched his escort smoke a 'green local leaf' through a used .303 cartridge case, each inhaling the fumes until 'his eyes rolled and his body swayed'; and compared the shape of a sand dune to the 'exquisite roundness of a girl's breast.'

Rashidi society, to the twentieth-century travellers, was egalitarian. Its members were unimpressed by Nasranis (whom they thought were a tribe from Aden) and pith helmets (Thomas always wore Bedouin clothes). They judged a man by their own high standards. Thomas, with his quietness and unobtrusiveness, passed that judgement.

At Shanna in January 1931, one-third of the way across, he changed escort to the Murra, reducing its number to thirteen (a lucky number in the Arab world). Their leader, Hamud, was dark and hawk-like. He had sharp eyes and an ironic grin. The veteran of many a blood feud, he was a marked man, and each night, when the caravan stopped, he slunk back over its tracks for a few miles to make sure they were not being followed. Raiders were his principle fear – after grazing and water – and as the caravan passed each hill or dune Hamud sent one of the escort to picket it until the caravan had passed by. It was a hard journey. There was neither water nor grazing. The landscape was utterly desolate, 'a hungry void and an abode of death to whoever should loiter there.'

After nearly three weeks through the central sands, over range after range of dunes, they arrived at Buraidan. They had crossed the worst. The thirsty and exhausted caravan straggled to the well. First to arrive were Hamud and Thomas. They waited until the others came up.

> It was their code after a thirsty day's march that when we arrived at a water-hole no drop should pass the lips of the advance party until those in the rear had come up, nor would any man eat a crust with me on the march unless his companions were to share it. If this precious condition of life produces savagery between enemies, it breeds none the less a fine humanity among friends.[6]

Four days later, on 2 February, he arrived at Doha on the Gulf.

'Damn and blast Thomas,' Philby wrote.

Thomas' route, as Philby never tired of pointing out, was the easiest one. Harry St John Philby was never one to take the easiest way. On Christmas Day 1931, with the permission of ibn Saud, he arrived at Hufuf to set out across the Empty Quarter. He left on 7 January 1932, first south-east to Salwah on the Gulf, then south-west to Jabrin. He had with him fourteen Bedouin, thirty-two camels, and three months' provisions. He was going well to the west of Thomas's route. Like Thomas, he encountered the 'singing sands' caused by the friction of millions of particles of shifting sands and sounding like a 'boom or drone with a sound not unlike that of a siren or perhaps an aeroplane engine – quite a musical pleasing rhythmic sound of astonishing depth.'

They continued zig-zagging south to Naifa, in the heart of the Empty Quarter, and from there they struggled on to Shanna, where Thomas had changed escorts. Philby's escort refused to go any further into the unknown. He rode west towards Sulayyil, but again his escort refused to continue without water. He was forced to return to Naifa again before continuing to Sulayyil. Over three hundred and fifty miles without water lay ahead. They were on a flat and featureless plain of gravel, the *Abu Bahr* (Father of the Sea). Only one of the escort had crossed it, and he had done that far to the north. Nothing grew and no one knew how far it extended. They started across it on 5 March, pouring dribbles of water down the camel's nostrils to keep them going, and rode day and night. By the time they reached Sulayyil they had travelled two hundred and fifty miles in six days. They had had no food for forty-eight hours and there were only three waterskins left. From Sulayyil, which Philby had passed through in 1918, he went on with his escort westwards until he arrived at Mecca in April. 'I think that I have done with desert exploration for good,' he wrote when it was over. 'It is hard work on short rations of dates and raw dried camel's meat. The skin on my hands is burnt through to the quick.'

Thomas's and Philby's journey's had opened up merely a fraction of the Empty Quarter; there were still tens of thousands of miles unknown and untouched. The man who crossed them, Wilfred Thesiger, was of a different generation to Philby. He belonged to the same generation as Philby's son Kim, who was at Cambridge while Thesiger won a Boxing Blue at Oxford. Over six foot tall with a crag of a face and fair hair, he was no stranger to desert travel. While still at Oxford he had crossed the Danakil Desert to Djibouti, and after Oxford he had served in the Sudan Political Service and trekked through the Tibesti and Sudan Deserts. The War provided him with

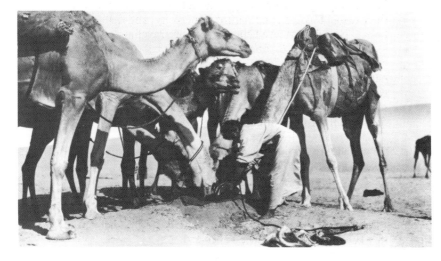

Left: *The last water hole before the Uraq el-Shaiba and Bani Maradh dunes in the heart of the Empty Quarter, photographed by Bertram Thomas.*

Right: *Thomas' camels resting and his* rafiks *praying with their faces turned towards Mecca, in the central Sands.*

more deserts in the Special Air Service in north Africa, but he travelled by jeep with other Englishmen, and felt isolated from both the desert and its people. In Addis Ababa after the War he was approached by O. B. Lean of the Middle East Locust Research Centre to go into the Empty Quarter, a suspected breeding-ground for locusts. 'The Empty Quarter offered me a chance to win distinction as a traveller; but I believed that it could give me more than this, that in those empty wastes I could find the peace that comes from solitude, and, among the Bedu, comradeship in a hostile world.'

In the years that followed he had only one disillusionment. Nomad encampments and caravan columns are about the noisiest and most crowded confined spaces on earth, as if by noise they can fill the surrounding void. To find solitude, Thesiger had to climb to the top of the nearest dune and lie down, a habit his Bedouin companions must have found quite extraordinary. It was impossible to be lonely in a community like that, and difficult even to be alone.

He made two journeys across the Empty Quarter. The first, with some twenty-four Bedouin, left Salalah, from where Bertram Thomas had set out, on 25 October 1946. Thesiger took with him two thousand pounds of flour, five hundred pounds of rice, clarified butter, coffee, tea, sugar, dates, a dozen .303 British Army rifles, a copy of Gibbon and *War and Peace*. Like Thomas's group they travelled at camel's pace, drifting with the terrain, not against it, and stopping wherever rare patches of grazing showed themselves. At Shisur, on the edge of the Empty Quarter, they were joined by some Rashidi who had travelled with Thomas.

> He was the first European to come among them and he won their respect by his good nature, generosity, and determination. They remembered him as a good travelling companion. When I went among these exclusive tribesmen sixteen years after he had left them, I was welcomed because I belonged to the same tribe as Thomas. I had only met him twice, in Cairo during the war, and then only for a few minutes. I should have liked to meet him again before he died to tell him how much I owed to him.[7]

For the actual crossing Thesiger reduced his party to twelve. Their destination was the Liwa Oases four hundred miles away. By the Wells of Mughshin seven of the twelve had abandoned him, leaving him with only five. He gave each a .303 rifle for their loyalty. They meandered northwards through brick-red dunes, ash-white gypsum flats and plains of gravel. He was a silent companion and in the endless hours of Bedouin chatter (the kind of thing Philby relished) he rarely uttered a word.

Left: *Sultan, a sheikh of the Bait Kathir, whose tribesmen refused to continue across the Empty Quarter, photographed by Wilfred Thesiger.*

The crossing of the Uruq el-Shaiba dunes was the hardest portion of the voyage. They had to lead their camels along crumbling knife-edge crests by foot. Range upon range of dunes stretched from horizon to horizon. 'Somewhere in the ultimate distance the sands merged into the sky, but in that infinity of space I could see no living thing, not even a withered plant, to give me hope.' Beyond the dunes a hare jumped out of a thicket. They had reached the other side of the Empty Quarter and were back among living things. A few days later they were at Liwa, from where they returned to Salalah by a semi-circular route along the edge of Oman.

He made his second crossing a year later, from Saiwun in the Hadramaut, north to Sulayyil, then east to Abu Dhabi on the Gulf. He spent the first fortnight waiting for his Rashidi companions, exploring the Hadramaut valleys with the Saar, the 'wolves of the desert'. Most southern Arabians feared them; Thesiger liked them. They had heard of his journey the year before and treated him like an old friend, but he found the terrain imprisoning. After two weeks his old Rashidi escort arrived by plane.

'When I got into the aeroplane the Christians tried to tie me with a rope. I would not let them,' said one of the Rashidis. Did he like flying? Yes, though when it grew dark he was frightened the pilot was going to lose his way.

They left on 17 December 1947 amid tribal wars and rumours of wars. It was unknown country to the Rashidis, and they could not find a guide. Ahead of them was a dune range of four hundred miles. Sixteen waterless days. Thesiger asked them if they could do it.

'We live in the Sands. We can take you across without a guide.'

Two hours after their departure from Minwakh, the last well before the emptiness, the Rashidis pointed to the tracks of five camels. They asked Thesiger to judge from the tracks which was the best. He pointed at random. They laughed. It was the weakest.

The world was cold and grey, and the wind came and went. The days repeated themselves. They started at dawn and walked for the first two hours,

Right: *A Bedouin of the Sands, photographed by Thesiger on his first crossing.*

then stretched their feet up onto the camel's bent neck and were lifted onto the saddles. As the day went on they alternated between walking and riding, varying their positions on the saddle from astride to side-saddle to kneeling. Whenever they saw the slightest protrusion of green they stopped for their camels to graze. Often they were hungry, and usually they were thirsty, for their pace was determined by grazing, not water. One day they came across the tracks of a pelican which had waddled in a straight line right across their path. At night they sheltered in the hollow valleys of dunes to protect themselves from wind and raiders.

Half way across they encountered the Bani Maradh dunes, as terrible as the Uruq el-Shaiba that they had crossed the year before. The dunes rose to four hundred feet, their colour golden red. Beyond the dunes lay Sulayyil, one of the last untouched *Ikhwan* communities in Arabia, where the Wahhabi elders spat on the ground as they walked past, the children chanted that ibn Saud would behead the Nasrani and the local governor locked him up in a castle.

He was saved by the omnipresent and omniscient Philby who, hearing of his fate, persuaded ibn Saud to release him and his escort and let them continue their journey, then motored down to Laila, their next stop, to see them on their way.

Thesiger and his party left Sulayyil on 29 January 1948 for Abu Dhabi, seven hundred and sixty miles away, twice the distance they had gone so far. The camels were still tired and the governor of Sulayyil had warned them that there was no grazing until Laila, one hundred and sixty miles away. It took a week to get there, where they found Philby cursing a broken axle and chattering about how he had interceded on Thesiger's behalf in Riyadh.

> I tried to put in a word for you but he wouldn't even let me open my mouth. I was worried what might happen to you and decided the best thing to do was to write him a letter. I gave it to him in the morning, saying as I did so that it was a man's duty to intercede for his friends. He was quite different from the night before; said at once that he would send off an order for your release.[8]

Laila was another *Ikhwan* stronghold. The governor was churlish and the local shopkeepers only accepted Thesigner's money after it had been publicly washed. He complained to Philby, who quickly put him in his place. Was it not their very adherence to their principles in a changing and superficial world, that made these people so attractive to the likes of Thesiger and Philby? Thesiger agreed. He recognized that these people realized their world was being destroyed by the twentieth century, which they saw as the 'Nasrani century'. They were not to know how little Thesiger himself sympathized with that century.

It took eight hot, hungry and thirsty days to reach Jabrin, on the northern edge of the Dahna Desert. Rain had fallen and the red dunes bloomed with green seedlings. On the eighth day they climbed the final ridge of sand and saw the bold green brush-strokes of Jabrin against the sandy plain below. They were half way.

They rode on across salt flats towards the well of Dhiby. No one had approached it from a western direction and they were without a guide, but it was marked on Thomas' map and both the Rashidi and Thesiger had confidence in Thomas. It was burning hot. The exhausted camels suffered from diarrhoea and their tails had to be tied to the saddles. Eight days out of Jabrin they reached the waters of Dhiby. The camels gulped greedily, the humans abstained. It was too brackish to drink.

Next day they crossed the Sabkhat Mutti salt-flats. The pan was covered in a salty crust that reflected the glare of the sun and crumbled with every camel's footfall. It took five hours to cross. Beyond were miles of barren silver-blue sand. Almost out of water they decided that their only course was to strike out east for Liwa where they had been the year before. It was a gamble. If they missed it they would be going straight back into the Empty Quarter. Another range of dunes, and then, on 28 February, one of the escort climbed to the summit of the last dune and shouted: 'I can see the sands of Liwa!' The last stage to Abu Dhabi, one hundred and fifty miles, was easy. The Empty Quarter had been unveiled. It was Thesiger's greatest moment.

The crossing of the Empty Quarter had been Philby's greatest moment, too. He continued his explorations, but by car, with a radio so he could follow the cricket commentaries. His lifelong battle against the forces of darkness, represented by the Foreign Office, continued as well, with Philby ensuring that most Saudi oil concessions went to American rather than British firms, on the mistaken assumption that Americans would be less imperialist.

The battle reached its highest point in 1937. Philby, who had come by car from the north, had been sent by ibn Saud to demarcate the new frontier with Yemen. The frontier lay astride the old Incense Road (one of the last unknown corners of Arabia), which continued right into the British territory of the Aden Protectorates. With a predictable disregard for other people's boundaries, Philby happily crossed the line in search of the mythical oases of Shabwa and Tarim. His car broke an axle and he had to go down to Mukalla on the coast. His arrival, with a seven-man Saudi escort, panicked the British into thinking ibn Saud had annexed the territory. The British were furious and ordered him out. 'Leaving today for advance GHQ to superintend evacuation of occupied territory,' he quipped back. It was another Philby triumph; he had outwitted everyone and made the first complete north-south crossing of the Peninsula. 'I could think of no better reward than the impotent rage of Aden.' The British in Aden were not the only ones suffering from impotent rage. In Jeddah the French seethed as the British Philby scored another First.

But for Harry St John Philby it was no First. He was rapidly becoming irrelevant to the world he lived in. Arabia had changed from a collection of Bedouin principalities to an oil-rich state run by men wearing 'spring-sided boots'. The eccentric Philby was only tolerated because of ibn Saud's loyalty to his old friend. When war came in 1939, Philby, convinced that he was Britain's only suitable warleader – and that the British were fools not to recognize it – was so damning in his criticism that his articles were reprinted in Mussolini's Nazi paper *Centro Tedesco d'Informazione*. When Philby arrived on British territory he was interned. He was put into a camp in the grounds of Bertram Mills' Circus at Ascot and spent his time reading philosophy, playing bridge and lecturing his captive audience of pacifists, fascists and bemused foreigners on anything and everything he wanted.

He appeared before an Appeals Tribunal made up of a diplomat, a barrister and a well-known cricketer. It was the usual confrontation. The forces of evil, to whit His Majesty's Government, argued that Philby had told ibn Saud that Britain was not a democracy. The forces of good, Harry St John Philby, proudly confirmed this, stating that there was no better way of securing the support of an absolute ruler than by being undemocratic. To the chagrin of the British Foreign Office Philby was released. It was the last of the great confrontations. The Foreign Office gave up on Philby and never tried to silence him again; some of them even began to like him in a patronizing sort of way. Age and the changing world had rendered him harmless.

Right: *Bin Anauf, a fifteen-year-old Bedouin boy of the Bait Kathir, photographed by Wilfred Thesiger.*

The passing years have pulled down, one by one, to their graves all the protagonists of that great struggle for Arabian hegemony – Hussain and Ali, Feisal and Lawrence, Gertrude Bell . . . Lord Curzon and Edwin Montagu, and many others of lesser calibre – leaving only ibn Saud and me, still alive together after nearly thirty years, to savour our triumph and to talk of 'long-remembered far-off things and battles long ago'.[9]

A few more journeys lay ahead, searching for pre-Islamic Arabia in Asir and the north, and leading a mining survey of Midian, where Richard Burton had searched for gold; but his active days were over. So too were ibn Saud's who, to Philby's disgust, had taken to a wheelchair, a present from President Roosevelt. He was in his seventies and dying. When the doctors prescribed a blood transfusion he whispered: 'Give me some of Philby's. He's never ill.' He died in 1953.

Philby continued until 1960, though part of him died with the man he had loved. He became more and more alienated from the petro-dollar society he saw growing up around him, and was disillusioned by the corruption, waste and materialism that he himself had introduced into Arabia with the *Sharqieh* agency and American oil companies. He moved to Beirut where his son Kim wrote for *The Observer* and *Economist*, and died there on 30 September. His last words were: 'God, I'm bored.'

GLOSSARY

Abba	cloak
Beyt	house
Caique	Greek sailing ship
Caravanserai	fortified inn where caravans sheltered overnight
Dakilah	protection
Delul	female dromedary or riding camel
Dey	Turkish governor
Dhow	Arab sailing vessel
Djinns	Spirits of the underworld
Dowla	Ottoman government or its local representative
Emir	king
fettoua	religious edict
Franji, Farrangi	European (from the 'Frank' of the Crusades)
Ghazu	raid
Grand Vizier	Prime Minister
Haj	the annual pilgrimage to Mecca which every Moslem should complete at least once
Haji	a Moslem who has completed the pilgrimage
Hakim	doctor
Ihram	pilgrim costume
Ikhwan	fanatical Wahhabi military elite, based on military-agricultural communes in the oasis of Nejd
Imam	religious leader (Islam has no priesthood), also used as title by the ruler of Yemen
Jibbeh, Jelaba	Arab coat
Kadi	judge
Kafir	unbeliever
Kella	fortified guardhouse over waterhole
Ksar	small castle
Kahwah	reception or coffee room
Kefiyeh	headdress
Mamelukes	Ottoman military caste, originating in south Russia
Meddeyyi	Wahhabi guardians (religious policemen)
Nasrani	Christian
Narghile	waterpipe or hookah
Pasha	Turkish governor, also used as a title
Rafik	travelling companion
Riyals	Arabian currency; same value as the Spanish or Marie Teresa dollar
Sambuk	small Arab sailing ship
Say	very small Arab sailing ship
Shiite	Moslem sect, strong in Iraq and Persia, followers of the reformer Ali, and awaiting the Twelfth Imam, the Expected One
Suk	market
Sunni	majority orthodox sect in Islam
Sublime Porte	Ottoman government in Constantinople

SOURCES

I The Early Travellers
[1] p. 17 Varthema, Ludovico di, *Itinerario de Ludovico di Varthema*, Rome, 1510, printed in England in Hakluyt's *Voyages*, London, 1863
[2] p. 18 ibid.
[3] p. 21 ibid.
[4] p. 22 Le Blanc, Vincent, *The World Surveyed*, London, 1660
[5] p. 25 Pitts, Joseph, *A true and faithful Account of the religion and manners of the Muhammadans*, Exeter, 1704
[6] p. 26 ibid.

II The Pioneers
[1] p. 31 Gibbon, Edward, *The Decline and Fall of the Roman Empire*, Oxford, 1828
[2] p. 33 Niebuhr, Carsten, *Reisebeschreibung nach Arabien und andern umliegenden Laendern*, Copenhagen, 1772
[3] p. 38 Hansen, Thorkild, *Arabia Felix*, Gregg International, London, 1964

[4] p. 38 Niebuhr, Carsten, *Reisebeschreibung nach Arabien und andern umliegenden Laendern*, Copenhagen, 1772
[5] p. 39 ibid.
[6] p. 43 ibid.

III The First Romantics
[1] p. 52 Bey, Ali, *Travels of Ali al Abbassi, alias Domingo Badia y Lieblich of Cadiz between 1803 and 1807*, London, 1816
[2] p. 53 Turner, William, *A Journal of a Tour in the Levant*, London, 1820
[3] p. 54 ibid.
[4] p. 54 ibid.
[5] p. 55 ibid.
[6] p. 56 Seetzen, U. J., *Beiträge zur Geographie Arabiens*, in von Zach's Correspondence, Vol. XVIII, 1808
[7] p. 60 Burckhardt, J. L., *Travels in Arabia*, London, 1829
[8] p. 62 ibid.

[9] p. 62 British Library MSS 27620, No. 24, 6 July 1813
[10] p. 66 Burckhardt, J. L., *Travels in Arabia*, London, 1829
[11] p. 71 Sadlier, G. F., *Diary of a Journey Across Arabia*, Bombay, 1866

IV The Opportunists

[1] p. 74 Wellsted, J. R., *Travels in Arabia*, London, 1838
[2] p. 75 von Wrede, A., *Reise in Hadhramut*, Brunswick, 1870
[3] p. 83 Burton, Sir Richard, *Pilgrimage to Al-Medinah and Meccah*, London, 1855
[4] p. 84 ibid.
[5] p. 85 ibid.
[6] p. 86 ibid.
[7] p. 87 ibid.
[8] p. 88 ibid.
[9] p. 89 ibid.
[10] p. 91 ibid.
[11] p. 91 ibid.
[12] p. 92 von Maltzen, Freiherr H., *Reisen in Arabien*, Brunswick, 1873

V Agents of Foreign Powers

[1] p. 97 Wallin, G. A., 'Report on a Journey to Hail in the Nejd', *Journal of the Royal Geographical Society*, Vol. XXIV, London, 1854
[2] p. 100 Palgrave, W. G., *Personal Narrative of a Year's Journey Through Central and Eastern Arabia*, Macmillan Ltd, London, 1865
[3] p. 101 ibid.
[4] p. 102 ibid.
[5] p. 104 ibid.
[6] p. 105 ibid.
[7] p. 107 ibid.
[8] p. 107 ibid.
[9] p. 108 ibid.
[10] p. 109 ibid.
[11] p. 110 ibid.
[12] p. 111 ibid.
[13] p. 112 ibid.
[14] p. 115 ibid.
[15] p. 115 ibid.
[16] p. 116 ibid.
[17] p. 117 ibid.
[18] p. 117 ibid.
[19] p. 121 Guarmani, Carlo, *Northern Nejd: Journey From Jerusalem to Anaiza in Kasim*, Press of the Franciscan Fathers, Jerusalem, 1866
[20] p. 124 ibid.
[21] p. 124 ibid.
[22] p. 126 ibid.
[23] p. 129 Saldana, J. A., *Précis of Nejd Affairs, 1804-1904*, Indian Political and Secret Department, Persian Gulf Gazetteer, Simla, 1906

VI The Wanderer

[1] p. 134 Doughty, C. M., *Travels in Arabia Deserta*, Cambridge University Press, 1888

[2] p. 134 ibid.
[3] p. 134 ibid.
[4] p. 136 ibid.
[5] p. 138 ibid.
[6] p. 140 ibid.
[7] p. 147 ibid.
[8] p. 149 ibid.
[9] p. 151 ibid.
[10] p. 152 ibid.
[11] p. 154 ibid.
[12] p. 160 ibid.
[13] p. 162 ibid.

VII The Last Romantics

[1] p. 166 Blunt, Lady Anne, *Bedouin Tribes of the Euphrates*, London, 1879
[2] p. 167 Blunt, Lady Anne, *A Pilgrimage to Nejd*, John Murray Ltd, London, 1881
[3] p. 168 ibid.
[4] p. 169 ibid.
[5] p. 171 ibid.
[6] p. 174 ibid.
[7] p. 174 ibid.
[8] p. 176 ibid.
[9] p. 176 ibid.
[10] p. 177 ibid.
[11] p. 177 ibid.
[12] p. 178 ibid.
[13] p. 179 ibid.
[14] p. 179 ibid.
[15] p. 180 ibid.
[16] p. 181 ibid.
[17] p. 182 ibid.
[18] p. 182 ibid.
[19] p. 182 ibid.
[20] p. 183 ibid.
[21] p. 185 ibid.
[22] p. 186 ibid.

VIII The Twentieth-Century Travellers

[1] p. 196 Burgyne, Elizabeth (ed.), *Gertrude Bell, From Her Personal Papers*, Benn, London, 1958
[2] p. 197 *Political and Secret File (1905-1919)*, Persian Gulf, India Office Library
[3] p. 199 Lawrence, T. E., *Seven Pillars of Wisdom*, Jonathan Cape Ltd, London, 1935
[4] p. 199 Sykes, Sir Mark, *Dar-al-Islam*, London, 1904
[5] p. 202 Philby, H. St J. B., *The Heart of Arabia*, Constable & Co. Ltd, London, 1922
[6] p. 211 Thomas, Bertram, *Arabia Felix*, Jonathan Cape Ltd, London, 1932
[7] p. 213 Thesiger, Wilfred, *Arabian Sands*, Longmans, Green & Co. Ltd, London, 1959
[8] p. 215 ibid.
[9] p. 217 Philby, H. St J. B., *Arabian Days*, Robert Hale Ltd, London, 1948

BIBLIOGRAPHY

General reference

Bidwell, Robin, *Travellers in Arabia*, Hamlyn Publishing Group Ltd, London, 1976

Freeth, Sandra, and Winstone, Victor, *Explorers in Arabia*, George Allen & Unwin Ltd, London, 1978

de Gaury, Gerald, *Rulers of Mecca*, London, 1951

Hogarth, D. G., *The Penetration of Arabia*, Lawrence & Bullen Ltd, London, 1904

Ralli, Augustus, *Christians in Mecca*, London, 1909

Ruthven, Malise, *Islam in the World*, Penguin Books Ltd, 1984

Said, Edward, *Orientalism*, Routledge and Kegan Paul Ltd, London, 1978

Tidrick, Kathryn, *Heart-Beguiling Araby*, Cambridge University Press, Cambridge, 1981

I The Early Travellers

Le Blanc, Vincent, *The World Surveyed*, London, 1660

Pitts, Joseph, *A true and faithful Account of the religion and manners of the Muhammadans*, Exeter, 1704

Varthema, Ludovico di, *Itinerario de Ludovico di Varthema*, Rome, 1510, printed in England in Hakluyt's *Voyages*, London, 1863

II The Pioneers

Hansen, Thorkild, *Arabia Felix*, Gregg International, London, 1964

Niebuhr, Carsten, *Reisebeschreibung nach Arabien und andern umliegenden Laendern*, Copenhagen, 1772. English edition, *Travels in Arabia*, London, 1792

III The First Romantics

Bankes, William, *Narrative of the Life and Adventures of Giovanni Finatti*, London, 1830

Bey, Ali, *Travels of Ali al Abbassi, alias Domingo Badia y Lieblich of Cadiz between 1803 and 1807*, London, 1816

Buckingham, J. S., *Travels in Assyria, Media, and Persia*, London, 1830

Burckhardt, J. L., *Travels in Arabia*, London, 1829

Burckhardt, J. L., *Notes on the Bedouins and Wahabys* (2 vols), London, 1831

Seetzen, U. J., *Beiträge zur Geographie Arabiens*, in von Zach's Correspondence, Vol. XVIII, 1808

Seetzen, U. J., *Reisen durch Syrien, Palestina, Phonicien, die Trans-Jordan-Lander, Arabia Petra und Unter-Aegyptum*, Berlin, 1854-9

Sadlier, G. F., *Diary of a Journey Across Arabia*, Bombay, 1866

Sim, Katharine, *Desert Traveller*, Victor Gollancz Ltd, London, 1969

IV The Opportunists

Burton, Sir Richard, *Pilgrimage to Al-Medinah and Meccah*, London, 1855

Burton, Lady, *Life of Sir Richard Burton* (2 vols), London, 1893

von Maltzen, Freiherr H., *Reisen in Arabien*, Brunswick, 1873

von Wrede, A., *Reise in Hadhramut*, Brunswick, 1870

Wellsted, J. R., *Travels in Arabia*, London, 1838

V Agents of Foreign Powers

Guarmani, Carlo, *Northern Nejd: Journey From Jerusalem to Anaiza in Kasim*, Press of the Franciscan Fathers, Jerusalem, 1866

Palgrave, W. G., *Personal Narrative of a Year's Journey Through Central and Eastern Arabia*, Macmillan Ltd, London, 1865

Pelly, Lewis, 'A Visit to the Wahabee Capital, Central Arabia', *Journal of the Royal Geographical Society*, Vol. XXXV, London, 1865

Saldana, J. A., *Précis of Nejd Affairs, 1804-1904*, Indian Political and Secret Department, Persian Gulf Gazetteer, Simla, 1906

Wallin, G. A., 'Report on a Journey to Hail and Nejd', *Journal of the Royal Geographical Society*, Vol XXIV, London, 1854

Winder, R. B., *Saudi Arabia in the Nineteenth Century*, Macmillan Ltd, London, 1965

VI The Wanderer

Burton, Sir Richard, *The Gold Mines of Midian and Ruined Midianite Cities*, Routledge and Kegan Paul Ltd, London, 1878

Burton, Sir Richard, *The Land of Midian Revisited*, London, 1879

Doughty, C. M., *Travels in Arabia Deserta*, Cambridge University Press, 1888

Hogarth, D. G., *The Life of Charles M. Doughty*, London, 1928

VII The Last Romantics

Blunt, Lady Anne, *Bedouin Tribes of the Euphrates*, London, 1879

Blunt, Lady Anne, *A Pilgrimage to Nejd*, John Murray Ltd, London, 1881

Blunt, Wilfrid Scawen, *My Diaries, Being a Personal Narrative of Events, 1888-1914*, New York, 1921

Longford, Elizabeth, *A Pilgrimage of Passion: The Life of Wilfrid Scawen Blunt*, Weidenfeld & Nicholson Ltd, London, 1979

VIII Twentieth-Century Travellers

Antonius, George, *The Arab Awakening*, London, 1938

Burgyne, Elizabeth (ed.), *Gertrude Bell, From her Personal Papers*, Benn, London, 1958

Carruthers, D., 'Captain Shakespear's Last Journey', *Journal of the Royal Geographical Society*, LIX, 1922

Kedourie, Elie, *England and the Middle East*, London, 1956

Lawrence, T. E., *Seven Pillars of Wisdom*, Jonathan Cape Ltd, London, 1935

Monroe, Elizabeth, *Britain's Moment in the Middle East*, Chatto & Windus Ltd, London, 1963

Monroe, Elizabeth, *Philby of Arabia*, Faber & Faber Ltd, London, 1973

Philby, H. St J. B., *The Heart of Arabia*, Constable & Co. Ltd, London, 1922

Philby, H. St J. B., *Arabia of the Wahhabis*, Constable & Co. Ltd, London, 1928

Philby, H. St J. B., *The Empty Quarter*, Constable & Co. Ltd, London, 1933

Philby, H. St J. B., *Sheba's Daughters*, Methuen Ltd, London, 1939

Philby, H. St J. B., *Arabian Days*, Robert Hale Ltd, London, 1948

Philby, H. St J. B., *Arabian Highlands*, Cornell, Ithaca, 1952

Philby, H. St J. B., *Forty Years in the Wilderness*, Robert Hale Ltd, London, 1957

Nolde, Eduard, *Reise nach Innerarabien, Kurdistan und Armenien*, Brunswick, 1895

Richmond, Lady (ed.), *The Letters of Gertrude Bell*, Penguin Books Ltd, London, 1953

Thesiger, Wilfred, *Arabian Sands*, Longmans, Green & Co. Ltd, London, 1959

Thomas, Bertram, *Arabia Felix*, Jonathan Cape Ltd, London, 1932

Winstone, H. V. F., *Captain Shakespear*, Jonathan Cape Ltd, London, 1976

Winstone, H. V. F., *Gertrude Bell*, Jonathan Cape Ltd, London, 1978

INDEX

Page numbers in italics refer to illustrations.

PICTURE ACKNOWLEDGEMENTS

Robert Adkinson Limited 8, 10, 11 above, 14, 28, 30, 32, 33 below, 34 below, 36, 37, 38, 39, 40, 40-1, 42, 45, 46, 48, 49, 56, 57, 59, 61 below, 64, 67, 68, 72, 74 above, 75, 77, 80, 81, 82, 83, 84, 85, 86, 88 above and below, 89, 90, 91, 93, 96, 97, 100, 103, 104 above and below, 106, 110, 112, 113, 115, 116, 117, 125, 129, 132, 133, 134, 136, 140, 141, 142, 143, 148, 153, 156, 157, 158, 159, 162, 163, 164, 166, 168, 169, 170, 171, 172, 173 above and below, 174, 176, 177, 178, 179, 180 above and below, 181, 182, 184, 185, 195, 211, 213; **Courtesy of the Fine Art Society** 79, 119, 175, 194 below; **Mansell Collection** title page, 12, 16, 18, 19, 20, 21, 24, 27, 33 above, 34 above, 44, 47, 48, 52, 53, 60, 61 above, 62, 65, 66, 71, 74 below, 76, 98, 101, 105, 109, 111, 120, 121, 122, 126, 127, 128, 135, 137, 144, 145, 149, 152, 161, 194 above, 196, 208; **Courtesy of the Mathaf Gallery, London** 13, 17, 22-3, 26, 31 below, 43, 54, 55, 70, 87, 92, 94, 107, 108, 114, 139, 146-7, 155, 160, 167, 190; **MEPhA** 199; **National Portrait Gallery, London** 159; **Royal Geographical Society** 188, 191, 192, 193, 197, 200, 201, 202, 204, 205, 206, 209, 210, 212, 215, 217; **Wilfred Thesiger** 6; **Courtesy of the Trustees of the Victoria & Albert Museum, photographer: Daniel McGrath** 11 below, 35, 50, 58, 63, 99, 102, 123, 130, 150, 183, 186, 203, 207.

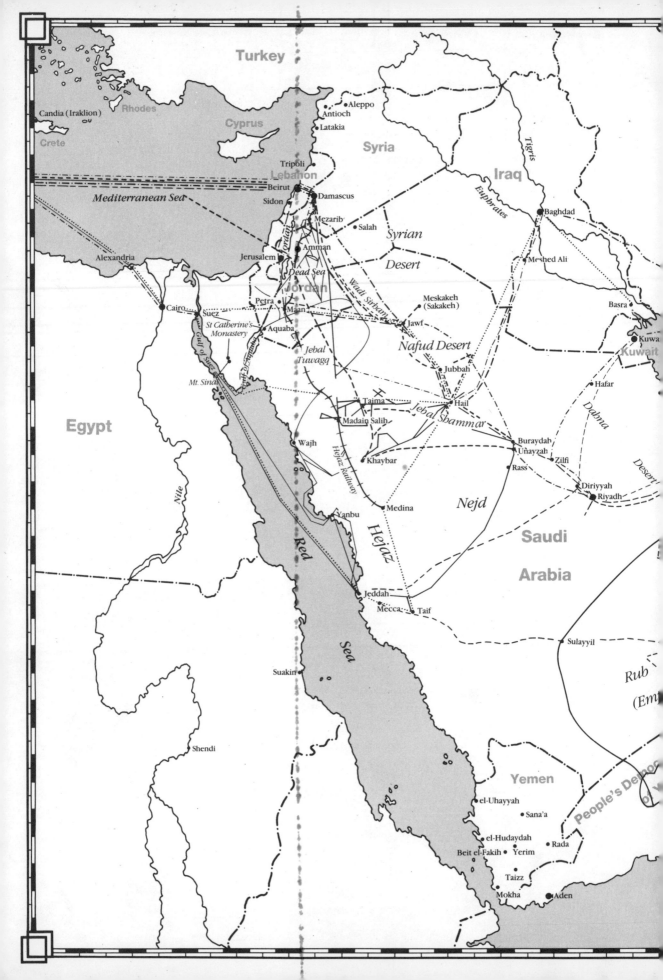